BLACK&DECKER®

THE COMPLETE GUIDE TO

DREAM
BATHROOMS

Design Yourself & Save

Features New Projects & Materials

Step-by-Step Instructions

**Creative Publishing
international**

MINNEAPOLIS, MINNESOTA
www.creativepub.com

Creative Publishing international

Library of Congress Cataloging-in-Publication Data

The complete guide to dream bathrooms : design yourself & save : features new products & materials : step-by-step instructions.
   p. cm. -- (Complete guide)
 Includes index.
 Summary: "Detailed step-by-step photos and text for more than two dozen bathroom remodeling projects, as well as a large inspirational gallery section"--Provided by publisher.
 ISBN-13: 978-1-58923-377-5 (soft cover)
 ISBN-10: 1-58923-377-8 (soft cover)
 1. Bathrooms. 2. Interior decoration. I. Creative Publishing International. II. Title. III. Series.

 NK2117.B33C58 2008
 643'.52--dc22

2008001536

President/CEO: Ken Fund
VP for Sales & Marketing: Kevin Hamric

Home Improvement Group

Publisher: Bryan Trandem
Managing Editor: Tracy Stanley
Senior Editor: Mark Johanson
Editor: Jennifer Gehlhar

Creative Director: Michele Lanci-Altomare
Senior Design Managers: Jon Simpson, Brad Springer
Design Managers: Sara Holle, James Kegley

Lead Photographer: Steve Galvin
Photo Coordinator: Joanne Wawra
Shop Manager: Bryan McLain
Shop Assistant: Cesar Fernandez Rodriguez

Production Managers: Linda Halls, Laura Hokkanen

Page Layout Artist: Danielle Smith
Copy Editor: Ruth Strother
Photographers: Andrea Rugg, Joel Schnell
Shop Help: Dan Anderson, Tami Helmer, John Webb

The Complete Guide to Dream Bathrooms
Created by: The editors of Creative Publishing international, Inc., in cooperation with Black & Decker.
Black & Decker® is a trademark of The Black & Decker Corporation and is used under license.

NOTICE TO READERS

For safety, use caution, care, and good judgment when following the procedures described in this book. The publisher and Black & Decker cannot assume responsibility for any damage to property or injury to persons as a result of misuse of the information provided.

The techniques shown in this book are general techniques for various applications. In some instances, additional techniques not shown in this book may be required. Always follow manufacturers' instructions included with products, since deviating from the directions may void warranties. The projects in this book vary widely as to skill levels required: some may not be appropriate for all do-it-yourselfers, and some may require professional help.

Consult your local building department for information on building permits, codes, and other laws as they apply to your project.

Contents

The Complete Guide to Dream Bathrooms

Introduction

Imagine having your own indoor oasis to ease you into your day or help you relax after stressful hours in the boardroom. You cross the threshold into your dream bathroom and you step into another world—one that makes you feel like royalty. The room is filled with luxury: lush towels warming on heated racks, soft lighting, a jetted tub. Everything is designed with pampering in mind.

Few rooms in the home serve as great a role in our daily routine, relaxation, and health as the bathroom. It must work with sanitary efficiency and, ideally, satisfy our cravings for privacy and luxury. Remodeling a bathroom, or building a brand-new one, can create a living space that better suits your needs. New hardware and fresh paint can transform a dingy half bath into a more attractive space. Changing the layout of fixtures can make a bathroom more usable for a growing family. Annexing the closet space of an adjacent room can provide the necessary space to add a sauna to a master bathroom. And an updated bathroom can be designed to be more hospitable for the physically challenged and the very young.

The Complete Guide to Dream Bathrooms is a comprehensive guide to remodeling bathrooms. With clear descriptions, step-by-step instructions, and full color photos and illustrations, this book gives you the knowledge to plan and complete your dream bathroom remodeling or addition project.

The book is divided into three sections to lead you through each phase of the bathroom remodeling process.

Planning & Designing Your Dream Bathroom: The first section guides you through each step of the planning stage, from initial concept to contacting building inspectors. No matter how simple or extravagant your new bathroom design may be, you will be able to create a working plan and budget that is right for you. This section also provides a gallery of dream baths to help generate practical and creative ideas you can use for redesigning your bathroom.

Dream Bathroom Projects: The second section shows you how to install bathroom fixtures, wall and floor surfaces, cabinets, lighting, and more. A short section, *Removal & Demolition,* gives helpful tips and techniques for the least glamorous part of a remodeling job: getting the old stuff out.

Even if you choose to hire professionals to do the demolition work or install the fixtures, *The Complete Guide to Dream Bathrooms* remains a useful tool. This book will give you an increased understanding of how to remodel a bathroom, work with contractors, and make the best use of your money.

PLANNING & DESIGNING
YOUR DREAM BATHROOM

Gallery of Dream Bathrooms

Modern dream bathrooms are designed with luxury and pampering in mind. But it hasn't always been this way. Traditionally, bathrooms have been all business—often white from floor to ceiling with only the essential fixtures. Happily, the dream of retreating from the stresses of work and long commutes by soaking in your jetted bath surrounded by walls of Italian marble is now attainable. Before you rush out to buy new fixtures or flooring, however, you'll want to consider your new bathroom's function, style, and color.

The three basic types of bathrooms, each with its own requirements for space and layout, are family baths, master (or luxury) baths, and half (or guest) baths. A bathroom should blend in with the overall style of your home. For optimum flexibility, choose neutral fixtures and tile, and then add easy-to-change color accents with wallpaper, paint, or towels.

The following gallery of dream bathrooms will inspire you to come up with practical and creative ideas.

A sunken tub is a perfect choice for this Japanese-inspired bathroom. The muted colors and simple natural accessories add a serene ambiance.

The natural stone deck lends a feeling of luxury to this bathroom along with the added benefit of water and mold resistance. The wood floor adds warmth, but is kept away from the tub and toilet areas. The large window bathes the room with natural light.

Shelving can provide useful and attractive storage space in a bathroom. Here, the rolled towels stored in open shelves contrast with the angular, modern feel of this bathroom, adding a bit of softness. The monochromatic color scheme provides a calm environment.

The built-in bathtub sunken into an elevated platform, the decorative tile work, and the stylized columns give this modern bathroom a Greek flavor.

The poured concrete bathtub with its low profile, simple lines, and soothing colors, sets the mood for a relaxing soak with a good novel. The windowsill serves as a handy bookshelf in this dream bathroom and is just right for those who can't put a book down.

The apron of this oval bathtub that's built into an alcove is decorated with mosaic tile. The larger mosaic wall tiles are set vertically to give this room a sense of height that enhances the feeling of luxury.

A freestanding bathtub is a great choice for a master bathroom. Glowing with ambient light, this bathroom is set up for soothing relaxation.

The streamlined floor faucet gives the old-time feel of this bathroom a modern twist. The hues of blue add to the relaxing atmosphere of this simple and elegant bathroom.

This deep freestanding tub is showcased on an elevated platform. The vessel sinks repeat the look in this peaceful, Zen-inspired retreat.

Toilets and bidets are offered in a variety of styles to match anyone's tastes. These conical fixtures add whimsy to this otherwise sober bathroom.

A bidet isn't always a masculine addition to a bathroom. Here, the Victorian details, light-colored walls and floor, and even the pink toilet tissue all give this bathroom a fresh and decidedly feminine twist.

A wall-mounted vanity cabinet gives a sleek look to any bathroom, but its space-saving design is especially well suited for powder rooms and other small bathrooms.

Vessel sinks mounted on a wall-hung countertop add a touch of elegance to a bathroom. Faucets that enhance the sinks' style complete the picture.

A wall-mounted vanity top of glass and wood contrasts beautifully with this industrial-looking bathroom. The glass adds brilliance to the otherwise matte room, while the wood contributes warmth.

A vessel sink is offset asymmetrically on a stone platform to surprise and delight. Water flowing from the wall-mounted faucet is easily contained in this deep sink. The tall, narrow mirror adds altitude to the otherwise horizontal design.

The widespread bathroom faucet is mounted to the countertop and is paired with a stainless steel under-mount sink, adding a high-tech look to the room. A striking backdrop of metal wall tiles reflects light and creates a bright atmosphere.

Vessel sinks add elegance and style to any bathroom. To minimize splash, the flow of water from the wall-mounted faucet is directed to the center of the sink.

Faucet styles are as varied as any other bathroom fixture. Here, the one-handled vessel faucet lends a contemporary look to the bathroom.

The integral sink/countertop paired with a sleek, stylized sensor faucet is distinctively modern.

This wall-hung sink with its traditional two-handled faucet reflects the deco style of the floor tiles. The glass-and-steel base is not structural.

This simple, square wall-mounted sink blends well with the bright colors of the walls and distinctively mid-century-modern décor. The rich, dark wood floor warms up the room, while the flokati rug adds contrast and texture.

A surface-mounted medicine cabinet adds to the traditional feel of this powder room.

The sleek, contemporary wall-mounted showerhead contrasts elegantly with the old-world stone tile.

The variety of materials here—natural stone, wood, glass, bamboo, and area rugs—create an eclectic look that can appeal to a variety of tastes.

Multiple showerheads are given a new twist with water tile body sprays. The spray face can be adjusted and the nozzles offer hydrotherapeutic benefits.

Storage space is at a premium in bathrooms. Employing some kitchen-style cabinet organizing tricks helps boost efficiency.

A towel warmer drawer built into a linen cabinet is a discreet yet extravagant addition to the bathroom.

Bathroom Elements

Bathroom fixtures and materials have changed dramatically in recent years. Tubs can rival healthclub spas, toilets and showerheads are more water efficient, and sinks run the gamut from stainless steel to wood basins.

Before you jump into a bathroom remodeling project, decide what's most important to you. Budget determines how luxurious you can get, but maybe it's worthwhile to splurge on that one item that would make you feel most pampered.

This chapter covers the most common bathroom fixtures and materials, but several other good resources are also available, such as magazines and websites.

Home centers and kitchen and bath showrooms have a variety of bathroom setups you can browse through to see how the products look and feel. It's always a good idea to see a product in person before doling out the cash.

In this chapter:

- Bathtubs & Whirlpools
- Showers
- Sinks
- Faucets & Showerheads
- Toilets, Bidets, & Urinals
- Cabinets & Vanity Cabinets
- Lighting
- Heating & Ventilation
- Walls & Ceilings
- Flooring
- Home Spa & Luxury Bathroom Amenities

Bathtubs & Whirlpools

The bathtub or whirlpool is often the largest component of the bathroom, so its placement anchors the room. You can find a wide variety of shapes, sizes, and materials to accommodate just about any situation. The three basic types of tubs are attached-apron, deck-mounted, and freestanding.

Attached-apron tubs are the most common. They are enclosed on three sides by alcove walls. Whirlpools (page 24) and one-piece tub-and-shower combinations (page 26) are also available to fit standard-size alcoves. See pages 94 to 97 for installing attached-apron bathtubs.)

Deck-mounted tubs and whirlpools generally rest on the subfloor and are surrounded by custom-built decks or platforms. Typically, these tubs have a larger capacity than attached-apron tubs. The deck makes these tubs more expensive than attached-apron models but the design possibilities are unlimited.

Freestanding tubs are available in both modern and traditional claw-foot styles. They're usually made of enameled cast iron, which retains heat well and is virtually indestructible. Though they are heavy and difficult to move, they are typically easy to install. The plumbing is exposed, so pipes need to have an attractive finish.

Rectangular tubs are the most common and are often combined with showers. They come in a wide range of lengths, widths, depths, and colors in addition to the traditional 30" × 60" × 14" white version.

Square and triangular tubs fit into corners to help open up small bathrooms, and they can also be combined easily with a shower.

Oval, round, and hourglass shapes are usually larger and work well in master or luxury bathrooms. Extra-deep tubs (as much as 22" to 24" in depth) are great for soaking, but can be difficult to get out of. For safety, set a deep tub into a deck so you can sit down for easier access.

This oval whirlpool is front and center in a room devoted to relaxation.

Freestanding tubs are available in the traditional claw-foot design as well as in the up-to-date modern models.

A deck-mounted tub is often the focal point of the bathroom, providing both visual appeal and a luxurious bathing experience.

Space-saving corner tubs are available for small bathrooms. Often these smaller tubs are deeper than standard tubs, which allows for more comfortable bathing.

(continued)

Tubs are manufactured from many different materials, each with its own advantages and disadvantages.

Fiberglass is an inexpensive, lightweight material that comes in a variety of colors. It is easily molded, so fiberglass tubs can have seats, grab bars, soap dishes, and shampoo shelves molded into the sides. Though fiberglass has many benefits, its surface can scratch easily and its color fades over time.

Acrylic, like fiberglass, can be molded into just about any size and shape required. Unlike fiberglass, however, the color runs through the entire substance rather than just on the surface coat, making it less likely to show scratches or to fade.

Enameled steel tubs are shaped from sheets of steel and coated with a baked-on enamel similar to that of cast-iron tubs. The enamel layer is usually thin, though, and is susceptible to chipping. In addition, enameled steel doesn't retain heat and tends to be noisy. When buying an enameled steel tub, check for a sprayed on undercoating that helps muffle sound and retain heat.

Cast iron is the most durable material available for tubs. Iron is cast into a tub shape, then coated with a baked-on enamel that is relatively thick (1/16"), resulting in a richly colored finish. The enamel is strong, durable, and resistant to chips, scratches, and stains.

The cast iron itself is almost impervious to dents and cracks. Cast iron is just about indestructible, but it's also heavy—a standard tub weighs between 300 and 400 lbs. In some cases, the floor framing must be reinforced to support the additional weight. Cast iron is used most commonly for claw-foot and other stand-alone bathtubs. A rapidly increasing number of tubs, both freestanding and alcove type, are now being made from composite materials that are solid like cast iron but much lighter in weight.

The enamel finish of old, scratched, or marred cast-iron tubs can be reglazed, but the finish doesn't last as long as the original and is more susceptible to chips and scratches. Reglazing a cast-iron tub is not a do-it-yourself project, so hire a contractor who is familiar with the process, look for a two-year guarantee, and ask to see examples of previous work.

The whirlpool for home use was developed by Roy Jacuzzi in 1968. A novelty at first, it became increasingly popular as prices dropped, systems became more reliable, and its practical benefits were realized.

Whirlpools circulate water mixed with air through jets mounted in the body of the tub. The pumps move as much as 50 gallons of water per minute to create a massaging effect that relieves stress and muscle pain. Some jets can be adjusted to alter both the stream's direction and the proportion of air and water (more air means a more vigorous massage).

Tub shapes and sizes vary dramatically to accommodate the space available and reflect the style you desire.

Whirlpools are almost always made of acrylic, and sizes and shapes vary tremendously. Prices also vary—whirlpools can range from $700 to $10,000 and up before installation. Price is determined by the number of jets (from four to ten or more), size of the water pump, and options such as a heater and emergency shut-off switch.

You can find a variety of accessories for whirlpools. A multispeed motor allows you to choose from various settings from a gentle, relaxing soak to a vigorous massage. An in-line heater maintains the water temperature. Grab bars, mood lights, pillows, timers, mirrors, and touch-pad controls are available for convenience and comfort.

Before you invest in a new whirlpool, review the maintenance requirements of the tub. Some whirlpools require elaborate upkeep of pumps, timers, and controls, and many roomy models require an extra large water heater.

Whirlpools can be installed by a skilled homeowner familiar with the basic techniques of carpentry, plumbing, and tile setting. Some whirlpools are small enough to fit in the alcove used for standard bathtubs, though most models require the construction of a surrounding deck or platform. See pages 114 to 115 for installing a deck-mounted whirlpool.

Deck-mounted whirlpools are the most widely available and come in many shapes to fit different needs.

Standard-size recessed tubs with whirlpool jets are available to fit into standard-size tub alcoves or short stub walls.

Showers

Showers can stand alone or be combined with tubs, and they come in a number of styles and materials.

The tub/shower combination is most common. It uses space efficiently, is generally cheaper to install than separate tub and shower units, and can easily be added to an alcove tub. One-piece molded fiberglass and acrylic tub-and-shower units are available, but they are often too large to fit through doors and are better suited for new construction.

Shower stalls are ideal for small bathrooms or as a supplement in master or luxury bathrooms. They can be purchased prefabricated or they can be custom-built.

One-piece alcove showers are the most common option for do-it-yourself installation. The seamless stall is molded from a single piece of fiberglass or acrylic, making it easy to clean and maintain. A wide range of shower stall sizes and styles are available, some complete with seats and steam bath capacity.

One-piece neo-angle showers are designed to fit into a corner. They are usually made of acrylic or fiberglass, and have doors that open at an angle.

Shower surround panels are used to construct simple, inexpensive shower stalls. They are built above a preformed shower base made of PVC plastic, fiberglass, acrylic, solid-surface material, quartz, or natural stone (pages 98 to 101). Three individual panels are bonded to the walls of the framed alcove, and the seams are sealed.

Freestanding showers are complete units that are not attached to walls. They range from inexpensive sheet metal or fiberglass units to elaborate glass block showers. The vast majority of showers, however, fit into corners or against one wall.

Custom shower stalls can be designed to fit into odd spaces (pages 78 to 85). The walls can be finished with ceramic tile, glass block, or a solid-surface material. Specialized options, such as seats, steam bath units, and soap dishes, can be incorporated into the design.

Barrier-free showers are designed for physically challenged users. The shower entrance has a low base curb or no curb at all, providing easy access to the shower. One-piece molded units are available, or barrier-free showers can be custom-built. Most have built-in shower seats and grab bars. See pages 48 to 53 for more information on barrier-free showers.

One-piece alcove showers made of fiberglass or acrylic fit between finished walls.

Neo-angle showers offer a unique look, and also save space.

A variety of shower accessories are available that can make a shower more convenient and comfortable.

Shower doors and curtains are usually purchased separately from the shower itself. Options range from simple plastic curtains costing a few dollars to custom-made tempered glass doors costing a thousand dollars or more.

An overhead light ensures safety in the shower. Make sure that any light installed in a shower area is moisture-resistant. Some lights include a heating element.

Multiple showerheads, shower towers, and steam showers (pages 124 to 125) can create a more luxurious shower. Steam showers require extra plumbing, wiring, and a shower stall with doors that seal tightly.

Solid-surface shower stalls are easy to install, clean, and maintain.

Custom-tiled showers can be built to accommodate unique spaces and desired options.

A glass block shower adds a distinctive and luxurious look that can brighten any bathroom.

Sinks

The variety of sinks available today ensures you will find one to match your space, budget, and taste. The most significant difference between the primary sink types, wall-mounted, countertop, and pedestal, is in how they are mounted.

Wall-mounted sinks are bolted to the wall, taking up little space and offering easy access to the plumbing hookups. They are a good option for utility bathrooms or half baths, where exposed plumbing and lack of storage space are not serious drawbacks.

Pedestal sinks are wall-mounted sinks that rest on decorative pedestals that partially hide the plumbing. A pedestal sink is an attractive choice for small guest bathrooms and half-baths, where space is at a premium.

Countertop sinks fit into a countertop cutout. They are often combined with vanity cabinets, which provide extra storage space and hide the plumbing.

The self-rimming sink drops into a cutout in the countertop with its rim overlapping the cutout's edges.

Integral sinks, usually made of solid-surface material or cultured marble, are molded into countertops (page 140) and are easy to install and maintain.

Undermounted sinks are attached with clips beneath a cutout in a solid-surface, stone, or concrete countertop.

Like bathtubs, sinks can be made of a number of materials. Cultured marble is an inexpensive material often used to create integral sink/countertop combinations to fit standard vanity sizes. Porcelain (vitreous china) is often used for self-rimming sinks. It has a durable glossy surface that is nonporous and easy to clean. Porcelain sinks are readily available in white and almond; you can special order other colors and designs.

Solid-surface material is long lasting and easy to clean; scratches can be buffed or sanded out. It is one of the more expensive choices for bathroom sinks, but its durability and ease of care help justify the price. Solid-surface sinks are available in self-rimming, undermounted, and integral models, with a variety of colors and patterns to choose from.

Stainless steel brings a high tech look and durability to bathroom sinks. It is available in either a satin or mirror finish. Price varies according to

A pedestal sink is attractive and doesn't consume large amounts of floor space.

Wall-mounted sinks are perfect for small bathrooms with limited space, such as half-baths.

thickness, or gauge—the lower the gauge number, the thicker the steel. Look for 18-gauge material with a noise-reducing undercoating. Because they are lightweight, stainless steel sinks are often used for undermounting.

Enameled cast iron is an extremely durable material. Made of thick, heavy iron with an enamel coating, these sinks are available in only a few shapes and sizes, and they are rather expensive. A low-cost alternative is enameled steel, but it is lightweight and not very durable—the enamel coat tends to chip easily.

Tempered glass is used to create stylish vessel sinks for bathrooms. Undermounted styles can be lit from underneath to create a mood-setting glow.

Other materials such as concrete, copper, carved stone, and wood can be used to create sinks for exotically styled bathrooms. Before you select a sink made of an unusual material, consider the shipping time, installation procedures, and day-to-day maintenance.

Self-rimming sinks mount into any type of countertop and are the most common style of bathroom sink.

An undermounted sink can be made of a contrasting color and material to achieve a specific look, or it can match the countertop.

A vessel sink creates a distinct visual effect in a bathroom.

Faucets & Showerheads

Faucets can significantly impact your bathroom's overall style. For instance, most traditional faucets have two handles, while more contemporary-looking faucets usually have one.

When selecting a spout, you'll want to coordinate its shape and length with the fixture. For example, a tall spout, which drops water from a greater distance, needs a deep sink basin to contain the additional splash. In bathrooms with multiple faucets, you may want to buy faucets within the same style suite. Look for faucets with antiscald valves (page 117), which are required by code for new construction.

Once you have chosen a style, examine the quality of the brands and models you're considering. Generally, a well-made faucet feels heavy and solid. The best choice for durability is a solid brass, corrosion-resistant faucet with a ceramic disc valve. These faucets are expensive but virtually indestructible.

The finish on a faucet affects its appearance, price, and maintenance. Polished chrome is durable and easy to maintain. Polished brass requires more maintenance than chrome. Colored epoxy on brass is long-lasting, easy to clean, and available in a variety of colors. Pewter, nickel, and gold finishes are also available, though somewhat expensive.

Two-handle faucets come in a variety of designs, from classic to ultramodern. The model above mounts on a single deckplate.

Single-handle faucets are the most common type of bathroom faucet, with many different designs to choose from.

Faucets with widespread handles can be mounted in any configuration you choose, allowing more design possibilities than single-body faucets.

Showerheads are available in many styles, from wall-mounted heads to handheld sprayers with adjustable spray settings.

Waterfall faucets deliver a large volume of water to bathtubs and whirlpools, and make a big design impact when used with lavatories.

Wall-mounted faucets are stylish fixtures for use with undermount and bowl sinks.

Toilets, Bidets, & Urinals

Toilets have changed in recent years. There's a toilet to fit every style. You can even get a square or stainless steel toilet, or one that has an aquarium built into its tank! The new designs are efficient, durable, and less susceptible to clogs.

A toilet's style is partly affected by the way it's built. You have a number of options from which to choose.

Two-piece toilets have separate water tanks and bowls.

One-piece toilets have a tank and bowl made of one seamless unit.

Elongated bowls are roughly 2" longer than regular bowls.

Elevated toilets have higher seats, generally 18", rather than the standard 15".

You have a choice of two basic types of flush mechanisms: gravity- and pressure-assisted.

Gravity-assisted toilets allow water to rush down from an elevated tank into the toilet bowl. Federal law mandates that new toilets consume no more than 1.6 gallons of water per flush, less than half the volume used by older styles.

Pressure-assisted toilets rely on either compressed air or water pumps to boost flushing power.

Dual-flush systems require the toilet to have two buttons on the top of the tank, allowing you to select either an 8-ounce flush for liquids or a 1.6-gallon flush for solids.

Toilets are available in a variety of styles and colors to suit almost any decor. Two-piece toilets are generally cheaper and come in a great assortment of styles and colors. Many high-end models have a matching bidet available.

Gravity-assisted toilets are now designed with taller tanks and steeper bowl walls to increase the effects of gravity.

Pressure-assisted toilets are more expensive than standard toilets, but they can reduce your water usage significantly. The flush mechanism of a pressure-assisted toilet boosts the flushing power by using either compressed air or water pumps.

Bidets & Urinals ▸

A bidet is a type of washbasin that allows for personal cleansing of the private areas. It is usually installed next to the toilet. A bidet needs its own water supply and drain. A storage space for towels and soap should be nearby.

Any institutional men's room is almost certain to have a urinal, and for good reason: urinals are sanitary and easy to use. Most fixture manufacturers are now producing urinals for home use. If there are a lot of men in your family, a urinal may be something to consider, if only for the green benefits of reduced water usage.

Cabinets & Vanity Cabinets

The typical bathroom lacks storage space. In fact, creating better storage is one of the most common reasons people remodel their bathrooms. As you design your dream bathroom, keep in mind three basic types of storage: cabinetry, open shelving, and linen closets.

If your bathroom is large enough for wall cabinets, decide what types and sizes you want. Then decide whether stock cabinets suit your needs, or if you want your dream cabinets custom-made.

Vanities hide plumbing, provide storage, and support the countertop and sink. A vanity is often a bathroom's visual focal point and can set the decorative tone for the whole room.

Medicine cabinets offer quick access to toiletries and keep storage items beyond the reach of young children. Most are designed with a mirror on the door or doors and are installed

Vanities can be combined with wall cabinets and medicine cabinets to get the look and storage space you desire.

above a sink. They can be either surface-mounted or recessed into walls between studs to exploit otherwise unused space (pages 174 to 175). Many incorporate lighting.

Linen cabinets are tall and narrow, taking advantage of floor-to-ceiling space.

Wall cabinets, because they are shallow, are versatile storage units for small spaces like bathrooms. They can be installed on any available wall space—the most popular spot is over the toilet. Some are freestanding units with legs that straddle the toilet tank. Wall cabinets can even be mounted low and topped with a counter.

A simple vanity provides convenient storage in a bathroom with limited space. Add a matching medicine cabinet for a classic combination.

Wall-mounted and recessed shelving are good ways to make use of space, such as above and behind a toilet.

(continued)

Whatever type of cabinet you're considering, you'll have the choice of stock or custom-made designs:

Stock cabinets are mass-produced in standard sizes and warehoused for quick delivery. They are less expensive than custom-made cabinets of comparable wood species, but a wide range of prices can be had within both categories.

Custom cabinets are built to order by a cabinetmaker or cabinet shop, so you get exactly the combination of size, style, material, and finish that you want. Start shopping for custom cabinets early and plan on at least six to eight weeks from design to delivery.

Other storage options for bathrooms include shelves and closets:

Shelves are a useful addition to bathrooms that don't have room for elaborate cabinetry. They can be recessed or surface-mounted and are often combined with baskets and storage bins.

Linen closets generally extend from floor to ceiling. Adding or relocating a closet requires significant construction—walls almost always have to be moved or built.

Medicine cabinets can be flush mounted or recessed to offer efficient storage right where it's needed.

Glide-out storage shelves make all items in your cabinet accessible, even those that are way in the back.

Linen closets with shelves can keep toiletries within easy reach.

Wall-mounted cabinets pull double duty as storage and as a vanity.

Lighting

Lighting can set the mood of any room. Dim lights and lit candles are perfect for a leisurely soak in the whirlpool. When it comes to shaving or applying makeup, though, bright lights are the ticket.

You can choose among three basic types of lighting to ensure personal safety, provide ambience, and permit various uses of your space:

General lighting usually involves an overhead fixture that illuminates the entire room.

Task lighting provides bright light for specific activities.

Accent lighting can be used to highlight points of interest, such as architectural details or artwork.

You can choose lighting fixtures to suit any decor. Surface-mounted fixtures are easy to install and are available in a variety of styles.

Recessed ceiling fixtures are mounted flush with the surface.

Track lighting ties into metal channels that supply power to several small lights that can be positioned as you wish.

Portable fixtures should be used only in bathrooms with plenty of counter or floor space. Avoid using extension cords in bathrooms, and never place electrical cords near water.

A combination of general lighting, task lighting, and natural lighting allows you to only use what is necessary.

Recessed light fixtures provide nondirectional lighting and have a fairly neutral design impact.

Heating & Ventilation

Consider room size, the number of windows, and the type of heat in the rest of the house when making decisions about your bathroom heating system. Consult a professional before making final decisions. You have four basic choices for auxiliary heat in bathrooms:

Electric heaters are mounted either by themselves or as part of light/vent/heating units.

Heat lamps use infrared light bulbs to provide radiant heat.

Radiant floor-heating systems are installed beneath the flooring and circulate either hot water or electricity.

Towel warmers keep towels toasty and can warm a small area of the room.

Good ventilation protects surfaces from moisture damage, deters mold and mildew, and keeps air fresh. Vents with electric fans (pages 194 to 197) are required by code in any bathroom without windows. It's best to install a vent with an exhaust system that carries stale or moist air outdoors.

Purchase a vent fan that's rated at least 5 cfm higher than the square footage of your bathroom. Local building codes may have specific requirements, so check with your building inspector or HVAC contractor before selecting a ventilation unit.

Radiant heat floor systems keep hard surfaces warm to the touch and heat the room.

Vent and light combinations serve the dual purpose of lighting the room and reducing moisture and odors. The more powerful heaters use infrared heat.

Walls & Ceilings

If you add, move, or replace walls in your bathroom, use moisture-resistant materials.

Drywall is adequate for most bathrooms, except for the area around tubs and showers.

Greenboard is a drywall with waterproof facing.

Cementboard is undamaged by water. It is required under tile in tub and shower surrounds.

Glass block can't bear loads, so use them only for interior walls.

You'll want the wall and ceiling finishes to be easy to maintain. Wall finishes for tub and shower surrounds, and behind sinks and toilets should be waterproof.

Paint finishes range from flat to glossy (enamel). Glossy finishes are best for areas that will be cleaned often. Latex (water-based) paints are more environmentally friendly than oil-based paints.

Wallpaper should be treated to withstand moisture. Choose smooth-textured, solid vinyl or vinyl-coated wallpaper.

Ceramic wall tiles are durable, easy to clean, and available in hundreds of styles.

Stone wall tiles are expensive, so consider using stone as an accent.

Solid-surface material is often used in tub or shower surrounds (pages 102 to 103).

Bathroom ceilings need moisture-resistant finishes. Avoid textured ceilings, which peel in humid conditions and are difficult to clean, repair, or paint.

Natural stone and ceramic tiles can be combined to create custom-designed wall surfaces.

Glass block allows light to penetrate the wall while serving as a partition.

Flooring

Bathroom floors should stand up to daily use, frequent cleaning, and moisture.

Resilient sheet vinyl flooring is inexpensive but is seldom the first choice of professional designers. It is simple to install, easy to clean, seamless, and available in a variety of colors, patterns, and styles.

Vinyl tile is easy to install but its seams allow moisture to soak through and ruin the adhesive bond.

Ceramic tile is available in a variety of sizes, patterns, and colors. You can choose among three main types of ceramic tile: glazed ceramic tile, quarry tile, and water-resistant porcelain tile. Although cleaning issues are created by the grout lines, mosaic ceramic tile is highly popular.

Natural stone tile is a premium flooring material. Granite, marble, and slate are the most common stone products for floors. Installation can be costly as natural stone requires a subbase of poured mortar or cementboard.

Hardwood floors are difficult to totally waterproof so they should be limited to half baths, where moisture is not a big problem.

Carpet typically doesn't have the water resistance required for bathroom floors, and it traps mold and mildew. Be sure to select a product that's designed especially for bathrooms.

The condition of your floor structure may affect the cost of installing new flooring. If the subfloor must be replaced or repaired, more time and money will be required. Consult a professional to assess the state of your subfloor.

Vinyl flooring is a popular choice for bathrooms because it is relatively inexpensive, durable, and easy to clean.

Ceramic floor tile, a popular choice for bathrooms, is durable and water-resistant.

Stone floor tile creates an inviting atmosphere with natural appeal.

Home Spa & Luxury Bathroom Amenities

Today's dream baths often include luxury amenities that bring home the therapeutic benefits of a trip to the spa. Master baths and luxury bathrooms are becoming larger to create a space that offers total relaxation and an escape from the rest of the world.

Jetted tubs have become a standard fixture in master baths. A jetted tub circulates water mixed with air through jets mounted in the body of the tub to deliver a soothing hydromassage. Newer models circulate air only, which has some advantages for a home spa.

A sauna in your dream bath allows you to sweat out the day's tension in the privacy of your home. Health professionals often prescribe saunas as a way to relieve joint problems and everyday aches and pains, and they are believed to have additional health benefits. Saunas are most commonly built of soft aromatic woods such as cedar, redwood, or white spruce. The temperature in a heated sauna ranges from 150° to 185°F.

Little space is required to accommodate a sauna; a 4-ft. × 4-ft. minimum size is recommended for comfort. A sauna can sometimes fit into a space not much bigger than a closet. Saunas can be custom-built in any size and shape to fit your bathroom design, or you can purchase a prefabricated kit that includes the heater and all precut parts. Some saunas are even sold completely preassembled. You just slide them in place and plug them in.

Steam showers and steam rooms are more recent luxury additions to the home bathroom. Steam heat speeds up all of the chemical processes in the body,

Some prefabricated saunas can rival custom-built saunas in style and quality, and they may be less expensive.

helping to rid the body of toxins. Some acrylic shower units are available with preinstalled steam capacity; custom-built steam rooms use separate steam generators. Steam rooms and steam showers require expanded or upgraded plumbing and wiring.

Shower towers are units that combine valves, multiple showerheads, handheld sprays, body sprayers, and water jets using only one water line connection. A shower tower is designed to provide therapeutic hydromassage for aching muscles. Most units require a ¾"-dia. dedicated hot water supply line.

The body spa system that is a variation of the shower tower, incorporates the tower design into a unit that forces a large volume of water quickly through jets for hydromassage therapy. The water collects in the basin and is recirculated back through the system. The amount of hot water required to run these systems may require you to upgrade your hot water heater before installing a shower tower or body spa system.

Many homeowners take their dream baths to an even higher level of luxury. They design their bathrooms with plenty of additional space to house exercise equipment or electronics to contribute entertainment, ambience, and convenience.

Use common sense and follow your local electrical codes when installing electronics in bathrooms. Devise an electrical plan that provides plenty of outlets for the appliances you will be using. Make sure to locate all cords and electrical items well away from tubs, showers, and sinks.

Steam rooms and steam showers must be fully enclosed units with doors that seal tightly to trap the steam produced by the generator. Steam therapy is said to provide many health benefits.

Shower towers are equipped with multiple shower heads and body sprayers to provide a therapeutic hydromassage for aching muscles.

Getting Started

Whether you are showering or shaving, a great bathroom enables you to take care of your needs in a comfortable, attractive, and convenient setting. It is a private retreat, where you can tend to your needs in a relaxed and pleasant fashion.

When designing a new bathroom or renovating an existing one, style can be as big a consideration as function. From the choice of materials to the layout of fixtures, the space should reflect your individual sense of style through the use of particular colors, textures, and patterns.

And yet, a bathroom does have to be functional. Without a strong foundation on which to express your style, you may spend more money and time creating your dream bath, and it may not turn out to be as well designed as you'd hoped. So the first step is to determine your needs and budget, and draw up some plans. Now you have a foundation on which to build the bathroom of your dreams!

In this chapter:

- Determining Your Needs
- Designing for Accessibility
- Design Standards
- Drawing Plans

Determining Your Needs

A typical bathroom is divided into three activity areas: the toilet, the sink, and the shower/tub. To create a successful bath design, you need to consider the relationship of these areas, allowing for accessibility and safety. This relationship varies depending on the type of bathroom being renovated: half bath, family bath, or master bath.

Half baths, also called powder rooms or guest baths, are small rooms near common areas of the home. They are designed largely for visitors to use. They can be as small as 20 sq. ft. and are often located near entrances or entertainment areas of a home. It's best to have their doors open into hallways.

Half baths typically feature a toilet and a vanity or pedestal sink finished with smaller fixtures and finer materials. When designed as a guest bath that includes a shower, these rooms require more space and are called three-quarter baths.

The family bath is usually located near the sleeping areas in a home. It is used by more than one family member, and it should provide storage for toiletries, towels, and laundry and cleaning supplies. It features at least one sink, one toilet, and a shower and tub or tub/shower combination.

The typical family bath can fit in a 5 × 7-ft. area. A larger bathroom allows space for extra features, such as a double-bowl sink or separate shower and tub area. A small family bath may conserve space by combining the tub and shower, incorporating recessed shelving, and featuring space-efficient fixtures and storage cabinets. Fixtures and finishes should be low-maintenance and highly durable, such as ceramic tile and enameled fixtures.

Bathrooms for children must be safe for them to use unsupervised and should be easy to adapt as the children grow. Features that make daily hygiene easier and safer for children include single-handle faucets with antiscald guards, adjustable showerheads, safety plugs in receptacles, grab bars, smaller toilets, lowered sinks, and vanities with built-in step stools.

The master bath is usually connected to the master bedroom and is a sanctuary for the owners of the house. It is typically quite large and may have separate activity centers containing features such as a jetted tub, shower, partitioned toilet, and multiple sinks and vanities. It may even feature a sauna or steam room. The fixtures and finishing materials generally feature ceramic, stone, or marble tiles; custom cabinets; and upscale accessories.

This half bath is well proportioned, featuring scaled-down fixtures and accessories.

Bathrooms are divided into three distinctive activity areas. Here, the shower and tub areas are set off from the vanity.

The family bath is used by multiple family members and benefits from ample storage space to accommodate everyone's needs.

The master bath is usually adjacent to the master bedroom and features top-quality fixtures and materials to give homeowners that sense of luxury.

Designing for Accessibility

The safety and accessibility of nearly all aspects of a bathroom can be improved.

For safer floors, add a slip-resistant glaze to ceramic tile, and add nonslip adhesive strips or decals to shower floors. If you're replacing your floor, look for mosaic tiles, vinyl, and cork materials. Matte finishes tend to be less slippery than polished surfaces and they reduce glare.

Toilets, faucets, sinks, cabinets, tubs, and showers can all be adapted or changed for increased usability by people who have experienced inflexibility or loss of strength.

Toilet height can be adjusted with the installation of a height adapter that raises a standard toilet seat 2" to 5". You can also consider an adjustable-height toilet or a model with a power-lift seat.

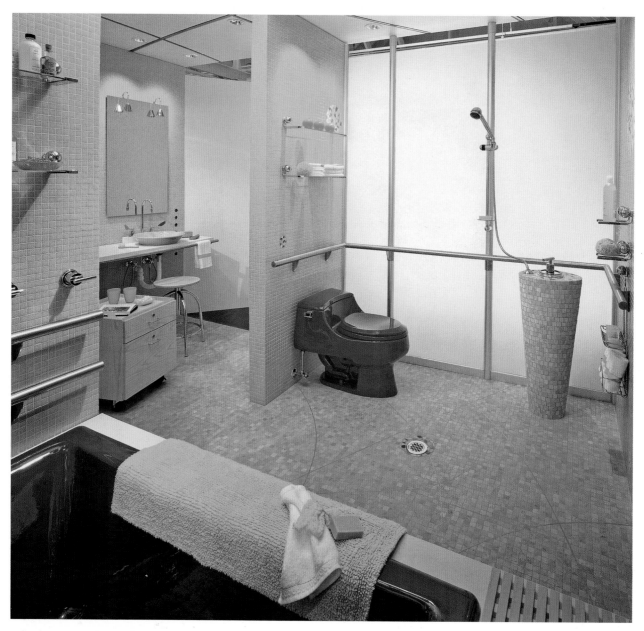

A bathroom designed for accessibility is an increasingly important element found in today's homes.

An integral personal hygiene system can be installed to help people with physical disabilities maintain independence.

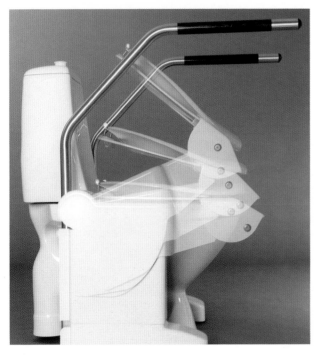

Power-lifts make toilet use easier for people with limited leg or joint strength.

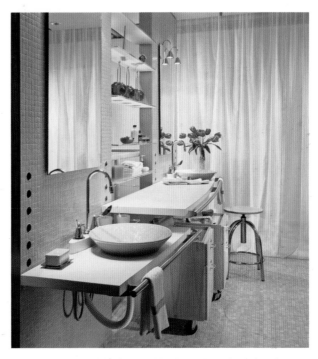

Roll-out base cabinets provide the option of seating space at the countertop.

(continued)

Consider replacing your toilet with a wall-hung style that can be installed at any height, providing additional clear space for maneuvering a wheelchair or walker. To help people with physical disabilities maintain independent personal hygiene, install either a bidet or a toilet with an integral personal hygiene system. Grab bars are a must on walls around the toilet.

Install antiscald guard and volume-control devices to faucets and showerheads. Replace double-handle faucets with single-lever models, which are easier to use. A faucet with motion-sensor operation for hands-free use is a plus.

Change a standard showerhead to an adjustable showerhead mounted on a vertical slide-bar to accommodate people of all heights. Look for handheld models for best control.

Vanities and cabinets with C-shaped pulls or magnetic touch latches are easy to use. Add pull-down hardware to cabinets to bring items within reach for seated people or those with limited mobility.

Install your countertops at varied heights to serve both seated and standing users. Also consider mounting the faucet controls at the side of the sink, rather than the back, for easier access.

If you are replacing your sink, choose a style that is shallower at the front and deeper at the drain. Or install a wall-mounted sink positioned at 30 to 32". Providing a clear space under sinks and low sections of countertop allows seated users to comfortably reach the vanity. Use fold-away doors, remove face frames on base cabinets, or install roll-out base cabinets to gain clear space. Always finish the floor under fold-away or roll-out cabinets. Then insulate hot-water supply pipes or install a protective panel to prevent burns to seated users.

Side-mounted faucet and drain pulls in combination with a wall-mounted sink are easily accessible.

A tilted mirror allows seated or short users to easily see themselves.

Install grab bars in and around the shower and tub. Adding a shower seat or installing a pull-down or permanent seat in the shower allows elderly or disabled family members to sit while bathing. Install a permanently mounted shower seat at 18" high, and be sure the seat is at least 15" deep.

Water controls and faucets on tubs repositioned toward the outside edge at a height of 38" to 48" allows the water to be turned on and adjusted before getting in to bathe. If you're buying a new bathtub, consider one with a side-access door.

Consider replacing a combination tub and shower with a stand-alone shower with a base that slopes gently toward the drain, rather than a curb to contain water. When fitted with a pull-down seat and an adjustable handheld showerhead, roll-in showers can accommodate people with a wide range of abilities.

Reverse door hinges so doors open out. That way, the door swing won't be blocked if someone falls.

If needed, widen doorways to 32 to 36" so wheelchair and walker users can enter the bathroom easily. Or, replace a swing door with a pocket door to gain clear space.

Roll-in shower designs, roll-under sinks, grab bars, adjustable slide-bar showers, and open floor space make bathing easier for people with disabilities.

(continued)

A swing-in door makes bathtubs accessible to practically anyone. The door creates a tight seal when closed and cannot be opened if the tub is full.

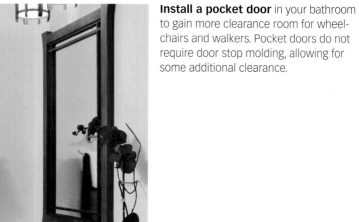

Install a pocket door in your bathroom to gain more clearance room for wheelchairs and walkers. Pocket doors do not require door stop molding, allowing for some additional clearance.

Recommended Clearances ▸

A bathroom should be planned with enough approach space and clearance room to allow a wheelchair or walker user to enter and turn around easily. The guidelines for approach spaces (patterned areas) and clearances shown here include some ADA guidelines and recommendations from universal design specialists.

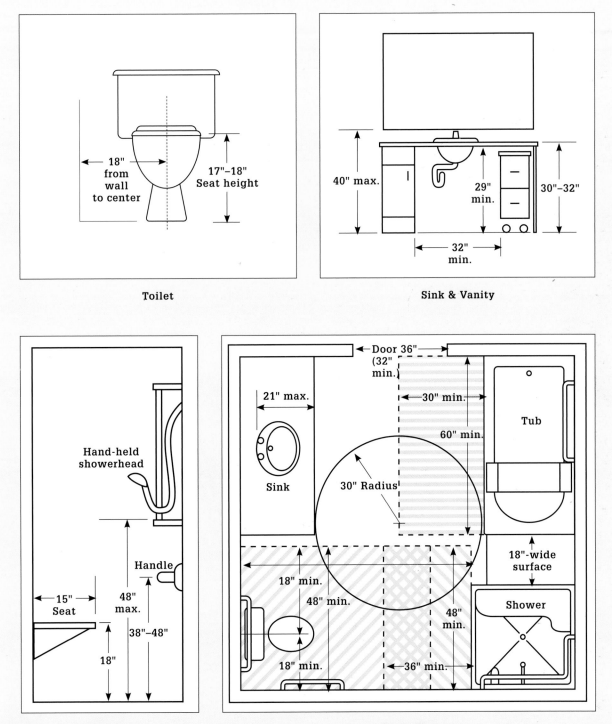

Toilet

Sink & Vanity

Shower

Floor Plan

Design Standards

Once you've drawn up your plan and created a materials list, you'll need to have them reviewed by your local building department. Getting approval early in the process can save you time and expense later. To help ensure success, here are some design standards for you to follow:

The National Kitchen and Bath (NKBA) publishes a list of bathroom design standards to help people plan rooms that are safe and accessible to all users (see Resources, page 284).

Your bathroom probably won't conform to all of the recommended standards, but they can help guide your overall plan. What your plan must include is everything prescribed by the local building codes, including plumbing and wiring codes (see pages 278 to 281).

Bathroom Design Standards ▸

Codes and permits are necessary to ensure safety in any remodel. They're not the most fun to focus on—not like choosing just the right floor covering or deciding between granite or marble countertops—but they are important.

- Plan doorways with a clear floor space equal to the door's width on the push side and greater than the door's width on the pull side. *Note: Clear floor spaces within the bathroom can overlap.*
- Design toilet enclosures with at least 36" × 66" of space; include a pocket door or a door that swings out toward the rest of the bathroom.
- Install toiletpaper holders approximately 26" above the floor, toward the front of the toilet bowl.
- Place fixtures so faucets are accessible from outside the tub or shower. Add antiscald devices to tub and sink faucets (they are required for shower faucets).
- Avoid steps around showers and tubs, if possible.
- Fit showers and tubs with safety rails and grab bars.
- Install shower doors so they swing open into the bathroom, not the shower.
- Use tempered glass or another type of safety glass for all glass doors and partitions.
- Include storage for soap, towels, and other items near the shower, located within 15" to 48" above the floor. These should be accessible to a person in the shower or tub.
- Provide natural light equal to at least 10% of the floor area in the room.
- Illuminate all activity centers in the bathroom with task and ambient lighting.
- Provide a minimum clearance of 15" from the centerline of sinks to any sidewalls. Double-bowl sinks should have 30" clearance between bowls from centerline to centerline.
- Provide access panels for all electrical, plumbing, and HVAC systems connections.
- Include a ventilation fan that exchanges air at a rate of 8 air changes per hour.
- Choose countertops and other surfaces with edges that are smoothed, clipped, or radiused.

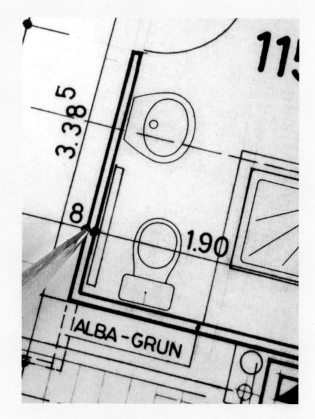

Building Codes for Bathrooms ▸

The following are some of the most common building codes for bathrooms. Contact your local building department for a list of all codes enforced in your area.

- The minimum ceiling height in bathrooms is 7 ft. (Minimum floor area is determined by clearances around fixtures.)
- Sinks must be at least 4" from side walls and have 21" of clearance in front.
- Sinks must be spaced 4" away from neighboring sinks and toilets, and 2" away from bathtubs.
- Toilets must be centered 15" from side walls and tubs, with 21" clearance in front.
- New and replacement toilets must be low-flow models (1.6 gal./flush).
- Shower stalls must be at least 30" × 30", with 24" of clearance in front of shower openings.
- Steps must be at least 10" deep and no higher than 7¼".
- Faucets for showers and combination tub/showers must be equipped with antiscald devices.
- Supply lines that are ½" in diameter can supply a single fixture, or one sink and one toilet.

- A ¾"-diameter supply line must be used to supply two or more fixtures.
- Waste and drain lines must slope ¼" per foot toward the main DWV stack to aid flow and prevent blockage.
- Each bathroom must be wired with at least one 20-amp circuit for GFCI-protected receptacles, and one 15-amp (minimum) circuit for light fixtures and vent fans without heating elements.
- All receptacles must be GFCI-protected.
- There must be at least one permanent light fixture controlled by a wall switch.
- Wall switches must be at least 60" away from bathtubs and showers.
- Toilet, shower, vanity, or other bathroom compartments must have adequate lighting.
- Light fixtures over bathtubs and showers must be vaporproof, with a UL rating for wet areas.
- Vanity light fixtures with built-in electrical receptacles are prohibited.
- Whirlpool motors must be powered by dedicated GFCI-protected circuits.
- Bathroom vent ducts must terminate no less than 10 ft. horizontally or 3 ft. vertically above skylights.

Note: Codes for accessible bathrooms may differ (see page 53).

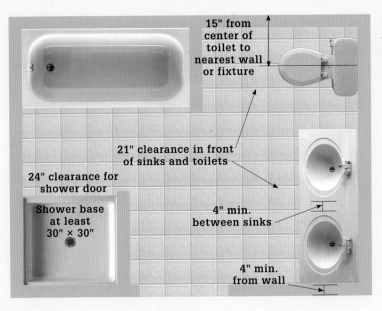

15" from center of toilet to nearest wall or fixture

21" clearance in front of sinks and toilets

24" clearance for shower door

Shower base at least 30" × 30"

4" min. between sinks

4" min. from wall

Follow minimum clearance and size guidelines when planning locations of bathroom fixtures. Easy access to fixtures is fundamental to creating a bathroom that is comfortable, safe, and easy to use.

Drawing Plans

If your new bathroom involves a layout change or expansion, you'll find it helpful to create floor plans and elevation drawings. A floor plan illustrates an overhead view, while an elevation drawing illustrates a face-on view. Your drawings will be the basis for obtaining permits, negotiating contracts with tradespeople, and ordering products.

To begin, make a rough sketch of the existing floor plan. Measure and record the size and location of all existing fixtures and mechanicals from a fixed point. Sketch an elevation of each wall.

Use these rough sketches to draft a precise scale drawing of your existing floor plan. You can now sketch variations of your new bathroom using the scale drawing of the floor plan as a guide.

Use the overall dimensions of your new floor plan to sketch elevation options. In the end, the elevations and floor plans must agree.

A scale drawing shows everything in accurate proportion. After measuring the dimensions of your existing bathroom, draft a floor plan, including any adjoining space that could be used for expansion of the layout (such as the storage closet shown below). The normal scale for bathroom plans is ½" = 1 ft.

The existing floor plan draft should contain dimension lines noting the accurate measurements of the space, including the location of all existing fixtures. This draft also shows the location of electrical circuits. It is the starting point for your remodeled bathroom plan.

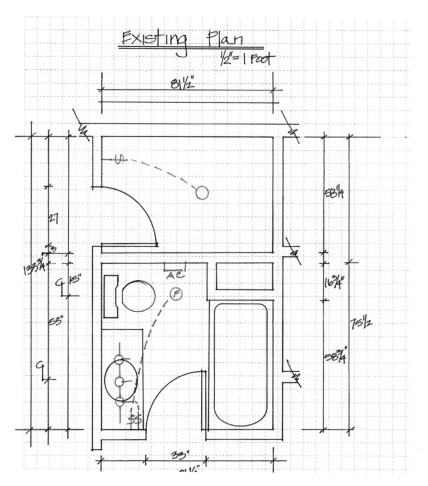

New Bathroom Floor Plan Samples ▸

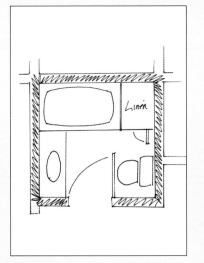

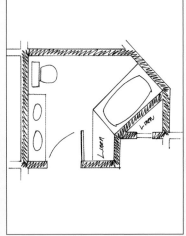

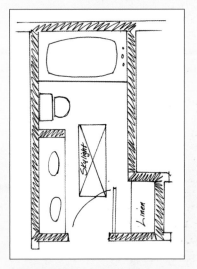

Option A: This floor plan option of the draft on the opposite page shows a layout change within the existing space. The sink and vanity stay in the same place, but the tub and toilet have been switched. There is room to add a linen cabinet, but the space is still very cramped.

Option B: This option explores expanding the room and experimenting with some interesting angles. There is now plenty of floor space for two people, plus room for a double vanity and a large linen cabinet for increased storage.

Option C: The existing room is expanded by annexing the adjacent closet. There's plenty of floor space, a double vanity, and a built-in linen cabinet. This plan has the practical benefits of Option B, but is less expensive to build.

Bathroom Elevation Options ▸

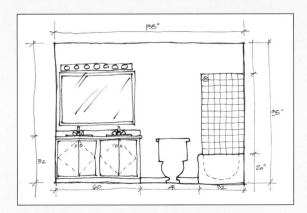

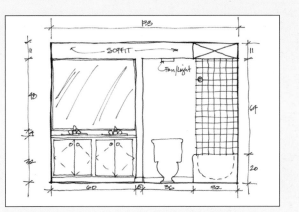

Option A: This elevation shows a simple arrangement with a standard mirror and light fixture. It also shows ceramic tile in the shower area, ending just above the shower curtain.

Option B: This variation shows a custom mirror framed in by a partition wall, and a soffit that runs above the vanity, toilet, and tub. Lights are recessed in the soffit.

DREAM BATHROOM PROJECTS

Showers, Tubs, & Whirlpools

Installing and hooking up plumbing for bathtubs and showers is a fairly simple job. Jetted tubs and saunas are more complicated because they also require electrical hookups, as well as structural frames.

The most difficult task you'll face when installing tubs, showers, and spas is moving the bulky fixtures and materials up stairways and through narrow doorways. With a two-wheel dolly and a little help, the job is much easier. Be sure to measure doorways and hallways.

If you do not plan to remove and replace your wall surfaces, you should still cut away at least six inches of wall surface above a tub or whirlpool to allow easier access during installation.

In this chapter:

- Installing Showers
- Shower Enclosure Kits
- Neo-Angle Showers
- Custom Shower Bases
- Glass Block Showers
- Tubs & Jetted Tubs
- Alcove Bathtubs
- 3-Piece Tub Surrounds
- Solid-Surface Surrounds
- Sliding Tub Doors
- Air-Jet Tubs
- Tub & Shower Fittings
- Adding a Shower to a Bathtub
- Dual Showerheads

Installing Showers

Showers can be built in a number of ways, from a number of materials, as discussed on pages 26 to 27. One of the easiest ways to build a shower is to frame an alcove and line it with prefabricated panels. Though water-resistant drywall is the standard backer for prefab panels, always check the manufacturer's recommendations. Some building codes also require a waterproof membrane between the studs and the backer material.

The type of shower base you use will affect the installation sequence. Some bases are made to be installed after the backer; others should be installed first. If your base is going in after the wall surface, be sure to account for the thickness of the surface material when framing the alcove.

Tools & Materials ▸

Circular saw	2 × 4 and 1 × 4 lumber
Drill	16d and 8d nails
Plumbing tools	Plumbing supplies
Hacksaw	Shower base
Channel-type pliers	Rag
Trowel	Dry-set mortar (optional)
Level	Soap

Ceramic tile for custom showers is installed the same way as in other applications. Ceramic shower accessories, such as a soap dish, are mortared in place during the tile installation.

Antiscald Valves

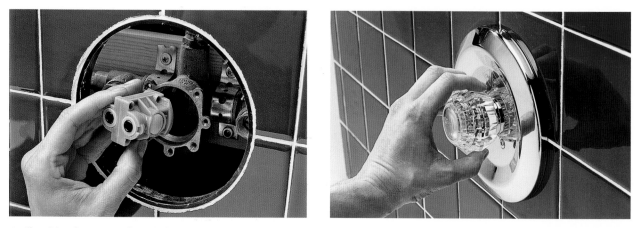

Antiscald valves are safety devices that protect against sudden water temperature changes. They are required by most building codes for faucets in showers and combination tub/showers. Once installed, faucets with antiscald valves look like standard faucets.

Anatomy of a Shower

Shower stalls are available in many different sizes and styles, but the basic elements are the same. Most shower stalls have a shower alcove, a supply system, and a drain system.

Shower alcove: The alcove is the frame for the stall, with 2 × 4 walls built to fit around a shower base and blocking to secure the plumbing. The base sets into a mortar bed for support, and water-resistant drywall or cementboard covers the alcove walls.

The supply system: The shower arm extends from the wall, where an elbow fitting connects it to the shower pipe. The pipe runs up from the faucet, which is fed by the hot and cold water supplies.

The drain system: The drain cover attaches to the drain tailpiece. A rubber gasket on the tailpiece slips over the drainpipe, leading to the P-trap and the branch drain.

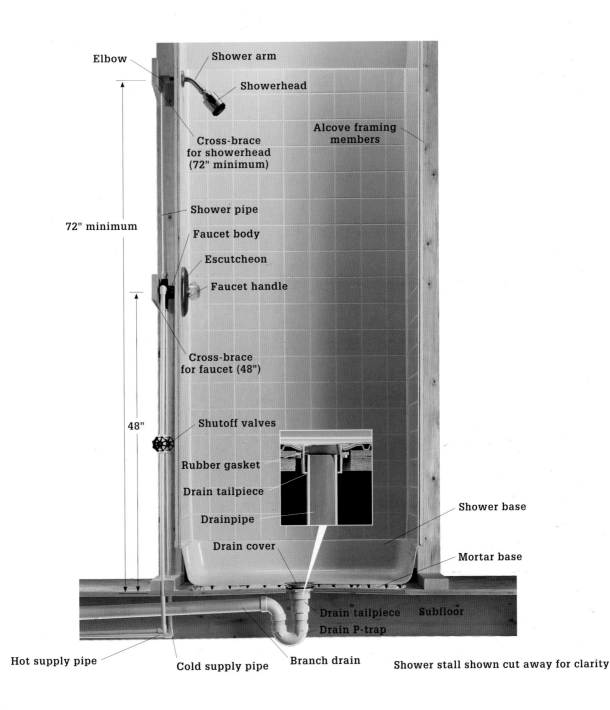

Elbow

Shower arm

Showerhead

Alcove framing members

Cross-brace for showerhead (72" minimum)

72" minimum

Shower pipe

Faucet body

Escutcheon

Faucet handle

Cross-brace for faucet (48")

48"

Shutoff valves

Rubber gasket

Drain tailpiece

Drainpipe

Shower base

Drain cover

Mortar base

Drain tailpiece   Subfloor

Drain P-trap

Hot supply pipe

Cold supply pipe

Branch drain

Shower stall shown cut away for clarity

Shower Enclosure Kits

The fastest and easiest way to create a new shower in your bathroom is to frame in the stall area with lumber and wallboard and then install a shower enclosure kit. Typically consisting of three fiberglass or plastic walls, these enclosure kits snap together at the corners and nestle inside the flanges of the shower pan to create nearly foolproof mechanical seals. Often, the walls are formed with shelves, soap holders, and other conveniences.

If you are on a tight budget, you can find extremely inexpensive enclosure kits to keep costs down. You can even create your own custom enclosure using waterproof beadboard panels and snap-together connectors. Or, you can invest in a higher grade kit made from thicker material that will last much longer. Some kits are sold with the receptor (and perhaps even the door) included. The kit shown here is designed to be attached directly to wall studs, but others require a backer wall for support. The panels are attached to the backer with high-tack panel adhesive.

Tools & Materials ▸

Tape measure
Pencil
Hammer
Carpenter's square
Screwdrivers
Pipe wrench
Level
Strap wrench
Adjustable wrench
Pliers
Drill/driver
Center punch
File
Utility knife
Hacksaw
Masking tape

Slicone caulk
  and caulk gun
Shower enclosure kit
Shower door
Showerhead
Faucet
Plumbing supplies

A paneled shower surround is inexpensive and easy to install. Designed for alcove installations, they often are sold with matching shower pans (called receptors).

How to Install a Shower Enclosure

Sill plate

Mark out the location of the shower, including any new walls, on the floor and walls. Most kits can be installed over wallboard, but you can usually achieve a more professional looking wall finish if you remove the wall covering and floor covering in the installation area. Dispose of the materials immediately and thoroughly clean the area.

If you are adding a wall to create the alcove, lay out the locations for the studs and plumbing on the new wood sill plate. Also lay out the stud locations on the cap plate that will be attached to the ceiling. Refer to the enclosure kit instructions for exact locations and dimensions of studs. Attach the sill plate to the floor with deck screws and panel adhesive, making sure it is square to the back wall and the correct distance from the side wall.

New wall stud

Align a straight 2 × 4 right next to the sill plate and make a mark on the ceiling. Use a level to extend that line directly above the sill plate. Attach the cap plate at that point.

Install the 2 × 4 studs at the outlined locations. Check with a level to make sure each stud is plumb and then attach them by driving deck screws toenail style into the sill plate and cap plate.

(continued)

5

Drain location

Cut an access hole in the floor for the drain, according to the installation manual instructions. Drill openings in the sill plate of the wet wall (the new wall in this project) for the supply pipes, also according to the instructions.

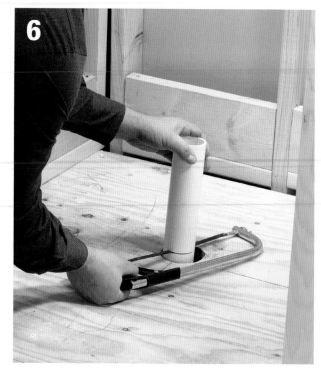

6

Install a drain pipe and branch line and then trim the drain pipe flush with the floor. If you are not experienced with plumbing, hire a plumber to install the new drain line.

7

Faucet body

Cross brace

Ball valves

Supply riser

Install new supply risers as directed in the instruction manual (again, have a plumber do this if necessary). Also install cross braces between the studs in the wet wall for mounting the faucet body and shower arm.

8

If the supply plumbing is located in a wall (old or new) that is accessible from the non-shower side, install framing for a removable access panel.

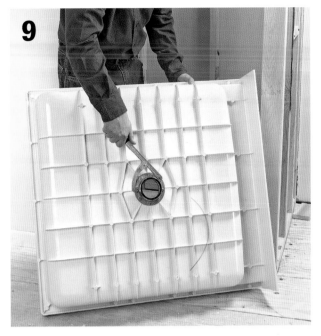

9

Attach the drain tailpiece that came with your receptor to the underside of the unit, following the manufacturer's instructions precisely. Here, an adjustable spud wrench is being used to tighten the tailpiece.

Option: To stabilize the receptor, especially if the floor is uneven, pour or trowel a layer of thinset mortar into the installation area, taking care to keep the mortar out of the drain access hole. Do not apply mortar in areas where the receptor has feet that are intended to make full contact with the floor.

10

Set the receptor in place, check to make sure it is level, and shim it if necessary. Secure the receptor with large-head roofing nails driven into the wall stud so the heads pin the flange against the stud. Do not overdrive the nails.

11

Lay out the locations for the valve hole or holes in the end wall panel that will be installed on the wet wall. Check your installation instructions. Some kits come with a template marked on the packaging carton. Cut the access hole with a hole saw and drill or with a jigsaw and fine-tooth blade. If using a jigsaw, orient the panel so the good surface is facing down.

(continued)

Position the back wall so there is a slight gap (about ¹⁄₃₂") between the bottom of the panel and the rim of the receptor— set a few small spacers on the rim if need be. Tack a pair of roofing nails above the top of the back panel to hold it in place (or use duct tape). Position both end walls and test the fits. Make clip connections between panels (inset) if your kit uses them.

Remove the end walls so you can prepare the installation area for them. If your kit recommends panel adhesive, apply it to the wall or studs. In the kit shown here, only a small bead of silicone sealant on the receptor flange is required.

Reinstall the end panels, permanently clipping them to the back panel according to the kit manufacturer's instructions. Make sure the front edges of the end panels are flush with the front of the receptor.

Once the panels are positioned correctly and snapped together, fasten them to the wall studs. If the panels have predrilled nail holes, drive roofing nails through them at each stud at the panel tops and every 4 to 6" along vertical surfaces.

Install wallcovering material above the enclosure panels and anywhere else it is needed. Use moisture-resistant materials, and maintain a gap of ¼" between the shoulders of the top panel flanges and the wallcovering.

Finish the walls and then caulk between the enclosure panels and the wallcoverings with silicone caulk.

Install the faucet handles and escutcheon and caulk around the escutcheon plate. Install the shower arm escutcheon and showerhead (see pages 120 to 129).

Access panel

Make an access panel and attach it at the framed opening created in step 8. A piece of ¼" plywood framed with mitered case molding and painted to match the wall is one idea for access panel covers.

How to Install a Hinged Shower Door

Measure the width of the shower opening. If the walls of the shower slope inward slightly before meeting the base, take your measurement from a higher point at the full width of the opening so you don't cut the door base too short. Cut the base piece to fit using a hack saw and a miter box. File the cut ends if necessary to deburr them.

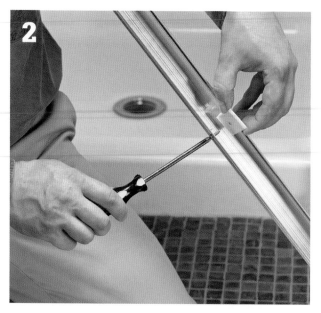

Identify which side jamb will be the hinge jamb and which will be the strike jamb according to the direction you want your hinged door to swing—an outward swing is preferred. Prepare the jambs for installation as directed in your instructions.

Place the base jamb on the curb of the shower base. If the joint where the wall meets the curb is sloped, you'll need to trim the corners of the base piece to follow the profile. Place a jamb carefully onto the base and plumb it with a level. Then, mark a drilling point by tapping a centerpunch in the middle of each nail hole in each jamb. Remove the jambs, drill pilot holes, and then attach the jambs with the provided screws.

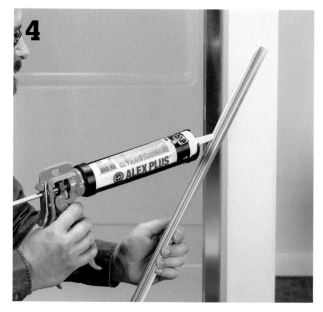

Remove the bottom track and prepare the shower base curb for installation of the base track, following the manufacturers directions. Permanently install the bottom track. Bottom tracks (not all doors have them) are usually attached to the side jambs or are held in place with adhesive. Never use fasteners to secure the tracks to the curb.

Working on the floor or another flat surface, attach the door hinge to the hinge jamb, if required. In most systems, the hinge is fitted over the hinge jamb after you attach it to the wall.

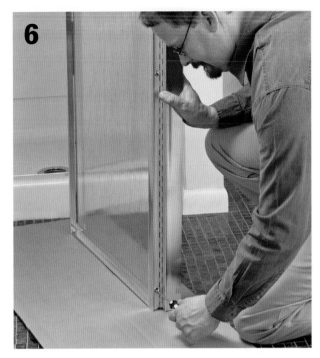

Attach the hinge to the door panel, according to the manufacturer's instructions. Attach any cap fitting that keeps water out of the jamb.

Fit the hinge jamb over the side jamb and adjust it as directed in your instruction manual. Once the clearances are correct, fasten the jambs to hang the door.

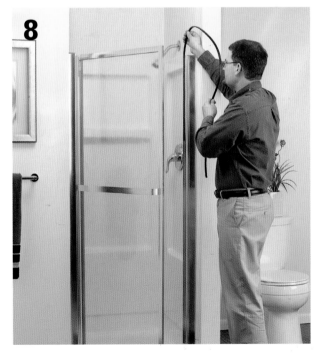

Install the magnetic strike plate and any remaining caps or accessories such as towel rods. Also attach the sweep that seals the passage, if provided.

Neo-Angle Showers

A neo-angle shower is the perfect choice when space is at a premium or when a corner is available. The shower surrounds are available as one-piece units or as two- or three-piece bases plus wall units. One-piece units are preferable because leakage is kept at a minimum, but they are so bulky that they are usually feasible only for new construction. The installation shown here features a neo-angle kit made by Kohler (see Resources, page 283). The specific steps for other models may slightly vary.

Tools & Materials ▸

Drill and bits	Basin wrench or large	Roofing nails	Silicone sealant
Hole saw	channel-type pliers	Scissors	Moisture-resistant wallboard
Hammer	Shims	File	Shower base
Level	Lath strips	Phillips screwdriver	Shower walls
Carpenter's square	Open-end wrenches	Drop cloth	Enclosure
Tape measure	Jigsaw	Center punch	Shower drain
C-clamps	Caulk gun	Masking tape	

Neo-angle showers make efficient use of bathroom floorspace by fitting into a corner. The real reason for their popularity, however, may well be the luxurious appeal of the contemporary glass wall design. Many neo-angle showers have frameless glass panels and doors, which further intensifies the contemporary appearance.

How to Install a Neo-Angle Shower

1

Remove existing wall and floor surfaces in the shower location, or remove the existing corner shower. Add additional wall studs and cross braces according to the manufacturer's instructions. All studs must be plumb and stud faces even to create a flat surface. The corner must also be square. Cut and install spacers and shims to create plumb and even corners.

2

Mark the position and size of the drain according to manufacturer's specifications and cut the drain hole through the subfloor. Install the rough plumbing to the drain hole. Install the plumbing for the faucet and showerhead. If you are not experienced with home plumbing, hire a plumber for this portion of the job.

3

On a level surface, position the walls upright. Use C-clamps to join them at the top and bottom. Mark drilling points on the flanges with a marker according to the manufacturer's instructions. At the marks, drill through both flanges with a 5/16" bit. Remove the clamps and apply a minimum 1/4" bead of mildew-resistant clear silicone sealant to one mating surface. Reposition the walls and fasten them together with a bolt and washer on one side and a washer, lock washer, and nut on the other. Tighten with a wrench, but do not overtighten.

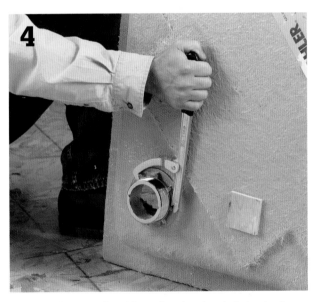

4

Hold the base on its side and apply a bead of plumber's putty around the underside of the strainer body flange. Position the strainer body through the shower drain hole. Fit the gasket and washer over the strainer body and secure it with the provided nut. Place the base over the drain hole. Check that the drain pipe extends 1¼" into the drain body.

(continued)

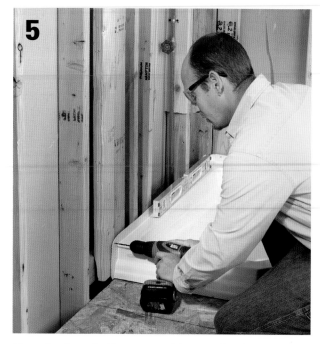

Shower arm hole

Place the base in the corner, tight up against the studs. The three front edges of the base should fit tightly to the floor. If not, you may need to use a leveling agent to level the floor. Check the base to make sure it's level along the two back sides and the angled front side. Shim along the back of the base to make the base level if needed. When level, drill holes through the base's nailing flanges at the stud locations, but do not nail it at this time.

Carefully cut the pipe entry holes in the shower walls. First, measure from the top ledge of the base to the valve stem of the faucet and the showerhead pipe. Be sure to measure carefully as misplaced holes cannot be repaired. Drill ¼" pilot holes, then use a hole saw to cut the outlets to the proper size. Refer to the faucet directions for sizing. Make all cuts from the inside of the shower walls.

Faucet cutout

Apply a minimum ¼" bead of silicone caulk around the back ledges of the base, where the walls will make contact with the base.

With a helper, carefully move and align the wall assembly onto the base. Check the walls for level and plumb and add shims if necessary. Drill pilot holes through the nailing flanges at the stud centers across the wall tops and every 8" down the nailing flanges on the sides.

9

Check that the shower base is still level. Nail through the pilot holes in the nailing flange using galvanized roofing nails. The nails should penetrate the studs to at least 1". Use longer nails if necessary due to shimming. Drive a nail at each stud location and every 4 to 6" on vertical edges.

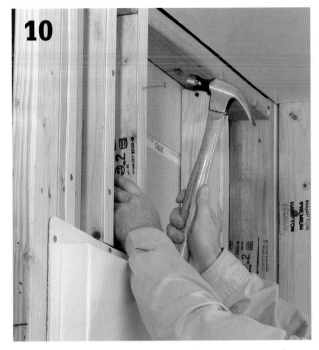

10

Nail lath strips the thickness of the shower's nailing flanges onto the studs so that the wallboard fits true. Apply silicone sealant to the nailing flanges before installing the wallboard.

11

Install wallboard so the finished paper edge is a maximum of ¼" above the top of the shower walls. Use greenboard or a mold- and moisture-resistant wallboard such as Sheetrock brand Humitek gypsum panels. Finish the wallboard by mudding and taping. Do not use metal tools to scrape mud spills from the shower surface. Use wood or plastic if necessary.

12

Lubricate the drain gasket connector with soapy water. Push the connector down into the strainer body so it fits tightly. With a hammer and thin piece of wood, drive the connector as far into the drain body as possible. You can now attach the shower arm and faucet.

(continued)

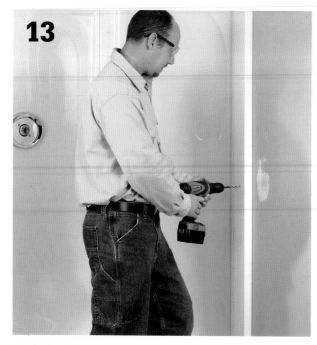

13

Mark the placement of the enclosure on the base ledge near the wall. Refer to the manufacturer's directions for the exact measurement. Align the outer edge of the wall jamb with the mark so that the sealing groove is on the outside edge. Use a level to check for plumb.

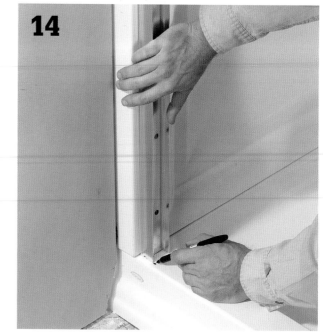

14

Mark the wall jamb screw locations onto the shower enclosure following the manufacturer's instructions. Then, predrill ⁵⁄₁₆" holes on the shower wall. Repeat for the second jamb.

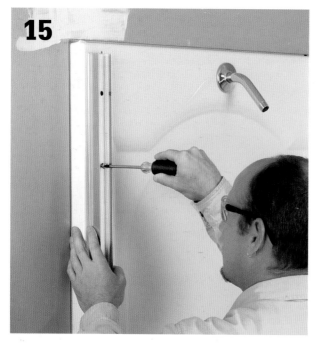

15

Align the jamb with the marks on the shower base and with the predrilled holes along the shower wall. Insert the wall anchors through the pilot holes in the shower walls. Slightly overfill the sealing groove with silicone sealant and reposition the jamb over the mounting holes. Drive three panhead screws through the holes that don't contain adjustment blocks. Drive screws by hand to avoid overtightening.

16

Carefully place the side panel expander jamb over the wall jamb. From inside the shower, use a phillips screwdriver to turn the adjustment blocks counterclockwise until they firmly contact the expander jamb. Repeat for the other side panel and check both panels for plumb.

17

Lay the shower door frame on a level surface with the beveled bridge members facing inward and the outside of the door frame facing up. Attach the flange and strike post to the bridge members with #8, 1" self-piloting screws. Place the doorframe between the side panels and align the flange lip and strike post lips with the column grooves. Push the lips into the grooves and secure with #8, ⅝" flat-head screws. Tighten by hand.

18

Decide whether the door will pivot to the left or to the right. Insert bushings into the holes on the pivot points and insert plugs into the opposite side. Insert the short end of the pivot pin into the bottom bushing and slide a nylon washer over the long end of the pivot pin. Push the door handle foam insert into the grooves of the door handle. Trim to fit.

19

Lift the door panel and place the pivot hole over the bottom pivot pin. Insert the long end of the second pivot pin through the top bushing and into the door. Open and close the door. If it rubs, make adjustments to the adjustment blocks as required. When adjustments are complete, drive a #8 × 3½" flat-head screw through the top and bottom adjustment holes to secure the side panels to the wall. Install column and post caps. Press the drain strainer plate into place.

20

Finish and seal the seams. Apply a bead of silicone sealant around the outside of the shower enclosure where it meets the base. Do not apply sealant to the inside of shower. Apply sealant on the top and outside of the bottom bridge member where it meets the door frame. Allow sealant to cure thoroughly before using the shower.

Custom Shower Bases

Building a custom-tiled shower base lets you choose the shape and size of your shower rather than having its dimensions dictated by available products. Building the base is quite simple, though it does require time and some knowledge of basic masonry techniques because the base is formed primarily using mortar. What you get for your time and trouble can be spectacular.

Before designing a shower base, contact your local building department regarding code restrictions and to secure the necessary permits. Most codes require water controls to be accessible from outside the shower and describe acceptable door positions and operation. Requirements like these influence the size and position of the base.

Choosing the tile before finalizing the design lets you size the base to require mostly or only full tiles. Consider using small tile and gradate the color from top to bottom or in a sweep across the walls. Or, use trim tile and listellos on the walls to create an interesting focal point.

Whatever tile you choose, remember to seal the grout in your new shower and to maintain it carefully over the years. Water-resistant grout protects the structure of the shower and prolongs its useful life.

Tools & Materials ▸

Tape measure	16d galvanized
Circular saw	common nails
Hammer	15# building paper
Utility knife	3-piece shower drain
Stapler	PVC primer & cement
2-ft. level	Galvanized finish nails
Mortar mixing box	Galvanized metal lath
Trowel	Thick-bed floor mortar
Wood float	Latex mortar additive
Felt-tip marker	CPE waterproof
Ratchet wrench	membrane &
Expandable stopper	preformed dam
Drill	corners
Tin snips	CPE membrane
Torpedo level	solvent glue
Tools & materials for	CPE membrane
installing tile	sealant
2 × 4 and 2 × 10	Cementboard &
framing lumber	materials

Choosing a custom shower base gives you myriad options for the shape and size of your shower.

Cross-Section of a Shower Pan

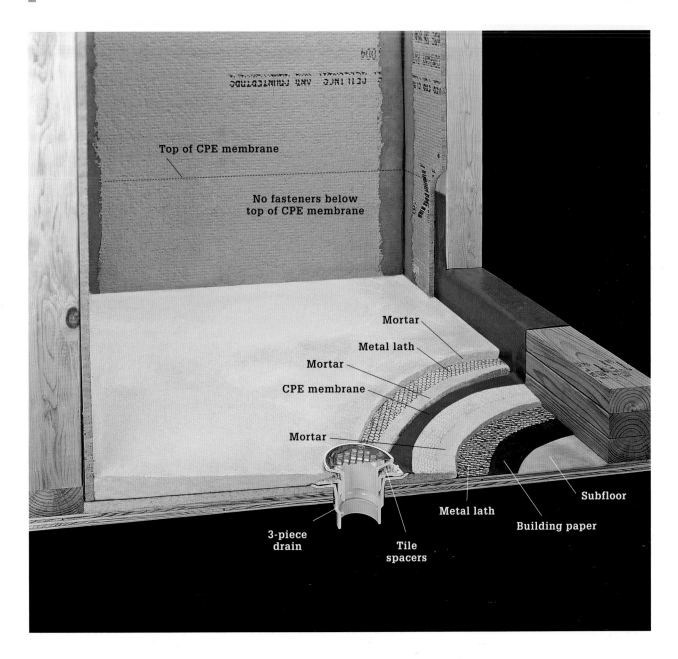

Top of CPE membrane

No fasteners below top of CPE membrane

Mortar

Metal lath

Mortar

CPE membrane

Mortar

Subfloor

Metal lath

Building paper

3-piece drain

Tile spacers

Tips for Building a Custom Shower Base ▸

A custom-tiled shower base is built in three layers to ensure proper water drainage: the pre pan, the shower pan, and the shower floor. A mortar pre pan is built first on top of the subfloor, establishing a slope toward the drain of ¼" for every 12" of shower floor. Next, a waterproof chlorinated polyethylene (CPE) membrane forms the shower pan, providing a watertight seal for the shower base. Finally, a second mortar bed reinforced with wire mesh is installed for the shower floor, providing a surface for tile installation. If water penetrates the tiled shower floor, the shower pan and sloped pre pan will direct it to the weep holes of the 3-piece drain.

One of the most important steps in building a custom-tiled shower base is testing the shower pan after installation. This allows you to locate and fix any leaks to prevent costly damage.

How to Build a Custom-tiled Shower Base

Remove building materials to expose subfloor and stud walls. Cut three 2 × 4s for the curb and fasten them to the floor joists and the studs at the shower threshold with 16d galvanized common nails. Also cut 2 × 10 lumber to size and install in the stud bays around the perimeter of the shower base. Install (or have installed) drain and supply plumbing.

Staple 15-pound building paper to the subfloor of the shower base. Disassemble the 3-piece shower drain and glue the bottom piece to the drain pipe with PVC cement. Partially screw the drain bolts into the drain piece, and stuff a rag into the drain pipe to prevent mortar from falling into the drain.

Mark the height of the bottom drain piece on the wall farthest from the center of the drain. Measure from the center of the drain straight across to that wall, then raise the height mark ¼" for every 12" of shower floor to slope the pre pan toward the drain. Trace a reference line at the height mark around the perimeter of the entire alcove, using a level.

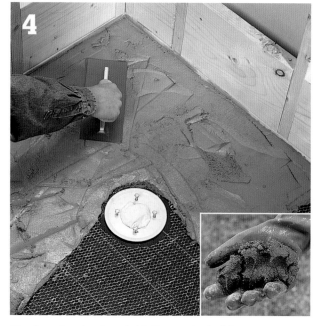

Staple galvanized metal lath over the building paper; cut a hole in the lath ½" from the drain. Mix thinset mortar to a fairly dry consistency, using a latex additive for strength; mortar should hold its shape when squeezed (inset). Trowel the mortar onto the subfloor, building the pre pan from the flange of the drain piece to the height line on the perimeter of the walls.

5

Continue using the trowel to form the pre pan, checking the slope using a level and filling any low spots with mortar. Finish the surface of the pre pan with a wood float until it is even and smooth. Allow the mortar to cure overnight.

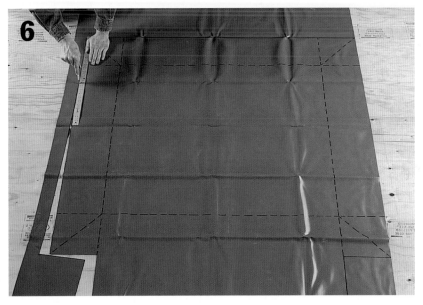

6

Measure the dimensions of the shower floor, and mark it out on a sheet of CPE waterproof membrane, using a felt-tipped marker. From the floor outline, measure out and mark an additional 8" for each wall and 16" for the curb end. Cut the membrane to size, using a utility knife and straightedge. Be careful to cut on a clean, smooth surface to prevent puncturing the membrane. Lay the membrane onto the shower pan.

7

Measure to find the exact location of the drain and mark it on the membrane, outlining the outer diameter of the drain flange. Cut a circular piece of CPE membrane roughly 2" larger than the drain flange, then use CPE membrane solvent glue to weld it into place and reinforce the seal at the drain.

8

Apply CPE sealant around the drain. Fold the membrane along the floor outline. Set the membrane over the pre pan so the reinforced drain seal is centered over the drain bolts. Working from the drain to the walls, carefully tuck the membrane tight into each corner, folding the extra material into triangular flaps.

(continued)

9

Apply CPE solvent glue to one side, press the flap flat, then staple it in place. Staple only the top edge of the membrane to the blocking; do not staple below the top of the curb, or on the curb itself.

10

Dam corner

At the shower curb, cut the membrane along the studs so it can be folded over the curb. Solvent glue a dam corner at each inside corner of the curb. Do not fasten the dam corners with staples.

11

At the reinforced drain seal on the membrane, locate and mark the drain bolts. Press the membrane down around the bolts, then use a utility knife to carefully cut a slit just large enough for the bolts to poke through. Push the membrane down over the bolts.

12

Use a utility knife to carefully cut away only enough of the membrane to expose the drain and allow the middle drain piece to fit in place. Remove the drain bolts, then position the middle drain piece over the bolt holes. Reinstall the bolts, tightening them evenly and firmly to create a watertight seal.

Test the shower pan for leaks overnight. Fill the shower pan with water, to 1" below the top of the curb. Mark the water level and let the water sit overnight. If the water level remains the same, the pan holds water. If the level is lower, locate and fix leaks in the pan using patches of membrane and CPE solvent.

Install cementboard on the alcove walls, using ¼" wood shims to lift the bottom edge off the CPE membrane. To prevent puncturing the membrane, do not use fasteners in the lower 8" of the cementboard. Cut a piece of metal lath to fit around the three sides of the curb. Bend the lath so it tightly conforms to the curb. Pressing the lath against the top of the curb, staple it to the outside face of the curb. Mix enough mortar for the two sides of the curb.

Overhang the front edge of the curb with a straight 1× board so it is flush with the outer wall material. Apply mortar to the mesh with a trowel, building to the edge of the board. Clear away excess mortar, then use a torpedo level to check for plumb, making adjustments as needed. Repeat for the inside face of the curb. *Note: The top of the curb will be finished after tile is installed (Step 19). Allow the mortar to cure overnight.*

Attach the drain strainer piece to the drain, adjusting it to a minimum of 1½" above the shower pan. On one wall, mark 1½" up from the shower pan, then use a level to draw a reference line around the perimeter of the shower base. Because the pre pan establishes the ¼" per foot slope, this measurement will maintain that slope.

(continued)

17

Spread tile spacers over the weep holes of the drain to prevent mortar from plugging the holes. Mix the floor mortar, then build up the shower floor to roughly half the planned thickness of this layer. Cut metal lath to cover the mortar bed, keeping it ½" from the drain (see photo in Step 18).

18

Continue to add mortar, building the floor to the reference line on the walls. Use a level to check the slope, and pack mortar into low spots with a trowel. Leave space around the drain flange for the thickness of the tile. Float the surface using a wood float until it is smooth and slopes evenly to the drain. When finished, allow the mortar to cure overnight before installing the tiles.

19

Install the tile. At the curb, cut the tiles for the inside to protrude ½" above the unfinished top of the curb, and the tiles for the outside to protrude ⅝" above the top, establishing a ⅛" slope so water drains back into the shower. Use a level to check the tops of the tiles for level as you work.

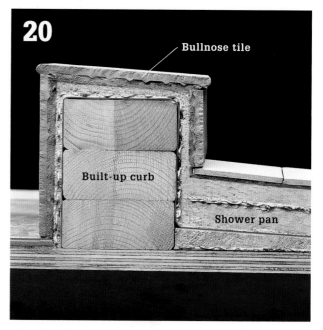

20

Mix enough mortar to cover the unfinished top of the curb, then pack it in place between the tiles, using a trowel. Screed off the excess mortar flush with the tops of the side tiles. Allow the mortar to cure, then install bullnose cap tile. Install the wall tile, then grout, clean, and seal all the tile. After the grout has cured fully, run a bead of silicone caulk around all inside corners to create control joints.

Textured surfaces improve the safety of tile floors, especially in wet areas such as this open shower. The shower area is designated effectively by a simple shift in color and size.

The raised curb on this open shower keeps most of the water headed toward the drain. But no matter, the entire bathroom is tiled, so stray droplets are no problem.

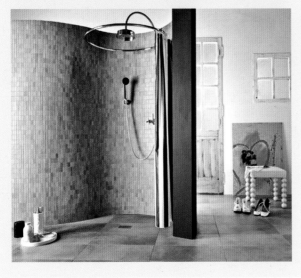

Mosaic tile, with its mesh backing and small shapes, often works well on curved walls such as the one that forms this shower. The rectangular shape of the individual mosaic tiles complements the shape of the post at the corner of the shower.

Glass Block Showers

A glass block shower is one of the most striking additions you can make to a bathroom. Creating an aura of elegance and luxury, glass block instantly adds a distinctive sparkle to a room, brightening even the dingiest corners.

In this project we are building our shower around a standard fiberglass shower base (receptor), modified to fit inside a concrete curb. Because glass block cannot be cut, it is crucial that the shower base fit the length of the glass block walls. We are using a 34" × 48" base to fit our shower design and 8" × 8" glass block. You can also consider building a custom-tiled shower base or using specially designed prefab shower bases built to hold and support glass block.

The key to any shower installation is making sure the base remains watertight. Concrete is a better option than wood for the curb in this project because it easily molds around the shower base, ensuring a tight fit, and it will not swell and produce gaps if water ever gets in. The curb is firmly anchored to the floor by pouring it over lag screws partially driven into the subfloor.

For best results when laying glass block, mix just enough mortar for about 30 minutes of work at a time. If possible, try to lay half of the courses on one day and finish on a second day. This will give the mortar in the first section time to harden, and will make the wall more stable as you climb higher.

The glass block wall needs to be secured to the adjoining wall using metal panel anchors. Add foam expansion strips between the glass block and the existing wall to allow for some independent movement of each as the house settles.

Because of its weight (each block weighs 6 pounds), a glass block shower requires a sturdy foundation. A 4"-thick concrete basement floor should be strong enough, but a wood floor may need reinforcing. Contact your local building department for requirements in your area. Also bear in mind that glass block products and installation techniques vary by manufacturer—ask a glass block retailer or manufacturer for advice about the best products and methods for your project.

Tools & Materials ▸

Jigsaw	Glass block
Straightedge	(standard,
Hammer	corner, end)
Plumb bob	Plastic sheeting
Chalk line	4" lag screws
Drill	Concrete
Mixing box	Asphalt roofing
Socket wrench	cement
Paintbrush	Panel anchors
Wire cutter	2½" drywall screws
Rubber-ended trowel	Foam expansion strips
Level	Glass block mortar
Jointing tool	Glass block spacers
Sponge	Straight board
Fiberglass	Ladder-type
shower base	reinforcement wire
Dry-set mortar	16-gauge wire
1 × 6 lumber	Silicone caulk
½" × 2" filler strips	Mortar sealer
Screed board	

A glass block shower can add dazzle to your bathroom, but it requires a strong foundation.

Construction & Plumbing Tip ▸

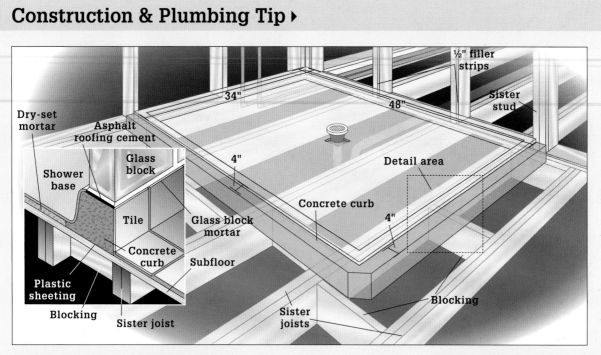

Install water supply and drain pipes before you begin the construction of the glass block shower. If you have to adjust the position of your base to fit the block wall (Step 2), take this into account as you mark the location for the shower drain.

How to Build a Glass Block Shower

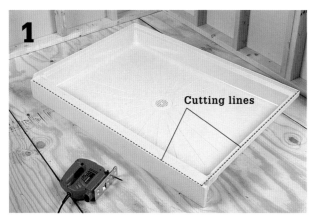

In order to create a watertight seal between the shower base, the concrete curb, and the glass block, use a jigsaw to remove the front edge of the shower base threshold. Remove any vertical flange along the glass block side of the base to create a smooth transition between the base and the curb. To ensure straight cuts, use a straightedge to guide your saw.

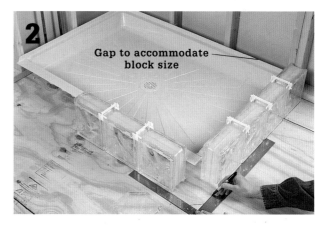

Set the shower base in place and dry-lay the first course of glass block and spacers. To allow for the wall material and expansion strips, include a gap between the stud wall and the first block. If there is space between the front block wall and the base, pull the base out from the wall slightly, so it is flush with the inside edge of the glass block, then mark reference lines for the curb outline. Attach ½" filler strips to the studs before you install the backerboard and wall material.

(continued)

Prepare the shower base drain for the installation (inset). Mix a batch of thin-set mortar, then apply a 1" layer to the subfloor, covering the shower base area. Install the base onto the drain pipe. Press the base into the mortar and adjust it so it is level. Allow the mortar to dry for 6 to 8 hours.

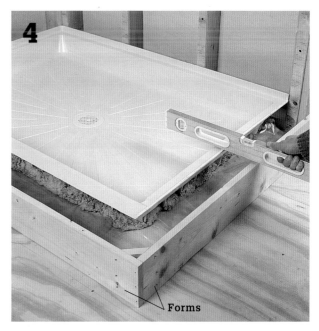

Build forms for the concrete curb from 1× lumber ripped even with the height of the shower base. Align the forms along the reference lines, check that they are level with the top edge of the base, then temporarily anchor them to the subfloor. Line the bottom of the forms with plastic to keep moisture from soaking into the subfloor. To provide anchoring for the curb, drive 4" lag screws 2" into the subfloor inside the forms, spaced every 12".

Mix a batch of concrete according to the manufacturer's directions. Pack the forms evenly with concrete. Rap the forms with a hammer to release air bubbles and settle the concrete. Run a 2 × 4 screed board over the forms to level off the concrete. Clean off concrete from walls of the shower pan. Cover the curb with plastic and allow it to harden for two days, then remove the forms.

Wall material, such as solid-surface or fiberglass shower surrounds or ceramic tile, can be installed either before or after the glass block installation, but will go more quickly without the walls in the way. However, it is best to wait to tile around the outside of the curb until the finished flooring has been installed.

7

Spread a thick layer of asphalt roofing cement over the top of the dry curb, just up to the lip of the shower base. This will help to ensure a watertight seal between the curb and shower base and provide a smooth base for the mortar bed. When the asphalt has completely dried, you can begin laying block.

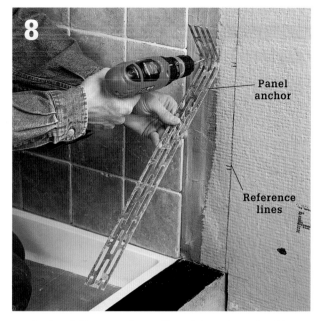

8

Panel anchor

Reference lines

Mark plumb lines on the wall, straight up from the sides of the curb. Mark the finished height of each course along the lines. Fasten a panel anchor to the anchor stud at the top of every second course using 2½" drywall screws. Cut foam expansion strips to size and adhere them to the wall between the anchors. *Note: When installing the glass block, do not mortar between the blocks and the expansion strips.*

9

Mix a batch of glass block mortar and lay a ⅜"-thick mortar bed along one side of the curb. Beginning at the corner, lay the first course. Use spacers at the mortar joint locations (follow the manufacturer's directions for modifying spacers for the corner blocks and the bottom and sides of the wall). Butter the leading edge of each block with enough mortar to fill the sides of both blocks. Make sure the faces of the block are plumb with the curb edge.

10

Expansion strips

Lay the remainder of the course, plumbing and leveling each block as you work. Then check the entire course using a flat board and a level. Tap the blocks into place using the rubber end of your trowel or a rubber mallet. At the top of the course, fill the joints with mortar. Then lay a ¼" bed of mortar for the second course.

(continued)

Lay the block for the second course, this time starting at the wall. For the remaining courses, install the corner block last. Check each block for level and plumb as you work. Apply a half bed of mortar (⅛") over the second course. Press the panel anchor into the mortar. Repeat this process at each anchor location.

Add reinforcement wire in the same joints as the panel anchors, overlapping the anchors by 6". At the corners, cut the inner rail of the wire, bend the outer rail to follow the corner, then tie the inner rail ends together with 16-gauge wire. Cover the wire and panel anchor with another ⅛" mortar bed, then lay the next course of block.

Check the mortar after each course: when it is hard enough to resist light finger pressure (usually within 30 minutes), twist off the T-spacer tabs (inset) and pack mortar in the voids. Then, tool all of the joints with a jointing tool. Clean the glass block thoroughly using a wet sponge, and rinse it often. Allow the surface to dry, then remove any cloudy residue with a clean, dry cloth.

Allow the mortar to dry for 24 hours, then run a thick bead of silicone caulk between the glass block and the shower base. Caulk the seams between the wall and the glass block, both inside and outside the shower. Install a door, if desired, according to the manufacturer's directions. After two weeks, apply a sealer to the mortar to prevent discoloration. *Note: The shower can be used before sealing as long as the mortar has dried.*

Variation: Building a Floor-to-Ceiling Glass Block Shower

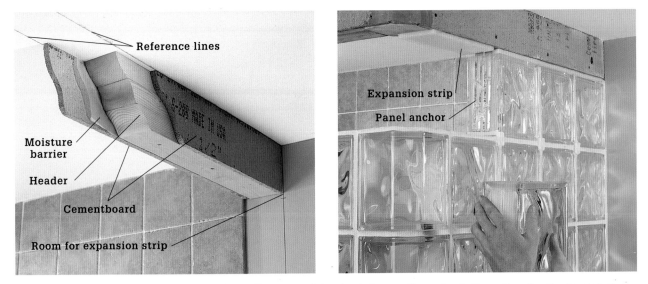

To extend your glass block shower to the ceiling, extend the plumb lines on the wall onto the ceiling directly above your curb. Snap chalk lines to mark the location for the header. To determine the height of the header, measure from the final course mark on the wall to the ceiling and then subtract ⅜" for expansion. Build the header from pressure-treated 2 × 4s, ripped to 3" in width, stacked and fastened with construction adhesive and 2½" screws. Attach ½" cementboard to the sides of the header, including a moisture barrier on the shower side (left). As you install the final course of glass block, attach panel anchors to the header, running vertically between every other block along the top row (right). Install expansion strips above the final course. Do not mortar between the block and the expansion strips. Caulk the gap between the header and the final course of block. Finish by installing tile along the sides of the header.

Glass Block Shower Variations

A glass block wall can work anywhere in the bathroom. Here, built between a tub and shower, glass block divides private areas while still bathing the room in light.

For a customized glass block shower, build a mortared and tiled shower base to fit your shower designs.

Glass block shower kits include a prefab shower base with a built-in support for the glass block. They are installed just like tradtional shower bases, but the need to modify the shower base and pour a concrete curb is eliminated.

Tubs & Jetted Tubs

Installing tubs and whirlpools is really more of an exercise in frame carpentry and wall finishing than it is a plumbing job.

If your tub is a standard alcove model with three open sides and a decorative front apron, then you'll have to do some considerable work to the wall—especially the wet wall and the floor. Generally, alcove tubs are supported by horizontal 1 × 4 ledgers that are attached to the wall studs. Tubs also can be installed in an island installation or against a flat wall. In each of these cases, the project involves constructing either two or three short 2 × 4 stub walls to support the edges of the top deck, or actually building a finished deck platform for support (platform decks usually are finished with tile).

Perhaps the best piece of advice to keep in mind as you prepare to install your tub or whirlpool tub is to install as many of the plumbing components as you possibly can before you move the tub into the installation area.

The construction techniques used to install tubs and jetted tubs are the same—but the plumbing and wiring for jetted tubs is more complex.

Choose the correct tub for your plumbing setup. Alcove-installed tubs with only one side apron are sold as either left-hand or right-hand models, depending on the location of the predrilled drain and overflow holes in the tub. To determine which type you need, face into the alcove and check whether the tub drain is on your right or your left.

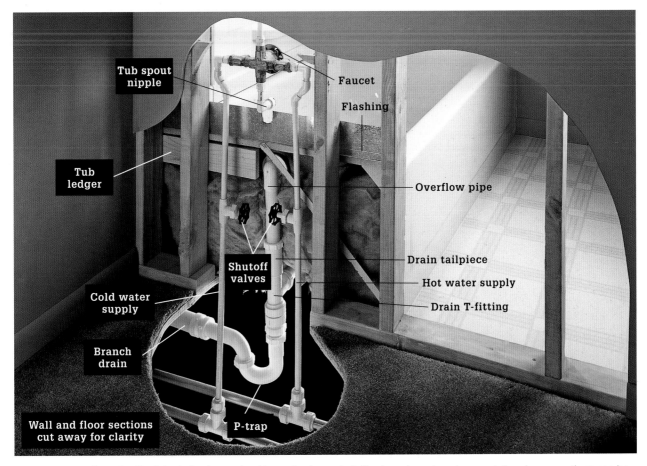

The plumbing for a bathtub labels:
- Tub spout nipple
- Faucet
- Flashing
- Tub ledger
- Overflow pipe
- Shutoff valves
- Drain tailpiece
- Hot water supply
- Drain T-fitting
- Cold water supply
- Branch drain
- P-trap
- Wall and floor sections cut away for clarity

The plumbing for a bathtub includes hot and cold supply pipes, shutoff valves, faucet, and a spout. Supply connections can be made before or after the tub is installed. The drain-waste-overflow system for a bathtub includes the overflow pipe, drain T-fitting, P-trap, and branch drain. The overflow pipe assembly is attached to the tub before installation.

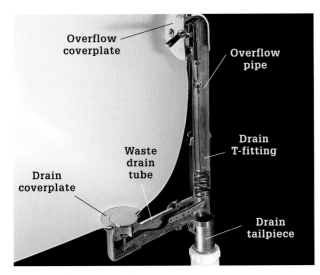

Labels:
- Overflow coverplate
- Overflow pipe
- Waste drain tube
- Drain T-fitting
- Drain coverplate
- Drain tailpiece

A drain-waste-overflow kit with a stopper mechanism must be attached to the tub before it is installed. Available in both brass and plastic types, most kits include an overflow coverplate, a height-adjustable overflow pipe, a drain T-fitting and tailpiece, a waste drain tube, and a drain coverplate that screws into the drain tube.

Add fiberglass insulation around the body of a steel bathtub to reduce noise and conserve heat. Before setting the tub in position, wrap unfaced batting around the tub, and secure it with string or twine. For showers, deck-mounted whirlpools, and saunas, insulate between the framing members.

Alcove Bathtubs

As with showers, standard bathtubs are typically installed in an alcove. If you are building a new alcove, follow the tub manufacturer's specifications regarding its size. Tub alcoves can be finished with ceramic tile or prefabricated panels.

Take care when handling a new bathtub, since the greatest risk of damaging it occurs during the installation. If the inside of your tub has a protective layer of removable plastic, leave it on until you've completed the installation. Also set a layer of cardboard into the bottom of the tub for added protection while you work.

Tools & Materials ▸

Channel-type pliers	Tub protector
Hacksaw	Shims
4-ft. level	Deck screws
Tape measure	Drain-waste-
Saw	overflow kit
Screwdriver	Lumber (1 × 3,
Drill	1 × 4, 2 × 4)
Adjustable wrench	Roofing nails
Hammer	Tub & tile caulk
Trowel	Dry-set mortar
Caulk gun	Plumber's putty

Ceramic tile is a popular wall finish for an alcove bathtub. With properly sealed grout, tile is virtually waterproof.

How to Install an Alcove Bathtub

Attach the faucet body and showerhead fittings to the water supply pipes, and secure the assemblies to 1 × 4 cross braces before installing the tub. Trim the drain pipe to the height specified by the drain-waste-overflow kit manufacturer.

Place a tub-bottom protector, which can be cut from the shipping carton, into the tub. Test-fit the tub by sliding it into the alcove so it rests on the subfloor, flush against the wall studs.

Check the tub rim with a level. If necessary, shim below the tub until it is level. Mark the top of the nailing flange at each stud. Remove the bathtub from the alcove.

Measure the distance from the top of the nailing flange to the underside of the tub rim (inset), and subtract that amount from the marks on the wall studs. Draw a line at that point on each wall stud.

(continued)

5

Cut ledger board strips from 1 × 4s, and attach them to the wall studs just below the marks for the underside of the tub rim (step 4) using deck screws. You may have to install the boards in sections to make room for any structural braces at the ends of the tub.

6

Adjust the drain-waste-overflow assembly to fit the drain and overflow openings. Attach the gaskets and washers as directed by the manufacturer, then position the assembly against the tub drain and overflow openings. Prop up the tub on 2 × 4s, if necessary.

7

Apply plumber's putty to the bottom of the drain coverplate flange, then insert the drain piece into the drain hole in the tub. Screw the drain piece into the waste drain tube, tightening until snug, then insert the pop-up drain plug. Insert the drain plug linkage into the overflow opening, and attach the overflow coverplate with long screws driven into the mounting flange on the overflow pipe. Adjust the drain plug linkage as directed by the manufacturer.

8

Use a trowel to apply a ½"-thick layer of thin-set mortar to the subfloor, covering the entire area where the tub will rest. Lay 1 × 4 runners across the alcove so they rest on the back wall's bottom plate. The runners will allow you to slide the tub into the alcove without disturbing the mortar base.

Slide the tub over the runners and into position, then remove the runners, allowing the tub to settle into the mortar. Press down evenly on the tub rims until they touch the ledger boards.

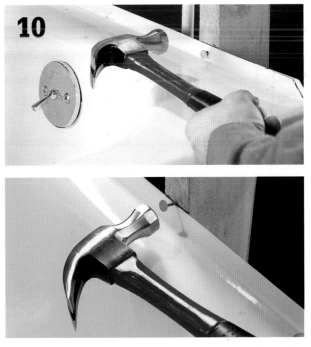

Before the mortar sets, nail the tub rim flanges to the wall studs. Attach the rim flanges either by drilling pilot holes into the flanges and nailing with galvanized roofing nails (top), or by driving roofing nails into the studs so the head of the nail covers the rim flange (bottom). After the rim flanges are secured, allow the mortar to dry for 6 to 8 hours.

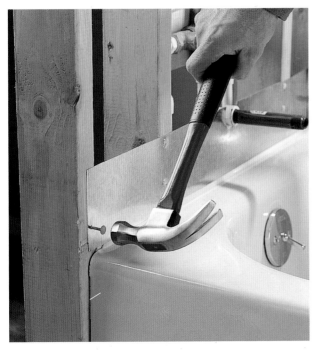

Option: Attach 4"-wide strips of galvanized metal roof flashing over the tub flange to help keep water out of the wall. Leave a ¼" expansion gap between the flashing and the tub rim. Nail the flashing to each wall stud using 1" galvanized roofing nails.

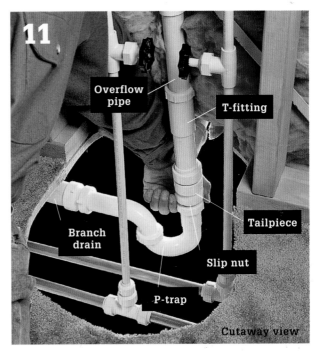

Overflow pipe · T-fitting · Tailpiece · Slip nut · P-trap · Branch drain · Cutaway view

Adjust the drain tailpiece so the overflow assembly will fit into the P-trap (you may have to trim it with a hacksaw), then connect it with a slip nut. Install the wall surfaces, then install the faucet handle and tub spout. Finally, caulk all around the bathtub.

3-Piece Tub Surrounds

No one wants bathroom fixtures that are aging or yellowed from years of use. A shiny new tub surround can add sparkle and freshness to your dream bath.

Tub surrounds come in many different styles, materials, and price ranges. Choose the features you want and measure your existing bathtub surround for sizing. Surrounds typically come in three or five pieces. A three-panel surround is being installed here, but the process is similar for five-panel systems.

Surface preparation is important for good glue adhesion. Plastic tiles and wallpaper must be removed and textured plaster must be sanded smooth. Surrounds can be installed over ceramic tile that is well attached and in good condition, but it must be sanded and primed. All surfaces must be primed with a water-based primer.

Tools & Materials ▸

Jigsaw	Adhesive
Hole saw	Screwdriver
Drill	Adjustable wrench
Measuring tape	Pry bar
Level	Hammer
Caulking gun	3-piece tub surround

Three-piece tub surrounds are inexpensive and come in many colors and styles. The typical unit has two end panels and a back panel that overlap in the corners to form a watertight seal. They are formed from fiberglass, PVC, acrylic, or proprietary resin-based polymers. Five piece versions are also available and typically have more features such as integral soap shelves and even cabinets.

How to Install a 3-Piece Tub Surround

1

Remove the old plumbing fixtures and wallcoverings in the tub area. In some cases you can attach surround panels to old tileboard or even tile, but it is generally best to remove the wallcoverings down to the studs if you can, so you may inspect for leaks or damage.

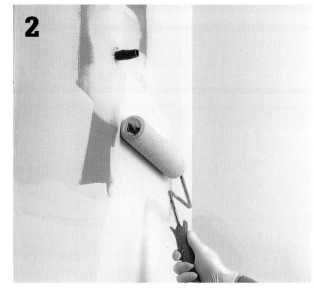

2

Replace the wallcoverings with appropriate materials, such as water and mold resistant wallboard or cementboard (for ceramic tile installations). Make sure the new wall surfaces are smooth and flat. Some surround kit manufacturers recommend that you apply a coat of primer to sheet goods such as greenboard to create a better bonding surface for the panel adhesive.

3

Test-fit the panels before you start; the tub may have settled unevenly or the walls may be out of plumb. Check the manufacturer's directions for distinguishing right and left panels. Place a panel in position on the tub ledge. Use a level across the top of the panel to determine if it is level. Create a vertical reference line to mark the edge of the panel on the plumbing end.

Test-fitting Tip ▸

Ensure a perfect fit by taping the surround panels to the walls in the tub area. Make sure the tops are level when the overlap seams are aligned and that you have a consistent gap between the panel bottoms and the tub flange. Mark the panels for cutting if necessary and, once the panels have been removed, make any adjustments to the walls that are needed.

(continued)

4

After performing the test-fit, check the fitting instructions to see if you need to trim any of the pieces. Follow the manufacturer instructions for cutting. Here, we had to cut the corner panels because the instructions advise not to overlap the back or side panel over the corner panels by more than 3". Cut panels using a jigsaw and a fine-tooth blade that is appropriate for cutting fiberglass or acrylic tileboard.

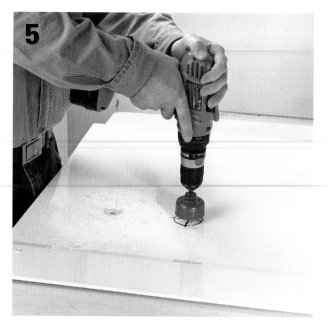

5

Lay out the locations of the faucets, spout, and shower arm. Measure in from the vertical reference line (made in Step 3) and up from the top of the tub ledge. Re-measure for accuracy, as any cuts to the surround are final. Place the panel face-up on a sheet of plywood. Mark the location of the holes. Cut the holes ½" larger than the pipe diameter. If your faucet has a recessed trim plate, cut the hole to fit the recess. Using a hole saw or a jigsaw, cut out the plumbing access holes.

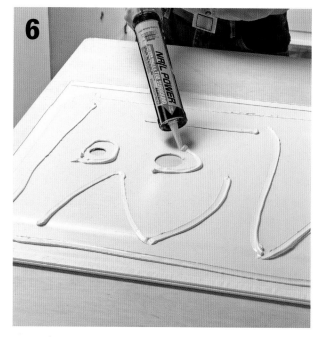

6

Apply the panel adhesive to the back of an end plumbing panel. Circle the plumbing outlet holes 1" from the edge. Follow the manufacturer's application pattern. Do not apply adhesive closer than 1" to the double-sided tape or the bottom edge of the panel.

7

Remove the protective backing from the tape. Carefully lift the panel by the edges and place against the corner and top of the tub ledge. Press firmly from top to bottom in the corner, then throughout the panel.

8

Test-fit the opposite end panel and make any necessary adjustments. Apply the adhesive, remove the protective backing from the tape, and put in place. Apply pressure to the corner first from top to bottom, and then apply pressure throughout.

9

Apply adhesive to the back panel following the manufacturer's instructions. Maintain a 1" space between adhesive tape and the bottom of the panel. Remove protective backing from the tape. Lift the panel by the edges and carefully center between the two end panels. When positioned, firmly press in place from top to bottom.

10

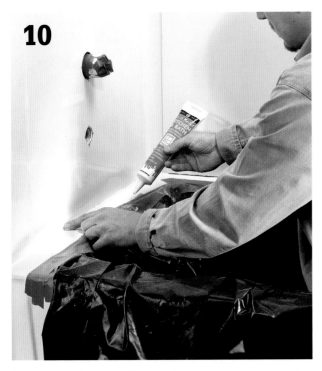

Apply caulk to the bottom and top edges of the panels and at panel joints. Dip your fingertip in water and use it to smooth the caulk to a uniform bead.

11

Apply silicone caulk to escutcheons or trim plates and reinstall them. Allow a minimum of 24 hours for caulk and adhesive to cure thoroughly before using the shower or tub.

Solid-Surface Surrounds

Bathtub surrounds are designed and installed in the same way as shower surrounds. Though fiberglass and plastic fabricated enclosures, as well as custom ceramic tile, are traditional materials for surrounds, the use of solid-surface materials—materials common to sinks and countertops—are growing in popularity.

Solid-surface surrounds are available in kits with ¼" panels that are installed much the same way as fiberglass enclosures. The panels can be fastened to any wall material—cementboard and greenboard are the most common in new construction. Walls must be free of debris and sealed with two coats of primer. Solid-surface panels can be installed over old tile, though you must chisel out any loose tiles and install filler strips the same thickness as the tiles (usually ¼") to fill any gaps between the walls and panels.

Solid-surface bathtub surrounds are becoming ever-more popular and are available as kits (see Resources, page 284).

Tools & Materials ▸

Tape measure	Sandpaper
4-ft. level	Pressure-sensitive
Jigsaw	tape
Drill with a hole saw	Panel adhesive
or spade bits	Tub & tile caulk
Caulk gun	Masking tape
Solid-surface	1× and 2× lumber
surround kit	

How to Install a Solid-Surface Bathtub Surround

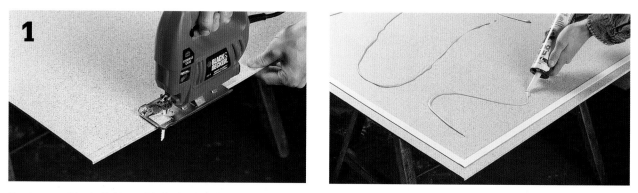

Begin panel installation with the back wall. Measure and mark the dimensions on the back side of the panel, then cut using a jigsaw (left photo). Remove rough edges with fine or medium sandpaper. Test-fit the panel to ensure a proper fit. On the back side of the panel, apply pressure-sensitive tape 1" from each edge, then apply panel adhesive in the field (right photo). Keep the adhesive 1" from the tape edges.

Remove the backing of the pressure-sensitive tape. Lift the panel into position, tight into one corner, then firmly press the panel to the wall. Using your hands, smooth across the entire panel while applying pressure to ensure firm contact with the wall. Follow the same procedures to install the panel on the side wall, opposite the plumbing outlets.

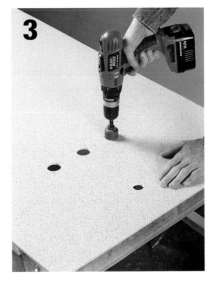

For the wall with the plumbing outlets, measure and trim the panel to size. Measure the location of the plumbing outlets on the wall, then transfer the dimensions to the finished side of the panel. Drill holes ½" larger than the plumbing outlets, using a drill and a hole saw or spade bits. Place a scrap board beneath the cutout area to ensure a clean cut.

Test-fit the panel and make any necessary adjustments, then install, following the same procedures as with the first two panels. After all the panels are installed, seal each joint, seam, and edge with a bead of caulk.

Follow the manufacturer's instructions to install any trim. For corner molding, test-fit each piece and trim to size, then apply a bead of panel adhesive down the corner joints and firmly press the moldings into position. Temporarily secure the molding with tape.

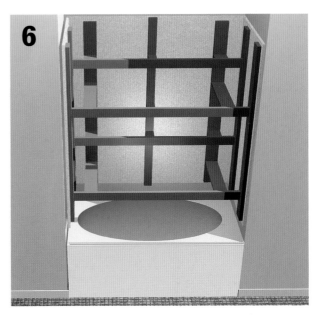

Use 1× and 2× lumber to construct temporary bracing to ensure a strong adhesive bond. Use soft cloth or carpet scraps to prevent the bracing from scratching the surround. Allow the adhesive to cure overnight, then remove the bracing. Wipe the surround clean with a damp cloth.

Sliding Tub Doors

Curtains on your bathtub shower are a hassle. If you forget to tuck them inside the tub, water flows freely onto your bathroom floor. If you forget to slide them closed, mildew sets up shop in the folds. And every time you brush against them they stick to your skin. Shower curtains certainly don't add much elegance or charm to a dream bath. Neither does a deteriorated door. Clean up the look of your bathroom, and even give it an extra touch of elegance, with a new sliding tub door.

When shopping for a sliding tub door, you have a choice of framed or frameless. A framed door is edged in metal. The metal framing is typically aluminum but is available in many finishes, including those that resemble gold, brass, or chrome. Glass options are also plentiful. You can choose between frosted or pebbled glass, clear, mirrored, tinted, or patterned glass. Doors can be installed on ceramic tile walls or through a fiberglass tub surround.

Tools & Materials ▸

Measuring tape
Pencil & marker
Hacksaw
Miter box
Level
Drill
Center punch

Masonry bit
  for tile wall
Phillips screwdriver
Caulk gun
Masking tape
Silicone sealant
Tub door kit

A sliding tub door in a metal frame gives the room a sleek, clean look and is just one of the available options.

How to Install Sliding Tub Doors

1

Remove the existing door and inspect the walls. Use a razor blade to cut sealant from tile and metal surfaces. Do not use a razor blade on fiberglass surfaces. Remove remaining sealant by scraping or pulling. Use a silicone sealant remover to remove all residue. Remove shower curtain rods, if present. Check the walls and tub ledge for plumb and level.

2

Measure the distance between the finished walls along the top of the tub ledge. Refer to the manufacturer's instructions for figuring the track dimensions. For the product seen here, ³⁄₁₆" is subtracted from the measurement to calculate the track dimensions.

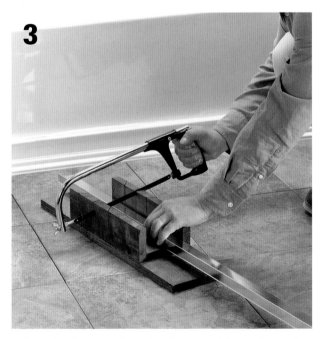

3

Using a hacksaw and a miter box, carefully cut the track to the proper dimension. Center the track on the bathtub ledge with the taller side out and so the gaps are even at each end. Tape into position with masking tape.

4

Place a wall channel against the wall with the longer side out and slide into place over the track so they overlap. Use a level to check the channel for plumb, and then mark the locations of the mounting holes on the wall with a marker. Repeat for the other wall channel. Remove the track.

(continued)

5

Drill mounting holes for the wall channel at the marked locations. In ceramic tile, nick the surface of the tile with a center punch, use a ¼" masonry bit to drill the hole, and then insert the included wall anchors. For fiberglass surrounds, use a ⅛" drill bit; wall anchors are not necessary.

6

Apply a bead of silicone sealant along the joint between the tub and the wall at the ends of the track. Apply a minimum ¼" bead of sealant along the outside leg of the track underside.

7

Position the track on the tub ledge and against the wall. Attach the wall channels using the provided screws. Do not use caulk on the wall channels at this time.

8

At a location above the tops of the wall channels, measure the distance between the walls. Refer to the manufacturer's instructions for calculating the header dimensions. For the doors seen here, the header dimension is the distance between the walls minus ¹⁄₁₆". Measure the header and carefully cut it to length using a hacksaw and a miter box. Slide the header down on top of the wall channels until seated.

9

Mount the rollers in the roller mounting holes. To begin, use the second from the top roller mounting holes. Follow the manufacturer's instructions for spacer or washer placement and direction.

10

Carefully lift the inner panel by the sides and place the rollers on the inner roller track. Roll the door toward the shower end of the tub. The edge of the panel should touch both rubber bumpers. If it doesn't, remove the door and move the rollers to different holes. Drive the screws by hand to prevent overtightening.

11

Lift the outer panel by the sides with the towel bar facing out from the tub. Place the outer rollers over the outer roller track. Slide the door to the end opposite the shower end of the tub. If the door does not contact both bumpers, remove the door and move the rollers to different mounting holes.

12

Apply a bead of silicone sealant to the inside seam of the wall and wall channel at both ends and to the U-shaped joint of the track and wall channels. Smooth the sealant with a fingertip dipped in water.

Air-Jet Tubs

A jetted spa is basically a bathtub that recirculates water, air, or a combination of the two to create an effect known as hydromassage. Hydromassage increases blood flow, relieves pressure on joints and muscles, and relieves tension. Indoor hydromassage tubs usually have a water pump that blows a mixture of air and water through jets located in the tub body. Many include an integral water heater.

The product you'll see installed on these pages is a bit different. It is an air-jet tub: a relatively new entry in the jetted spa market that circulates only warm air, not water. This technology makes it safe to use bath oils, bubble bath, and bath salts in the spa. A model with no heater requires only a single 120-volt dedicated circuit. Models with heaters normally require either multiple dedicated 120-volt circuits or a 240-volt circuit.

Like normal bathtubs, jetted tubs can be installed in a variety of ways. Here, we install a drop-in tub (no nailing flange) in a 3-wall alcove. This may require the construction of a new stub wall, like the short wall we plumbed as the wet wall for this installation. Unless you have a lot of wiring and plumbing experience, consider hiring professionals for all or parts of the project.

Tools & Materials ▸

Plumbing tools & supplies	Drain-waste-overflow assembly
Utility knife	Shims
4-foot level	1 × 4 lumber
Square-edge trowel	Deck screws
Drill or power driver	Roofing nails
Channel-type pliers	Plumber's putty
Hacksaw	Dry-set mortar
Level	Trowel
Circular saw	Silicone caulk
Screwdriver	Jetted tub
Adjustable wrench	Faucet set

Air-jet tubs create massaging action, stirring the water with warm air. Air-jets eliminate concerns about stagnant water and bacteria that can remain in the pipes of whirlpool tubs.

How to Install an Air-jet Tub

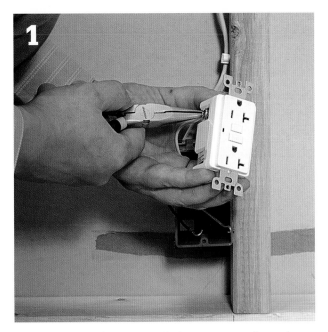

Prepare the site for the installation. Remove wall coverings in the installation area to expose bare studs. Provide a dedicated electrical circuit or circuits to the tub area according to the specifications in your installation manual (hire an electrician if you are not comfortable with wiring). This model plugs into a GFCI-protected receptacle on a dedicated 120-volt, 20-amp circuit.

Make framing improvements such as adding 1 × 4 bracing at supply risers and the faucet body location. For drop-in tubs that do not have nailing flanges, you may need to add short stub walls to provide a stable resting point. Here, a short stub wall was installed at one end to serve as the tub wet wall.

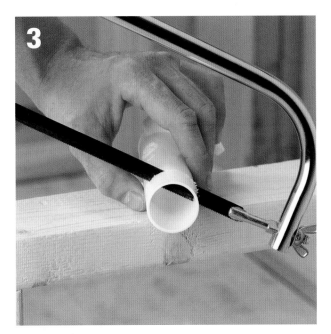

Cut the drain tailpiece to length depending on the distance you'll need to span to the trap. Use a hacksaw or tubing cutter to make the cut.

Prepare the floor or subfloor. Check with a level and fill any dips with floor leveling compound or mortar. If there is a joint in the subfloor in the installation area, make sure the sides are level. (The floor has to be level in order to support the weight of the tub, the water, and bathers.) Also make sure there is no rot or disrepair in the structural elements.

(continued)

5

Test the tub fit. First, cut a piece of the shipping carton to fit inside the tub and protect its surface. Have someone help you slide the tub into the installation area, flush against the wall studs, so you can check the fit. *Tip: Lay a pair of 1 × 4s perpendicular to the tub opening and use them as skids to make it easier to slide the tub in. Remove the skids and lower the tub on the floor.*

6

Set a 4-ft. level across the rim of the tub and check it for level. If it is not level, place shims under the tub until it is.

7

Mark the top of the tub's rim or nailing flange at each stud as a reference for installing additional supports or ledgers. Remove the tub from the alcove.

8

Add support frames or ledgers as directed by the manufacturer and secure them in the installation area so the top of the tub or nailing flange will be at the height you scribed in Step 7.

9

Assemble the drain-waste-overflow kit to fit the drain and overflow openings, following the tub manufacturer's directions. Install the D-W-O kit (it is virtually impossible to attach it once the tub is in place).

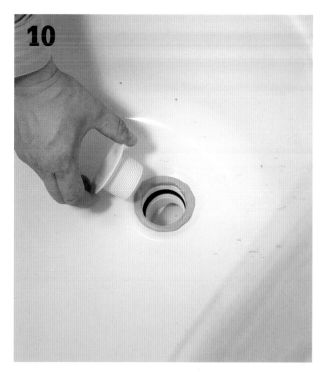

10

Fasten the threaded parts of the drain assembly. A ring of plumber's putty between the drain coverplate and the tub will help create a good seal. If you will be installing a pop-up drain, install it now as well.

11

Attach the overflow coverplate so it conceals the overflow opening. Adjust the pop-up drain plug linkage as directed by the manufacturer.

12

Begin the actual installation. For some tubs, it is recommended that you trowel a layer of thinset mortar in the installation area. But read your instructions carefully. Many tubs feature integral feet that are meant to rest directly on the floor.

(continued)

13

Slide the tub back into the opening. Remove the skids, if you are using them. Press down evenly on the tub rims until they make solid contact with the ledgers or frames.

14

Provide support for the tub on the open side if it does not have a structural skirt. Here, a 2 × 4 stub wall is built to the exact height of the underside of the rim and then attached in place. Screw it to both end walls and to the floor.

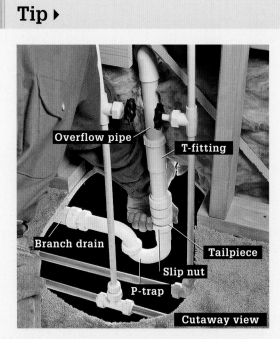

Tip ▶

Overflow pipe

T-fitting

Branch drain

Tailpiece

Slip nut

P-trap

Cutaway view

Make the plumbing drain connections before you proceed further. To connect the drain tailpiece to the trap you will need access either from below or from an access panel. The photo above shows a typical tub drain configuration seen cutaway through the floor.

15

Cover the gaps in the wallcoverings around the tub. Here, cementboard is installed in preparation for a tile backsplash. If your tub has nailing flanges, attach strips of metal flashing to the wall so they extend down to within about ¼" of the tub rim. If your tub has a removable apron, install it.

16

Make wiring connections according to the tub manufacturer's instructions. The requirements vary greatly among jetted spas. Some municipalities may require that a licensed professional do this work. Here, the airflow regulator is being wired. Note that most codes have a safety requirement that the on/off switch must be located so it cannot be reached by a bather in the tub.

17

Test the operation of the jetted spa before you finish the walls or deck in case there is a hidden problem. Fill it with a hose if you have not installed the faucet (the faucet normally is installed after the wall surfaces, unless you are deck-mounting the faucet on the tub rim). Run the spa. If it works, go ahead and drain the water.

18

Finish the wall surfaces. Here, a tile surround and backsplash is being installed over the cementboard backer.

19

Hook up the faucet to the water supply plumbing according to the manufacturer's directions (or have your plumber do the job). Remove the aerator from the tip of the spout and run water through it to clear out any debris. Attach the aerator, fill the tub, and have yourself a nice, relaxing soak.

Whirlpools ▸

Installing a whirlpool is very similar to installing a bathtub, once the rough-in is completed. Completing a rough-in for a whirlpool requires that you install a separate GFCI-protected electrical circuit for the pump motor. Some building codes specify that a licensed electrician be hired to wire whirlpools; check with your local building inspector.

Select your whirlpool before you do rough-in work, because exact requirements will differ from model to model (pages 22 to 25). Select your faucet to match the trim kit that comes with your whirlpool. When selecting a faucet, make sure the spout is large enough to reach over the tub rim. Most whirlpools use "widespread" faucets because the handles and spout are separate, and can be positioned however you like, even on opposite sides of the tub. Most building centers carry flex tube in a variety of lengths for connecting the faucet handles and spout.

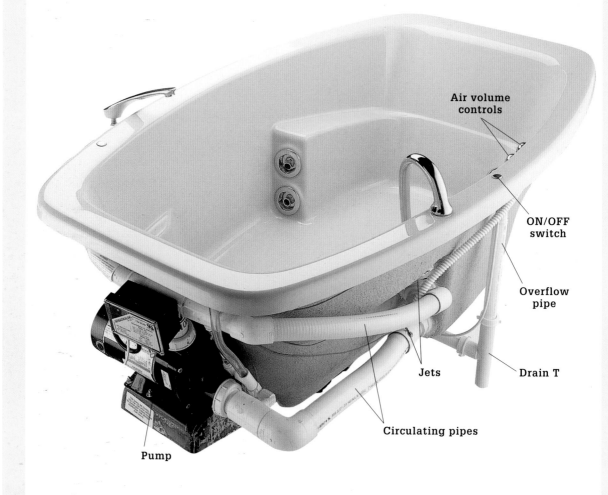

A whirlpool circulates aerated water through jets mounted in the body of the tub. Whirlpool pumps move as much as 50 gallons of water per minute to create a relaxing "hydromassage" effect. The pump, pipes, jets, and most of the controls are installed at the factory, making the actual hookup in your home quite simple.

OPTIONAL WHIRLPOOL ACCESSORIES

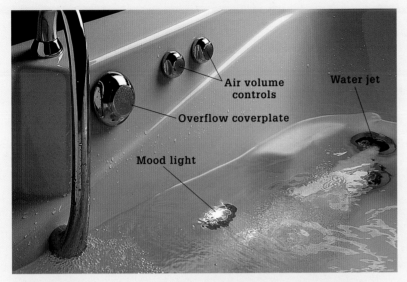

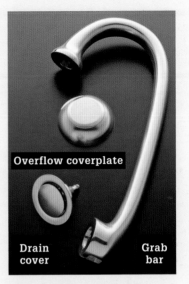

Mood lights are sold as factory-installed accessories by many manufacturers. Most are available with several filters to let you adjust the color to suit your mood. Mood lights are low-voltage fixtures wired through 12-volt transformers. Do not wire mood lights or other accessories into the electrical circuit that supplies the pump motor.

Trim kits for whirlpools are ordered at the time of purchase. Available in a variety of finishes, all of the trim pieces except the grab bar and overflow coverplate are normally installed at the factory.

REQUIREMENTS FOR MAKING ELECTRICAL HOOKUPS

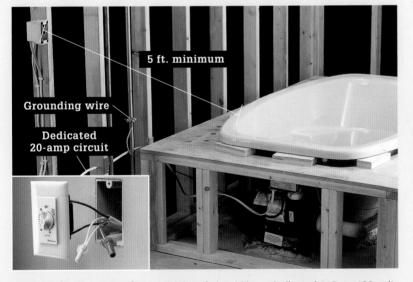

The electrical service for a whirlpool should be a dedicated 115- to 120-volt, 20-amp circuit. The pump motor should be grounded separately, normally to a metal cold water supply pipe. Most whirlpool motors are wired with 12/2 NM cable, but some local codes require the use of conduit. Remote timer switches (inset), located at least 5 ft. from the tub, are required by some codes, even for a tub with a built-in timer.

A GFCI circuit breaker at the main service panel is required with whirlpool installations. Hire an electrician to connect new circuits at your service panel if you are uncomfortable installing circuit cables on your own.

Tub & Shower Fittings

In many situations, replacing a bathtub spout can be almost as easy as hooking up a garden hose to an outdoor spigot. There are some situations where it is a bit more difficult, but still pretty simple. The only time it's a real problem is when the spout is attached to a plain copper supply nipple, rather than a threaded nipple. You'll know this is the case if the spout has a setscrew on the underside where it meets the wall. Many bathtub spouts are sold in kits with a matching showerhead and handle or handles. But for a simple one-for-one replacement, spouts are sold separately. You just need to make sure the new spout is compatible with the existing nipple (see page 121).

Tub spouts can be relatively complicated plumbing fittings, often performing three or four important functions. The spout itself is simple enough, since its only function is to deliver bathwater to the tub. But the diverter network and pop-up drain contain multiple moving parts that require precise adjustment and occasional repair or replacement (see photo, next page). The diverter is basically a stop valve that's activated by a lever or knob to block flow of water from the spout, forcing it up to a showerhead or out through a handheld showerhead, as seen here.

— Diverter lever

— Gate diverter

In many bathtub/shower plumbing systems, the spout has the important job of housing the diverter—a gate inside the spout that is operated by a lever with a knob for pulling. An open gate allows water to come out of the spout when the faucet is turned on. When the diverter is pulled shut, the water is redirected up a riser pipe and to the showerhead. Failure of the diverter is one of the most common reasons for replacing a spout.

Tools & Materials ▸

Pliers
Adjustable pliers
Channel-type pliers
Rags
Masking tape
Screwdrivers
Allen wrenches
Replacement spout

Measuring tape
Teflon tape
Utility knife

Installation Tip ▸

If you are installing a brand new tub/shower faucet, it likely contains an antiscald device. Most of these devices work by sensing a decrease in cold water flow and compensating by stemming the hot water flow too. As you install the new plumbing, be aware that faucets with antiscald protection will not function at all if both water supply tubes are not turned on at the stop valve. In other words, you can't test the hot and cold supply independently.

How to Install a Slip-Fit Spout

Slip fitting: Check underneath the tub spout to look for an access slot or cutout, which indicates the spout is a slip-fit style that is held in place with a setscrew and mounted on a copper supply nipple. Loosen the screw with a hex (Allen) wrench. Pull off the spout.

Clean the copper nipple with steel wool. If you find any sharp edges where the nipple was cut, smooth them out with emery paper. Then, insert the O-ring that comes with the spout onto the nipple (see the manufacturer's instructions) and slide the spout body over the nipple in an upside-down position.

With the spout upside down for ease of access, tighten the setscrews on the clamp, working through the access slot or cutout, until you feel resistance.

Spin the spout so it's right-side up and then tighten the setscrew from below, making sure the wall end of the spout is flush against the wall. Do not overtighten the setscrew.

How to Install a Threaded Spout

1

If you see no setscrew or slot on the underside of the spout, it is attached to a threaded nipple. Unscrew the tub spout by inserting a heavy-duty flat screwdriver into the spout opening and spinning it counterclockwise.

Tool Tip ▸

Alternatively, grip the spout with a padded pipe wrench or channel-type pliers. Buy a compatible replacement spout at a home center or hardware store.

2

Copper nipple with threaded adapter

Wrap several courses of Teflon tape clockwise onto the pipe threads of the nipple. Using extra Teflon tape on the threads creates resistance if the spout tip points past six o'clock when tight.

3

Twist the new spout onto the nipple until it is flush against the wall and the spout is oriented properly. If the spout falls short of six o'clock, you may protect the finish of the spout with tape and twist it a little beyond hand tight with your channel-type pliers—but don't overdo it; the fitting can crack.

Adding a Shower to a Bathtub

Your dream bath remodel may include adding a shower to your old built-in bathtub—finally you will be able to enjoy the ease of waking up and hopping into a steamy shower. All you need to do is remove the spout and replace it with one equipped with an adapter hose outlet to which you can screw a flexible shower hose. Then you need to install a mounting bracket so you can hang the showerhead and free your hands. Add a telescoping shower curtain rod and a shower curtain and your new shower stall is ready for duty.

Tools & Materials ▸

Pipe Wrench
Drill
Glass and tile drill bit
Measuring tape
Screwdriver
Marker
Teflon tape
Brass nipple
Spout with diverter outlet
Hand-held mountable showerhead
   with flexible hose
Mounting hardware

Converting a plain bathtub into a tub/shower is a relatively easy task when you use a flexible shower adapter that fits onto a special replacement tub spout.

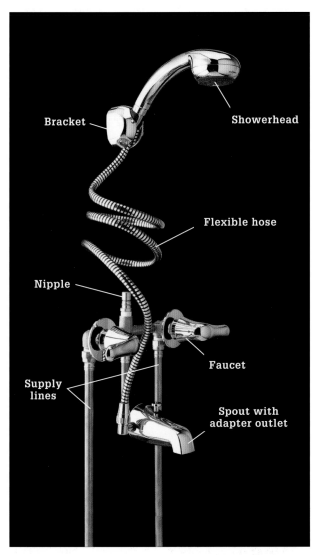

Bracket

Showerhead

Flexible hose

Nipple

Faucet

Supply lines

Spout with adapter outlet

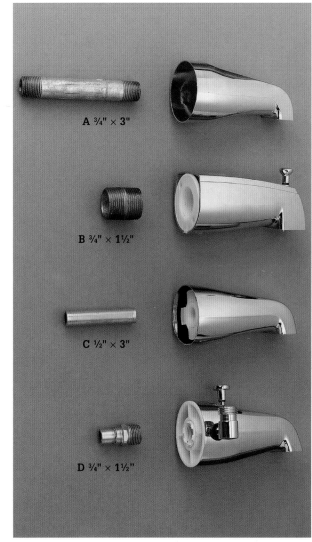

A ¾" × 3"

B ¾" × 1½"

C ½" × 3"

D ¾" × 1½"

A shower adapter kit lets you add shower functionality to a bathtub. The parts include a replacement spout that includes a diverter (usually located farther back on the spout) and an outlet port that's connected to a flexible shower hose. The other end of the hose is connected to a showerhead, which is usually a handheld model that can be set into a bracket to work like a normal showerhead. Obviously, if you wish to use the showerhead in a mounting bracket, your tub must have suitable shower walls and a door or curtain.

The appearance of the spout gives good clues as to which kind of nipple it is connected to. A) A spout with no diverter is probably connected to a 3"-long threaded nipple. To install a diverter spout you'll need to replace the 3" threaded nipple with a shorter threaded nipple that sticks out no more than ½" from the wall—not too big of a job. B) If the spout already has a diverter knob, it already has a showerhead, and you're doing the wrong project (although there is no reason you couldn't hook up a shower adapter if you want a handheld shower). C) If the spout has a small setscrew in a slot on the underside, it is probably attached with a slip fitting to a ½" copper supply nipple. Unless you are able to solder a new transition fitting onto the old pipe after cutting it, call a plumber to install the new spout here. D) Spouts with outlets for shower adapters require a short threaded nipple (or comparable union) that sticks out from the wall no more than ¾".

How to Add a Shower with an Adapter Spout

1

Make sure the old spout is not held in place with a setscrew (see previous page) and then remove it by wrapping it with a cloth and turning the spout with channel-type pliers or a pipe wrench.

(see previous page)

Tool Tip ▸

A long-bladed screwdriver or a dowel inserted into the mouth of the spout can be used to spin the spout free from the nipple.

2

If you have a long iron or brass nipple like this, you need to replace it with a short one. Threaded nipples have threads at each end, so you can usually unscrew the old ones. Mark the nipple at the face of the wall and write "front" on your side. Unscrew it counterclockwise with a pipe wrench. Get a threaded brass nipple of the same diameter that is about half an inch longer than the distance from the back of your old nipple to your line.

3

Wrap six layers of Teflon tape clockwise on the nipple and thread into the wall. Thread the reducing bushing onto the nipple if it will fit. Thread the adapter spout on. Tighten farther with a screwdriver or dowel to orient the spout correctly.

4

Attach a flexible shower hose to the adapter hose outlet. Tighten with an adjustable wrench.

5

Determine the location of the showerhead bracket. Use the hose length as a guide, and make sure the showerhead can be lifted off the bracket with ease.

6

Mark hole locations. Obtain a glass-and-tile drill bit for your electric drill in the size recommended by the shower bracket manufacturer. Put on eye protection and drill holes in the ceramic tile on your marks.

7

Insert anchors into the holes and tap in place with a wooden or rubber mallet. Fasten the showerhead holder to the wall using a Phillips screwdriver and the mounting screws.

Dual Showerheads

What's more luxurious than a hot shower? Two hot showers at one time. That's what you get with a dual-head, multifunction shower such as the one shown in this project. Multiple showerheads let you aim the pulsing action at your neck and shoulders, your chest and legs, your hair and torso—you decide where you need it most.

Although some multifunction showerheads require elaborate and painstaking installation, others, such as the one shown here, take less than an hour, start to finish. This showerhead produces a lot of enjoyment in return for a reasonable investment of time and money.

At a flow of 2.5 gallons per minute, this showerhead won't overwhelm a water heater, either. Unless you and your family members take longer showers to extend your enjoyment of its pleasures, it shouldn't radically increase your water usage or your utility bills.

Tools & Materials ▸

Pipe wrench
Dual-head
    multifunction
    showerhead

Fine-grit sandpaper
    or stiff bristle brush
Teflon tape
Soft rag or cloth
Electrical tape

Gentle streams, invigorating massage, soothing pulses—they're all available at the touch of a finger after you replace a standard showerhead with a two-head model.

How to Replace a Showerhead with a Multi-head fitting

Place electrical tape on the jaws of a pipe wrench to protect the metal showerhead parts from the teeth of the pipe wrench.

Grasp the end of the existing showerhead. Using a pipe wrench, turn the collar nut counterclockwise to remove the showerhead. Leave the shower arm and flange in place.

Carefully clean the threads at the end of the shower arm with fine-grit sandpaper or a stiff bristle metal brush. Be careful not to damage the threads. Run the water for a few seconds to flush debris from the arm.

Make sure the pre-installed rubber washers are in place inside each showerhead as well as the shower arm's swivel nut.

Wrap Teflon tape clockwise around the shower arm threads, making three or four loops of tape. Thread the shower arm extension from the new, dual-head showerhead onto the shower arm, turning clockwise. Hand-tighten firmly.

Wrap three or four loops of Teflon tape clockwise around the threads at each end of the shower arm extension.

Install one showerhead on each end of the arm, hand tightening them by turning clockwise. Wrap several courses of electrician's tape around the pipe wrench jaws and gently tighten the showerhead nut. Do not overtighten.

Adjust and rotate the showerheads as desired. Turn on the water and check for leaks. Gently tighten if necessary.

Low-Flow Upgrades ▶

Replacing a toilet or adding a urinal are good ways to reduce your water consumption, but you needn't embark on ambitious plumbing projects to make a difference. Very simple projects like replacing a showerhead with a more efficient model or adding a flow restrictor to a faucet take only minutes to do.

SHOWERHEADS

The perfect showerhead is subject to personal taste. Some people like a strong, pulsating spray, while others prefer a gentle shower of water that falls vertically like rain. Some even claim to enjoy the piercing-needle sensation delivered by showerheads in budget hotels. But whatever your idea of a good spray may be, you can be sure of finding it in a new showerhead that uses no more than 2.5 gallons per minute.

The same federal act that limits water consumption in toilets (the Energy Policy Act of 1992) also requires that all showerheads made in the U.S. have a flow rate of 2.5 gpm or less. This has had several positive effects. It reduces household water consumption, of course, but it also leveled the playing field so that manufacturers must now compete by improving the spray of a showerhead without taking the easy route by adding more water. Unfortunately,

This showerhead (above) and this handshower (left) are engineered to operate with full performance at only 2.0 gallons per minute (gpm), saving 20 percent on water usage versus showerheads with a flow rate of 2.5 gpm. Made by Kohler (see Resources, page 284), they come with three spray options – soft coverage, rhythmic pulse, and aerated sprays.

Low-flow faucet aerators reduce water flow rates from a typical 2.2 gpm to 1.5 gpm. You may be able to find a low-flow aerator that fits your current faucet—check with the manufacturer.

the law does not restrict the number of showerheads a shower can have.

Showering accounts for about 17% of household water use, and while 2.5 gpm is a decent benchmark for general conservation, there's plenty of room for improvement. Many showerheads offer lower flow rates, such as 1.0 gpm to 2.25 gpm. You can also choose a head with a built-in ON/OFF switch that allows you to conveniently shut off the water while you soap up. When the switch is turned back on for rinsing, the water is still mixed at the desired temperature. It's important to remember that most of what you're paying for when showering is not the water itself but the gas or electricity used to heat the water. Shower water is typically about three quarters hot water and one quarter cold.

Replacing an old showerhead is an incredibly simple and usually inexpensive upgrade that can save water at the same time that it improves your showering experience and lowers your utility bill. There really aren't a lot of recommendations to follow when choosing a showerhead. Just take your time shopping around, ask your friends, maybe read some reviews, then take the plunge. You might find your ideal spray in a product that costs $15.

MEASURING SHOWERHEAD FLOW

Here's a simple method for testing the flow rate on an old showerhead: Turn on the shower full-blast with both hot and cold water and direct it into a 5-gallon bucket. Let the water run for exactly two minutes. If the bucket overflows before the time is up, it's not a low-flow showerhead.

A manual ON/OFF switch lets you stop the flow while you shampoo and soap up but keeps the water at the right temperature.

Today's showerhead designs use advances like air-inducing vacuum holes to provide a forceful spray that emits as little as 1.0 gpm.

Slide-bar Showerheads

The slide-bar showerhead is an attractive and practical shower addition for any bathroom. It combines the flexibility of a handheld sprayer with a sliding mounted showerhead. This convenient height adjustability makes it perfect for all family members, including children or disabled users who must sit to shower. The model shown uses a slide-lock mechanism that allows you to easily set the sprayer height anywhere along the 2-ft. span of the bar.

Slide-bar showerheads are generally sold as a kit that includes the bar, sprayer, hose, and mounting hardware. Many basic kits contain only a simple coupling that attaches the hose to the end of the shower arm. For a cleaner look, purchase a matching supply elbow that attaches to the pipe stub at the wall via a galvanized nipple connector, as shown in this project.

Tools & Materials ▸

Pipe wrench
³⁄₁₆" masonry drill bit
½" masonry drill bit
Screwdriver
Level
Nailset
Hammer
Drill
Caulk gun
Slide-bar
   showerhead kit

½"-diameter
   × 1½"-long
   galvanized nipple
Teflon tape
Chrome
   supply elbow
Wall anchors
   or toggle bolts
¼"-20 stainless steel
   machine bolt
Silicone caulk

A slide-bar showerhead allows you to set the spray at varying heights, which makes it a perfect choice for the family bathroom.

How to Install a Slide-bar Showerhead

Remove the existing showerhead.
Wrap the threads of a galvanized nipple with Teflon tape and thread it into the stub-out, leaving about ⁹⁄₁₆" of the nipple protruding from the wall. Thread the supply elbow onto the nipple. Cover the elbow with a soft cloth and tighten it with a pipe wrench.

Attach a mounting bracket to each end of the slide-bar. Place the bar 4" to 6" to the side of the wall supply elbow to avoid the water pipes. Locate the lower end of the bar about 48" from the bottom of the tub or shower. Use a level to make sure the bar is plumb, then mark the location of the mounting holes.

Drill holes in the tile using a masonry bit. If you hit a stud, attach the slide-bar to the wall, using the screws and wall anchors provided with the kit.

Anchoring to the Wall ▶

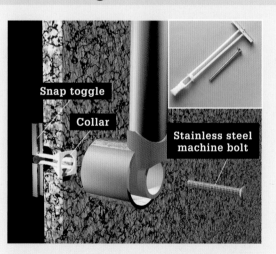

If you don't hit a stud, enlarge the hole, using a ½" masonry bit, then insert a toggle anchor (inset) into the hole. Slide the collar forward to hold the toggle against the back of the wall, then snap off the plastic straps. Attach the slide-bar to the wall with ¼"-20 stainless steel machine bolts.

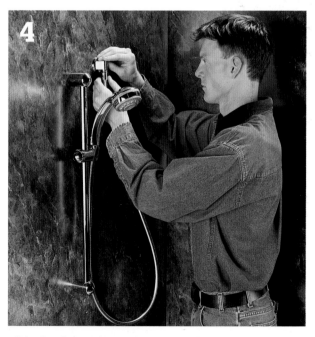

Slide the decorative end caps onto the mounting brackets. Thread the shower hose onto the wall supply elbow. Clip the showerhead into the slide-lock mechanism. Apply silicone caulk around the supply elbow and mounting brackets.

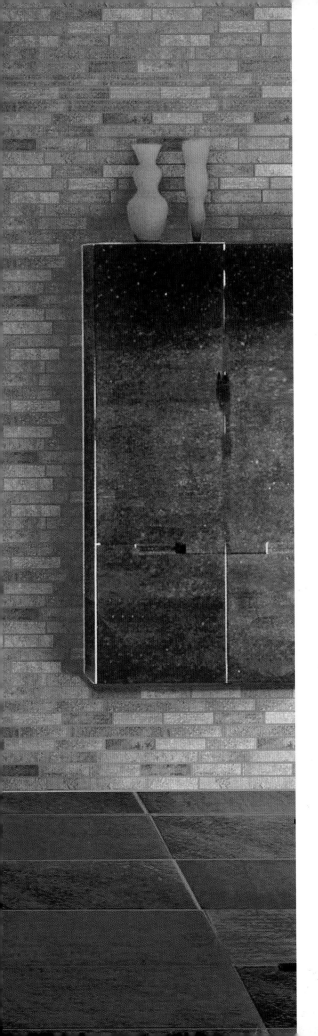

Sinks & Vanities

When discussing bathroom sinks ("lavatories") and vanities it is sometimes difficult to decide if the conversation is about cabinetry or plumbing. In some cases, such as installing a traditional vanity cabinet, you'll definitely need to do work in both areas. But for other sink types, such as a wall-hung lavatory, the job is mostly about plumbing. Regardless of what type of sink you're installing, all of the information is here.

Until recently, wood vanity cabinets with integral sinks have been the standard in residential bathrooms. But changing design standards have given rise to newer, more modern-looking options. Wall-hung vanity bases made from alternative materials are one new choice. And instead of an integral cultured marble top, they are often fitted with gleaming glass countertops and intriguing vessel sinks—sometimes with a high-end wall-mounted faucet and spout. Drop-in sinks and pedestal sinks are familiar options that continue to enjoy popularity.

In this chapter:

- Pedestal Sinks
- Wall-Hung Vanities
- Vessel Sinks
- Integral Vanity Tops
- Lavatory Faucets
- Wall-Mount Faucets
- Lavatory Drains

Pedestal Sinks

Pedestal sinks move in and out of popularity more frequently than other sink types, but even during times they aren't particularly trendy they retain fairly stable demand. You'll find them most frequently in small half baths, where their little footprint makes them an efficient choice. Designers are also discovering the appeal of tandem pedestal sinks of late, where the smaller profiles allow for his-and-hers sinks that don't dominate visually.

The primary drawback to pedestal sinks is that they don't offer any storage. Their chief practical benefit is that they conceal plumbing some home-owners would prefer not to see.

Pedestal sinks are mounted in two ways. Most of the more inexpensive ones you'll find at home stores are hung in the manner of wall-hung sinks. The pedestal is actually installed after the sink is hung and its purpose is only decorative. But other pedestal sinks (typically on the higher end of the design scale) have structurally important pedestals that do most or all of the bearing for the sink.

Pedestal sinks are available in a variety of styles and are a perfect fit for small half baths. They keep plumbing hidden, lending a neat, contained look to the bathroom.

How to Install a Pedestal Sink

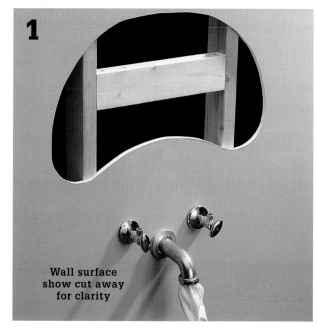

Install 2 × 4 blocking between the wall studs, behind the planned sink location. Cover the wall with water-resistant drywall.

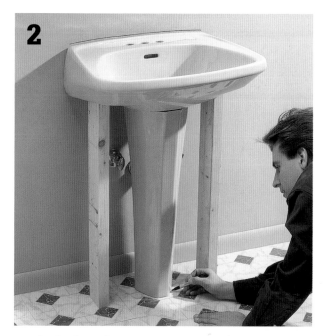

Set the basin and pedestal in position and brace it with 2 × 4s. Outline the top of the basin on the wall, and mark the base of the pedestal on the floor. Mark reference points on the wall and floor through the mounting holes found on the back of the sink and the bottom of the pedestal.

Set aside the basin and pedestal. Drill pilot holes in the wall and floor at the reference points, then reposition the pedestal. Anchor the pedestal to the floor with lag screws.

Attach the faucet, then set the sink on the pedestal. Align the holes in the back of the sink with the pilot holes drilled in the wall, then drive lag screws and washers into the wall brace using a ratchet wrench. Do not overtighten the screws.

Hook up the drain and supply fittings. Caulk between the back of the sink and the wall when installation is finished.

Wall-Hung Vanities

Think of a wall-mounted sink or vanity cabinet and you're likely to conjure up images of public restrooms, where these conveniences are installed to improve access for floor cleaning. However, wall-hung sinks and vanities made for home use are very different from the commercial installations. Often boasting high design, beautiful modern vanities and sinks come in a variety of styles and materials, including wood, metal, and glass. Some attach with decorative wall brackets that are part of the presentation; others look like standard vanities, just without legs. Install wall-hung sinks and vanities by attaching them securely to studs or wood blocking.

Tools & Materials ▸

Studfinder   Pencil
Drill   Vanity
Level

Today's wall-hung sinks are stylish and attractive, but they require mounting into studs or added blocking to keep them secure.

How to Install a Wall-hung Vanity Base

1

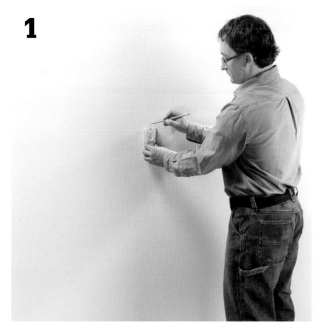

Remove the existing sink or fixture (pages 270 to 271) and inspect the wall framing. Also determine if plumbing supply and waste lines will need to be moved to accommodate the dimensions of the new fixture. Locate the studs in the sink location with a stud finder.

2

Hold the sink or cabinet in the installation area and check to see if the studs align with the sink or sink bracket mounting holes. If they do, skip to Step 3. If the studs do not align, remove the wallboard behind the mounting area. Install 2 × 6 blocking between studs at the locations of the mounting screws. Replace and repair wallboard.

3

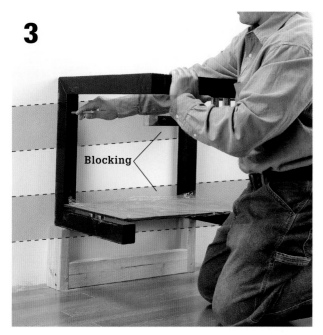

Mark the locations of the mounting holes on the wall using a template or by supporting the sink or vanity against the wall with a temporary brace (here, made from scrap 2 × 4s) and marking through the mounting holes.

4

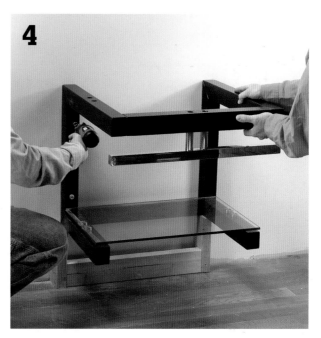

Drill pilot holes at the marks. Have a helper hold the vanity in place while you drive the mounting screws. Hook up the plumbing.

Vessel Sinks

The vessel sink harkens back to the days of washstands and washbowls. Whether it's round, square, or oval, shallow or deep, the vessel sink offers great opportunity for creativity and proudly displays its style. Vessel sinks are a perfect choice for a powder room, where they will have high visibility.

Most vessel sinks can be installed on any flat surface—from a granite countertop to a wall-mounted vanity to an antique dresser. Some sinks are designed to contact the mounting surface only at the drain flange. Others are made to be partially embedded in the surface. Take care to follow the manufacturer's instructions for cutting holes for sinks and faucets.

A beautiful vessel sink demands an equally attractive faucet. Select a tall spout mounted on the countertop or vanity top or a wall-mounted spout to accommodate the height of the vessel. To minimize splashing, spouts should direct flow to the center of the vessel, not down the side. Make sure your faucet is compatible with your vessel choice. Look for a centerset or single-handle model if you'll be custom drilling the countertop—you only need to drill one faucet hole.

Tools & Materials ▸

Jigsaw	Drill
Trowel	Vanity or countertop
Pliers	Vessel sink
Wrench	Pop-up drain
Caulk gun and caulk	P-trap and drain kit
Sponge	Faucet

Vessel sinks are available in countless styles and materials, shapes and sizes. Their one commonality is that they all need to be installed on a flat surface.

Vessel Sink Options

This glass vessel sink embedded in a "floating" glass countertop is a stunning contrast to the strong and attractive wood frame anchoring it to the wall.

The natural stone vessel sink blends elegantly into the stone countertop and is enhanced by the sleek faucet and round mirror.

The stone vessel sink is complemented by the wall-hung faucet. The rich wood vanity on which it's perched adds warmth to the room.

Vitreous china with a glazed enamel finish is an economical and durable choice for a vessel sink (although it is less durable than stone). Because of the flexibility of both the material and the glaze the design options are virtually unlimited with vitreous china.

How to Install a Vessel Sink

Secure the vanity cabinet or other countertop that you'll be using to mount the vessel sink (see pages 136 to 137).

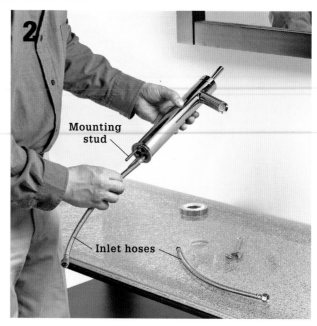

Begin hooking up the faucet. Insert the brass mounting stud into the threaded hole in the faucet base with the slotted end facing out. Hand tighten, and then use a slotted screwdriver to tighten another half turn. Insert the inlet hoses into the faucet body and hand tighten. Use an adjustable wrench to tighten another half turn. Do not overtighten.

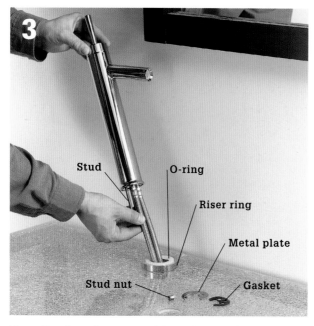

Place the riser ring on top of the O-ring over the faucet cutout in the countertop. From underneath, slide the rubber gasket and the metal plate over the mounting stud. Thread the mounting stud nut onto the mounting stud and hand tighten. Use an adjustable wrench to tighten another half turn.

To install the sink and pop-up drain, first place the small metal ring between two O-rings and place over the drain cutout.

Place the vessel bowl on top of the O-rings. In this installation, the vessel is not bonded to the countertop.

Put the small rubber gasket over the drain hole in the vessel. From the top, push the pop-up assembly through the drain hole.

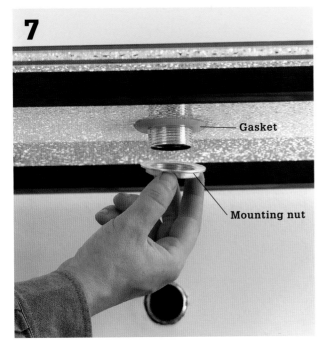

From underneath, push the large rubber gasket onto the threaded portion of the pop-up assembly. Thread the nut onto the pop-up assembly and tighten. Use an adjustable wrench or basin wrench to tighten an additional half turn. Thread the tailpiece onto the pop-up assembly.

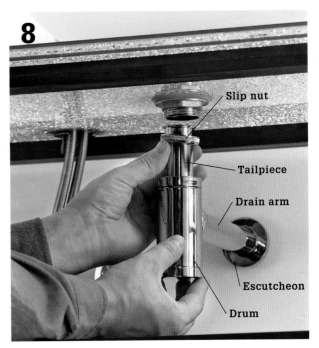

Install the drum trap. Loosen the rings on the top and outlet of the drum trap. Slide the drum trap top hole over the tailpiece. Slide the drain arm into the side outlet, with the flat side of the rubber gasket facing away from the trap. Insert the drain arm into the wall outlet. Hand tighten the rings.

Integral Vanity Tops

Most bathroom countertops installed today are integral (one-piece) sink/countertop units made from cultured marble or other solid materials, like solid surfacing. Integral sink/countertops are convenient, and many are inexpensive, but style and color options are limited.

Some remodelers and designers still prefer the distinctive look of a custom-built countertop with a self-rimming sink basin, which gives you a much greater selection of styles and colors. Installing a self-rimming sink is very simple.

Tools & Materials ▶

Pencil	Basin wrench
Scissors	Cardboard
Carpenter's level	Masking tape
Screwdriver	Plumber's putty
Channel-type pliers	Lag screws
Ratchet wrench	Tub & tile caulk

Integral sink/countertops are made in standard sizes to fit common vanity widths. Because the sink and countertop are cast from the same material, integral sink/countertops do not leak, and do not require extensive caulking and sealing.

How to Install a Vanity Cabinet

Set the sink/countertop unit onto sawhorses. Attach the faucet and slip the drain lever through the faucet body. Place a ring of plumber's putty around the drain flange, then insert the flange in the drain opening.

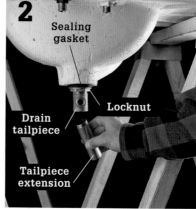

Thread the locknut and sealing gasket onto the drain tailpiece, then insert the tailpiece into the drain opening and screw it onto the drain flange. Tighten the locknut securely. Attach the tailpiece extension. Insert the pop-up stopper linkage.

Apply a layer of tub & tile caulk (or adhesive, if specified by the countertop manufacturer) to the top edges of the cabinet vanity, and to any corner braces.

Center the sink/countertop unit over the vanity, so the overhang is equal on both sides and the backsplash of the countertop is flush with the wall. Press the countertop evenly into the caulk.

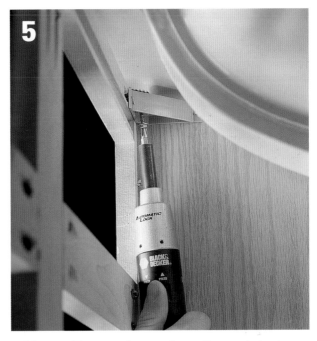

Cabinets with corner braces: Secure the countertop to the cabinet by driving a mounting screw through each corner brace and up into the countertop. *Note: Cultured marble and other hard countertops require predrilling and a plastic screw sleeve.*

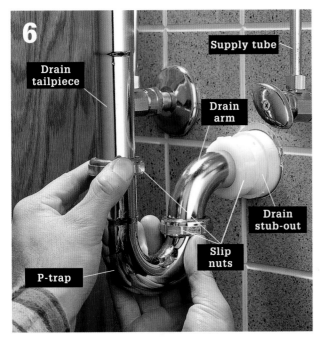

Attach the drain arm to the drain stub-out in the wall, using a slip nut. Attach one end of the P-trap to the drain arm, and the other to the tailpiece of the sink drain, using slip nuts. Connect supply tubes to the faucet tailpieces.

Seal the gap between the backsplash and the wall with tub & tile caulk.

Lavatory Faucets

Widespread faucets come in three pieces instead of one: a hot tap, a cold tap, and the spout. Each piece is mounted separately in its own hole in the sink. The hot and cold taps (valves) are connected to hot and cold water supplies respectively. The spout is connected to the valves with reinforced flexible hoses. The great advantage to this configuration is that you gain flexibility when locating your spout and handles. If your faucet set has a long enough hose, you can even create arrangements such as locating the handles near one end of the tub and the spout near the other so you can turn the water on and off or adjust the temperature without getting up. Even models made for bathroom lavatories, like the one you see here, offer many creative configuration options.

Tip: Save your paperwork. Should you ever need to service your faucet, the product literature will be useful for troubleshooting and identifying and replacing parts.

Three-piece (widespread) faucets are as classy as a good three-piece suit, and the styles are virtually unlimited.

Tools & Materials ▸

Heatproof grease	Pipe joint compound	Adjustable wrench	Standing flashlight
Teflon tape	Plumber's putty	Basin wrench	Eye protection
Measuring tape	New 3-piece faucet	Channel-type pliers	
Loctite	Supply lines	Screwdriver	

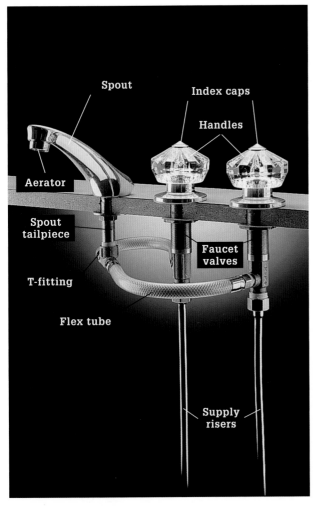

Widespread faucets come in three pieces, a spout and two valves. Supply risers carry hot and cold water to the valves, which are turned to regulate the amount of water going to the spout, where the water is mixed. Water travels from the valves to the spout through flex tubes, which in turn attach to the spout tailpiece via a T-fitting. Three-piece faucets designed to work with a pop-up stopper have a clevis and a lift rod. The handles attach with handle screws that are covered with index caps. An aerator is screwed on the faucet spout after debris is flushed from the faucet.

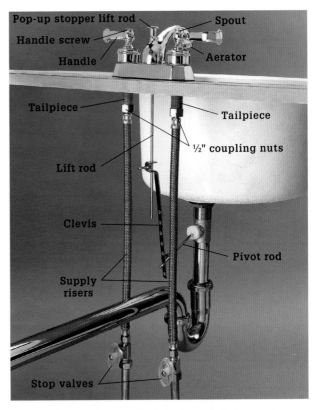

The tailpieces of a standard deck-mounted, one-piece bathroom sink faucet are 4" apart on center. As long as the two outside holes in the back of your sink measure 4" from center to center, and you have a middle hole for a pop-up stopper, you can put in any standard one-piece bathroom faucet with pop-up stopper. The faucet is secured to the sink with mounting nuts that screw onto the tailpieces from below. Also get two flexible stainless steel supply risers for sinks, long enough to replace the old tubes. These typically attach to the stop valves with ⅜-inch compression-sized coupling nuts and to the faucet with standard faucet coupling nuts. But take your old tubes and the old compression nuts from the stop valves to the store to ensure a match. The clevis, lift rod, and pivot rod are parts of the pop-up stopper assembly. The handles attach with handle screws that are covered with index caps. An aerator is screwed on the faucet spout after debris is flushed from the faucet.

How to Install a Widespread Faucet

1 Spout shank / Plumber's putty

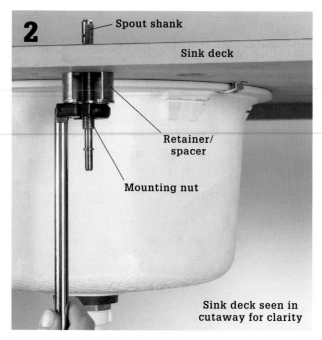

2 Spout shank / Sink deck / Retainer/spacer / Mounting nut

Sink deck seen in cutaway for clarity

Insert the shank of the faucet spout through one of the holes in the sink deck (usually the center hole but you can offset it in one of the end holes if you prefer). If the faucet is not equipped with seals or O-rings for the spout and handles, pack plumber's putty on the undersides before inserting the valves into the deck. *Note: If you are installing the widespread faucet in a new sink deck, drill three holes of the size suggested by the faucet manufacturer.*

In addition to mounting nuts, many spout valves for widespread faucets have an open retainer fitting that goes between the underside of the deck and the mounting nut. Others have only a mounting nut. In either case, tighten the mounting nut with pliers or a basin wrench to secure the spout valve. You may need a helper to keep the spout centered and facing forward.

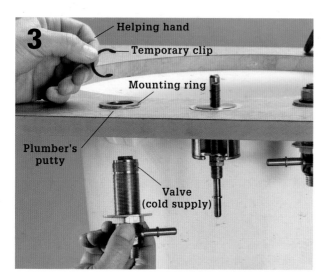

3 Helping hand / Temporary clip / Mounting ring / Plumber's putty / Valve (cold supply)

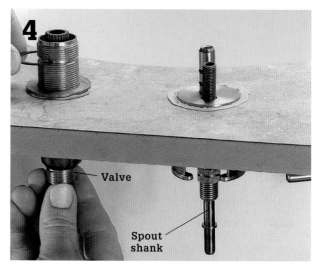

4 Valve / Spout shank

Mount the valves to the deck using whichever method the manufacturer specifies (it varies quite a bit). In the model seen here, a mounting ring is positioned over the deck hole (with plumber's putty seal) and the valve is inserted from below. A clip snaps onto the valve from above to hold it in place temporarily (you'll want a helper for this).

From below, thread the mounting nuts that secure the valves to the sink deck. Make sure the cold water valve (usually has a blue cartridge inside) is in the right-side hole (from the front) and the hot water valve (red cartridge) is in the left hole. Install both valves.

5

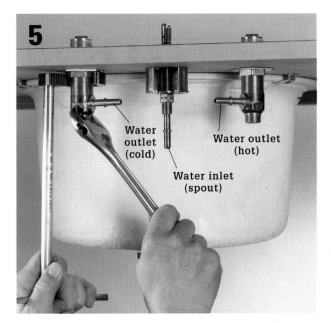

Water outlet (cold)
Water outlet (hot)
Water inlet (spout)

Once you've started the nut on the threaded valve shank, secure the valve with a basin wrench squeezing the lugs where the valve fits against the deck. Use an adjustable wrench to finish tightening the lock nut onto the valve. The valves should be oriented so the water outlets are aimed at the inlet on the spout shank.

6

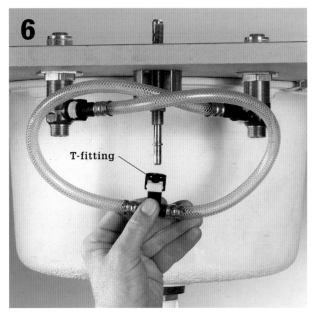

T-fitting

Attach the flexible supply tubes (supplied with the faucet) to the water outlets on the valves. Some twist onto the outlets, but others (like the ones above) click into place. The supply hoses meet in a T-fitting that is attached to the water inlet on the spout.

7

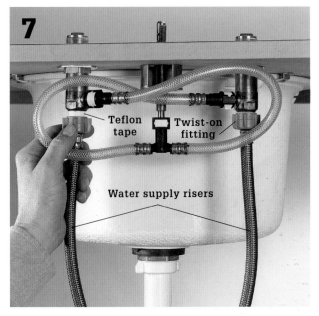

Teflon tape
Twist-on fitting
Water supply risers

Attach flexible braided metal supply risers to the water stop valves and then attach the tubes to the inlet port on each valve (usually with Teflon tape and a twist-on fitting at the valve end of the supply riser).

8

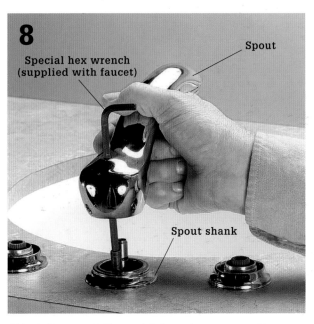

Special hex wrench (supplied with faucet)
Spout
Spout shank

Attach the spout. The model shown here comes with a special hex wrench that is threaded through the hole in the spout where the lift rod for the pop-up drain will be located. Once the spout is seated cleanly on the spout shank you tighten the hex wrench to secure the spout. Different faucets will use other methods to secure the spout to the shank.

(continued)

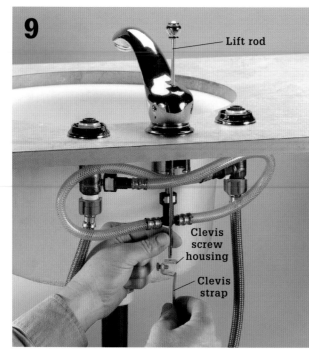

9 Lift rod

If your sink did not have a pop-up stopper, you'll need to replace the sink drain tailpiece with a pop-up stopper body (often supplied with the faucet). Insert the lift rod through the hole in the back of the spout and, from below, thread the pivot rod through the housing for the clevis screw.

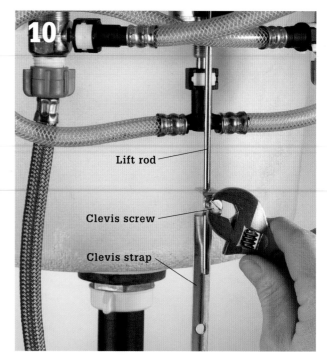

10 Lift rod

Clevis screw

Clevis strap

Attach the clevis strap to the pivot rod that enters the pop-up drain body and adjust the position of the strap so it raises and lowers properly when the lift rod is pulled up. Tighten the clevis screw at this point. It's hard to fit a screwdriver in here, so you may need to use a wrench or pliers.

11

Attach the faucet handles to the valves using whichever method is required by the faucet manufacturer. Most faucets are designed with registration methods to ensure that the handles are symmetrical and oriented in an ergonomic way once you secure them to the valves.

12 Aerator

Turn on the water supply and test the faucet. Remove the faucet aerator so any debris in the lines can clear the spout.

Variation: Single-piece Faucets

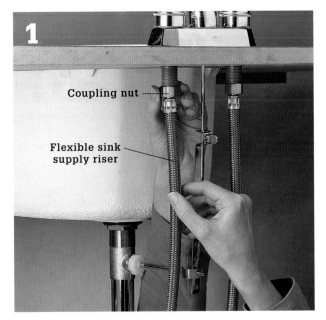

Insert the faucet tailpieces through the holes in the sink. From below, thread washers and mounting nuts over the tailpieces, then tighten the mounting nuts with a basin wrench until snug. Put a dab of pipe joint compound on the threads of the stop valves and thread the metal nuts of the flexible supply risers to these. Wrench tighten about a half turn past hand tight. Overtightening these nuts will strip the threads. Now tighten the coupling nuts to the faucet tailpieces with a basin wrench.

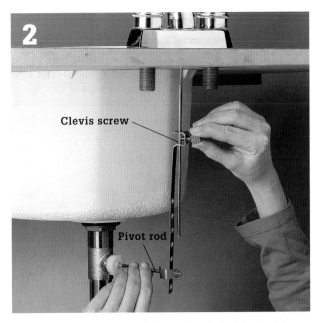

Slide the lift rod of the new faucet into its hole behind the spout. Thread it into the clevis past the clevis screw. Push the pivot rod all the way down so the stopper is open. With the lift rod also all the way down, tighten the clevis to the lift rod.

Grease the fluted valve stems with heatproof grease, then put the handles in place. Put a drop of Loctite on each handle screw before tightening it on to keep your handles from coming loose. Cover each handle screw with the appropriate index cap—Hot or Cold.

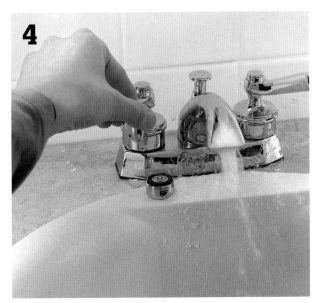

Unscrew the aerator from the end of the spout. Turn the hot and cold water taps on full. Turn the water back on at the stop valves and flush out the faucet for a couple of minutes before turning off the water at the faucet. Check the riser connections for drips. Tighten a compression nut only until the drip stops.

Wall-Mount Faucets

A wall-mounted faucet adds a touch of elegance to your bathroom. It's perfect for vessel sinks and hanging vanities, because the hoses and shut-off valves are out of view.

A wall-mounted sink faucet is similar to a shower or bathtub faucet. The main difference is that the handles and faucet are usually in a line, rather than at a distance from each other. Like the shower or bathtub faucet, you will need to have an access door behind the sink, or have the plumbing easily accessible in the basement for a first floor bathroom.

The valve unit and the faucets and spout will likely need to be made by the same manufacturer, as the parts are generally not interchangeable.

Tools & Materials ▸

Tubing cutter	Lead-free solder
Tape measure	Flux
Level	2 × 4 lumber
Torch	#10, 1" wood screws
Channel-type pliers	Two-handle valve
Allen wrench	Wall-mount faucet
Wallboard	Plumber's putty
finishing tools	Wallboard

Wall-mounted faucets have a spare, futuristic appeal that many high-end designers prefer. Functionally, they have the added advantage of keeping the sink deck clear.

How to Install a Wall-Mounted Sink Faucet

1

Determine the location for the faucet. Make reference marks for the faucet location on walls that will not be removed or create a cardboard template. Remove the wallboard between the studs at the faucet location and where necessary to run supply and drain lines. Install 2 × 4 bracing according to the faucet manufacturer's instructions.

2

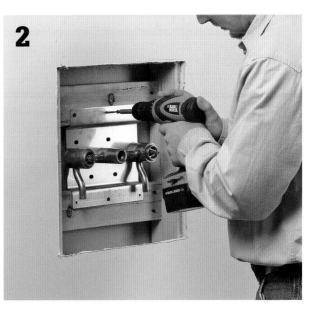

Attach the wall plate from the faucet kit to the studs with #10, 1" wood screws. Check the installation for level and correct it if necessary. Solder the lines from the valve assembly to ½" copper supply lines using couplings (left is hot, right is cold). Turn the water on and check for leaks.

3

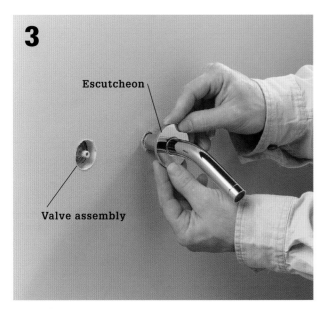

Replace the wallboard and finish the wall surface. The circular cutouts for the handles and spout should be no more than 1½" in diameter. Remove the plaster guards from the valve. Thread the spout into the spout stub until tight. Back off the spout until it faces downward and tighten the screws. Apply plumber's putty to the back of the escutcheon and slide it into place.

4

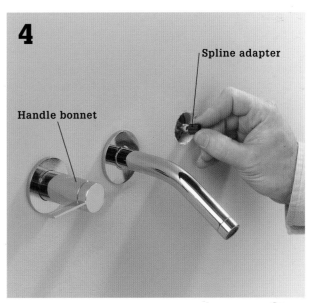

Thread the handle assemblies onto the valve bodies and tighten. If the handles are not horizontal when closed, remove them. Remove the spline adapter and give it a quarter turn. Repeat until the handles are horizontal when closed. Remove the handles. Apply plumber's putty to the back of the escutcheons and slide over the handle bonnets. Securely hand tighten the handles and slide escutcheons into place. Remove excess putty from escutcheons.

Lavatory Drains

Pop-up stoppers are those chrome-plated long-legged plugs in bathroom sinks that are opened and closed with a knob behind the spout. The stopper itself is just the glory guy for a behind-the-scenes assembly that makes sure the stopper sits and stands on cue. New faucets come with their own pop-up stopper assemblies, assuming they use one, but you may also purchase one by itself. This will include everything from the stopper to the pipe that drops into the trap (the trap is that drooping piece of drainpipe under your sink). Choose a pop-up stopper assembly that's heavy brass under the chrome finish. This will hold up better to time and abuse than a plastic or light-gauge metal model.

Installing a lavatory drain is a bit trickier than installing a kitchen sink drain because most have a pop-up stopper with linkage.

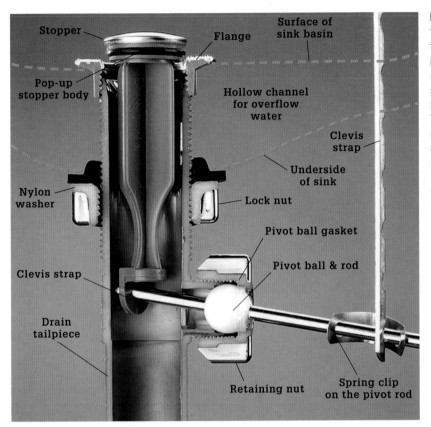

Stopper

Flange

Surface of sink basin

Pop-up stopper body

Hollow channel for overflow water

Nylon washer

Clevis strap

Underside of sink

Lock nut

Pivot ball gasket

Pivot ball & rod

Clevis strap

Drain tailpiece

Retaining nut

Spring clip on the pivot rod

Pop-up stoppers keep objects from falling down the drain, and they make filling and draining the sink easy. When you pull up on the lift rod, the clevis strap is raised, which raises the pivot rod, which seesaws on the pivot ball and pulls the pop-up stopper down against the flange. This blocks water through the sink drain, but water may still overflow into the overflow channel and get into the stopper body and down the drain through overflow ports in the pop-up body. This is a nice feature if you leave the water running in a plugged basin by mistake.

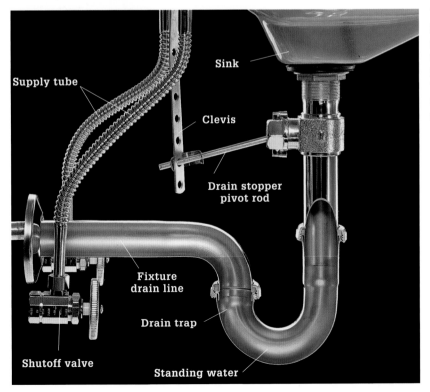

Supply tube

Sink

Clevis

Drain stopper pivot rod

Fixture drain line

Drain trap

Shutoff valve

Standing water

The lavatory drain trap holds water that seals the drain line and prevents sewer gases from entering the home. Each time a drain is used, the standing trap water is flushed away and replaced by new water. The shape of the trap and fixture drain line may resemble the letter P, and sink traps sometimes are called P-traps.

How to Replace a Pop-up Stopper

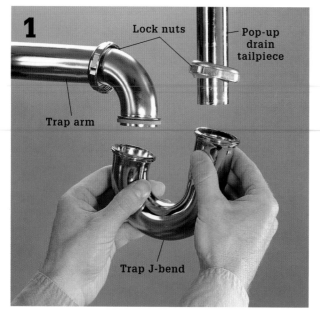

1

Lock nuts

Pop-up drain tailpiece

Trap arm

Trap J-bend

Put a basin under the trap to catch water. Loosen the nuts at the outlet and inlet to the trap J-bend by hand or with channel-type pliers and remove the bend. The trap will slide off the pop-up body tailpiece when the nuts are loose. Keep track of washers and nuts and their up/down orientation by leaving them on the tubes.

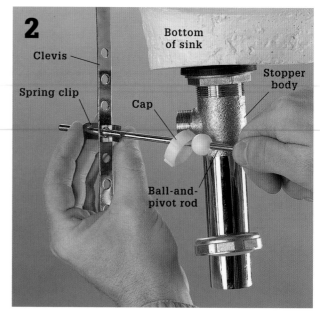

2

Bottom of sink

Clevis

Spring clip

Cap

Stopper body

Ball-and-pivot rod

Unscrew the cap holding the ball-and-pivot rod in the pop-up body and withdraw the ball. Compress the spring clip on the clevis and withdraw the pivot rod from the clevis.

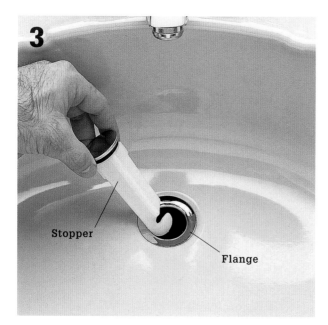

3

Stopper

Flange

Remove the pop-up stopper. Then, from below, remove the lock nut on the stopper body. If needed, keep the flange from turning by inserting a large screwdriver in the drain from the top. Thrust the stopper body up through the hole to free the flange from the basin, and then remove the flange and the stopper body.

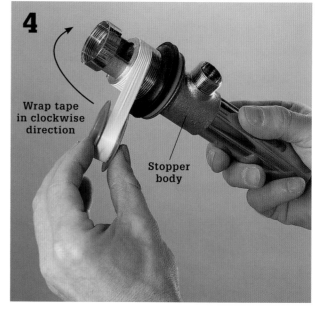

4

Wrap tape in clockwise direction

Stopper body

Clean the drain opening above and below, and then thread the locknut all the way down the new pop-up body followed by the flat washer and the rubber gasket (beveled side up). Wrap three layers of Teflon tape clockwise onto the top of the threaded body. Make a ½"-dia. snake from plumber's putty, form it into a ring, and stick the ring underneath the drain flange.

From below, face the pivot rod opening directly back toward the middle of the faucet and pull the body straight down to seat the flange. Thread the locknut/washer assembly up under the sink, then fully tighten the locknut with channel-type pliers. Do not twist the flange in the process, as this can break the putty seal. Clean off the squeezeout of plumber's putty from around the flange.

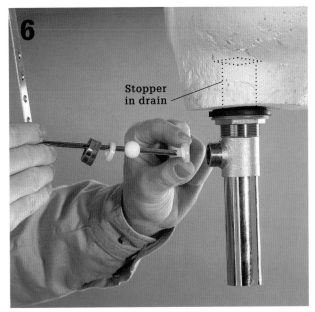

Drop the pop-up stopper into the drain hole so the hole at the bottom of its post is closest to the back of the sink. Put the beveled nylon washer into the opening in the back of the pop-up body with the bevel facing back.

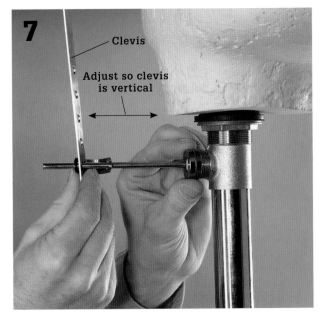

Put the cap behind the ball on the pivot rod as shown. Sandwich a hole in the clevis with the spring clip and thread the long end of the pivot rod through the clip and clevis. Put the ball end of the pivot rod into the pop-up body opening and into the hole in the the stopper stem. Screw the cap on to the pop-up body over the ball.

Loosen the clevis screw holding the clevis to the lift rod. Push the pivot rod all the way down (which fully opens the pop-up stopper). With the lift rod also all the way down, tighten the clevis screw to the rod. If the clevis runs into the top of the trap, cut it short with your hacksaw or tin snips. Reassemble the J-bend trap.

Toilets, Bidets, & Urinals

Since the invention of the original water closet in the 19th Century, toilets have become (arguably) the most indispensable piece of household equipment. If your toilet is not functioning acceptably, no one is happy. Advancing technology has given us toilets that perform more reliably and more efficiently than ever, but it is still estimated that toilets are responsible for as many as half of all home plumbing repair calls. It is worth installing a quality fixture and taking the time to do it right.

The toilet has two close relatives that are becoming increasingly popular in modern homes: the bidet and the urinal. A longtime standard in Europe, the bidet is positioned directly next to the toilet and is used for personal sanitation after the toilet. The warm water stream is a much more effective sanitation solution than paper alone, and is also useful for people with limited mobility.

The urinal has become a very trendy piece of bathroom equipment (and it is not limited only to the bathroom). As water becomes more scarce, expect to see more and more urinals being installed in homes. They use just a fraction of the water that a toilet consumes per flush, and some types use no water at all.

In this chapter:

- Toilets
- Bidets
- Urinals

Toilets

You can replace a poorly functioning toilet with a high-efficiency, high-quality new toilet for under two hundred and fifty dollars, but don't. As Ben Franklin would say, be penny wise and pound foolish. All toilets made since 1996 have been required to use 1.6 gallons or less per flush, which has been a huge challenge for the industry. Today, the most evolved 1.6-gallon toilets have wide passages behind the bowl and wide (3") flush valve openings—features that facilitate short, powerful flushes. This means fewer second flushes and fewer clogged toilets, which were common complaints about the first generation of 1.6-gallon toilets that continue to beleaguer inferior models today. See what toilets are available at your local home center in your price range, then go online and see what other consumers' experiences with those models have been. New toilets often go through a "de-bugging" stage when problems with leaks and malfunctioning parts are more common. Your criteria should include ease of installation, good flush performance, and reliability. With a little research, you should be able to purchase and install a high-functioning economical gravity-flush toilet that will serve you well for years to come.

Replacing a toilet is simple, and the latest generation of 1.6-gallon water-saving toilets has overcome the performance problems of earlier models.

Buy a toilet that will fit the space. Measure the distance from the floor bolts back to the wall (if your old toilet has two pairs of bolts, go by the rear pair). This is your rough-in distance and will be either 10" or approximately 12". Make note of the bowl shape, round or oval (long). Oval bowls (also called elongated bowls) are a few inches longer for greater comfort, but may be too big for your space. The safest bet is to buy a replacement with the same bowl shape.

Round front

Rough-in distance 10", 12", or 14" (12" most common)

Floor bolt (cap on)

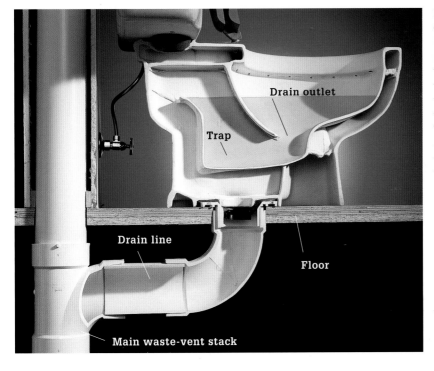

Drain outlet

Trap

Drain line

Floor

Main waste-vent stack

Knowing how a toilet works isn't essential to successful installation, but it helps. This cutaway photo features a pre-1.6 gallon law model, so your new toilet will have a much smaller trap. When the flush handle on the tank is depressed, the water in the tank rushes out through the hole in the underside of the bowl rim. The onrushing water forces the contents of the bowl and the trap out through the closet flange and into the drain line, while the fresh tank water refills the bowl and trap.

How to Install a Toilet

1

Clean and inspect the old closet flange. Look for breaks or wear. Also inspect the flooring around the flange. If either the flange or floor is worn or damaged, repair the damage. Use a rag and mineral spirits to completely remove residue from the old wax ring.

Replacing a Flange Tip ▸

If the old flange is solvent-welded to the closet pipe, cut the pipe flush with the floor. Dry-fit the new flange into the pipe. Turn the flange until the side cut-out screw slots are parallel to the wall. (Do not use the curved keyhole slots, as they are not as strong.) Attach the new flange with solvent glue.

2

Insert new closet bolts (don't reuse old ones) into the openings in the closet flange. Make sure the heads of the bolts are oriented to catch the maximum amount of flange material.

3

Remove the wax ring and apply it to the underside of the bowl, around the horn. Remove the protective covering. Do not touch the wax ring. It is very sticky.

4

Lower the bowl onto the flange, taking care not to disturb the wax ring. The holes in the bowl base should align perfectly with the tank bolts. Add a washer and tighten a nut on each bolt. Hand tighten each nut and then use channel-type pliers to further tighten the nuts. Alternate back and forth between nuts until the bowl is secure. DO NOT OVERTIGHTEN.

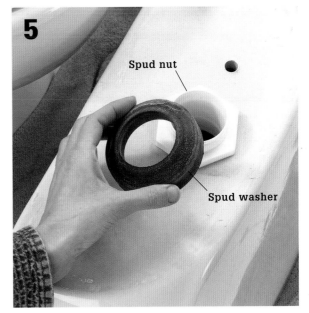

5

Spud nut

Spud washer

Attach the toilet tank. Some tanks come with a flush valve and a fill valve preinstalled, but if yours does not, insert the flush valve through the tank opening and tighten a spud nut over the threaded end of the valve. Place a foam spud washer on top of the spud nut.

6

Adjust the fill valve as directed by the manufacturer to set the correct tank water level height and install the valve inside the tank. Hand-tighten the nylon lock nut that secures the valve to the tank (inset photo) and then tighten it farther with channel-type pliers.

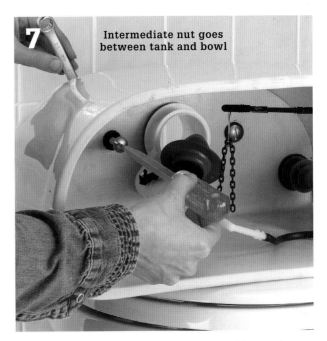

7

Intermediate nut goes between tank and bowl

With the tank lying on its back, thread a rubber washer onto each tank bolt and insert it into the bolt holes from inside the tank. Then, thread a brass washer and hex nut onto the tank bolts from below and tighten them to a quarter-turn past hand tight. Do not overtighten.

(continued)

8

Intermediate
nut

Position the tank on the bowl, spud washer on the opening, bolts through bolt holes. Put a rubber washer followed by a brass washer and a wing nut on each bolt and tighten these up evenly.

9

You may stabilize the bolts with a large slotted screwdriver from inside the tank, but tighten the nuts, not the bolts. You may press down a little on a side, the front, or the rear of the tank to level it as you tighten the nuts by hand. Do not overtighten and crack the tank. The tank should be level and stable when you're done.

10

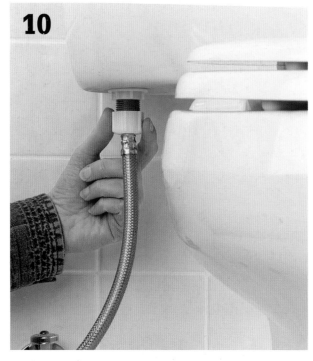

Hook up the water supply by connecting the supply tube to the threaded fill valve with the coupling nut provided. Turn on the water and test for leaks.

11

Attach the toilet seat by threading the plastic or brass bolts provided with the seat through the openings on the back of the rim and attaching nuts.

Toilet Height Extenders ▸

Although today's toilets are being made with higher seats than in the past, physically challenged and elderly people often find it difficult to use standard toilets, especially compact toilets (most of the more inexpensive toilets are compact). To address the problem of low toilet seats, you can retrofit your toilet with a seat riser or reinstall the toilet on a platform. See Resources, page 284.

Hinged Seat Risers: By replacing your old toilet seat with a riser seat, you can raise the functional height of the toilet by 3" to 4". Look for models that are hinged or removable for easy cleaning.

Platforms: It is possible to use a closet flange extender and plywood to rig up a DIY toilet platform so you can install a standard toilet with the seat higher. A cleaner and simpler option is to purchase a tall toilet platform that is designed to fit over your existing closet flange and is predrilled with holes for the closet flange bolts.

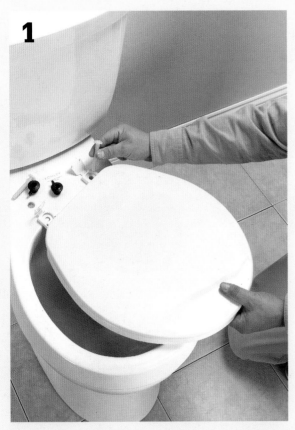

Remove the old seat. If the nuts for the seat bolts are corroded, slip a hack saw blade between the hinge plates and stool and cut the bolts.

Install the new height extender by bolting it to the stool through the seat bolt holes. Attach a standard toilet seat to the extender.

Bidets

Bidets are becoming ever more popular in the United States. Maybe that's because they can give a dream bath that European flare so many of us find alluring. Go to Europe, Asia, or South America and you'll see how much people can come to rely on bidets. Some fans of this bathroom fixture think those who don't use bidets are unhygienic.

With the trend moving toward larger and more luxurious bathrooms, many Americans are becoming intrigued by this personal hygiene appliance. The standard model features hot and cold faucets, and either a movable nozzle located by the faucet handles or a vertical sprayer located near the front of the bowl. Most bidets are outfitted with a pop-up drain. You can also buy a combination toilet and bidet if space is an issue.

Installing a bidet is very much like installing a sink. The only difference is that the bidet can have the waste line plumbed below the floor, like a shower. But like sinks, bidets may have single or multiple deck holes for faucets, so be certain to purchase compatible components.

Tools & Materials ›

Tape measure	P-trap
Drill	Tubing cutter
Adjustable wrench	Plumber's putt
Level	Thread tape
Silicone sealant	Bidet
(2) ⅜" shut off valves	Bidet faucet
(2) ⅜" supply lines	Marker

A bidet is a useful companion to a toilet, and it is a luxury item you and your family will appreciate. It's also a bit of a novelty you will enjoy sharing. For people with limited mobility, a bidet is an aide to independent personal sanitation.

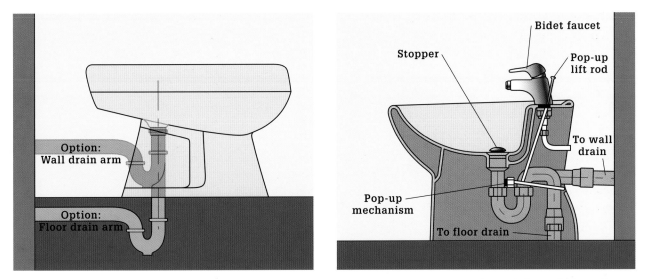

Bidet drains have more in common with sink drains than with toilet drains. Some even attach to a drain arm in the wall, with a P-trap that fits between the fixture drain tailpiece and the arm. Other bidets drain into a floor drain outlet with a trap that's situated between the tailpiece and the branch drain line.

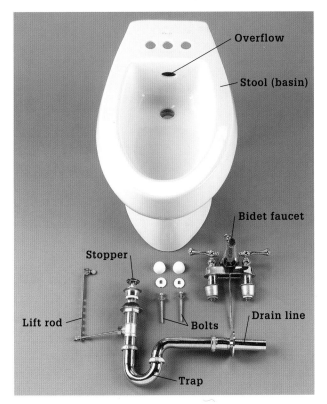

A bidet requires a special faucet that allows you to mix hot and cold water to a temperature you find comfortable. It has a third knob to control the water pressure. The aerator and spout pivot to allow you to adjust the spray to a comfortable height.

You can get all the features of a bidet on your existing toilet with a number of aftermarket bidet seats. These seats feature heaters, sprayers, and dryers in basic or deluxe versions. Installation takes less than an hour and no additional space is needed.

How to Install a Bidet

Rough-in the supply and drain lines according to the manufacturer's specifications. If you do not have experience installing home plumbing, hire a plumber for this part of the job. Apply a coil of plumber's putty to the base of the bidet faucet, and then insert the faucet body into the mounting holes. Thread the washers and locknut onto the faucet body shank and hand tighten. Remove any plumber's putty squeeze out.

Apply a coil of plumber's putty around the underside of the drain flange. Insert the flange in the drain hole, place the gasket and washer, and then thread the nut onto the flange. Do not fully tighten.

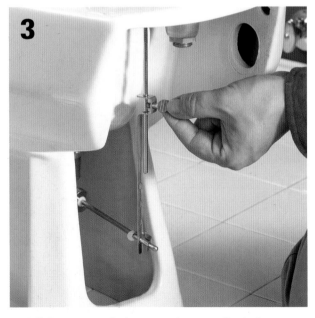

Install the pop-up drain apparatus according to the manufacturer's instructions.

Place the bidet in its final location, checking that supply and drain lines will be in alignment. Mark the locations of the two side-mounting holes through the predrilled holes on the stool and onto the floor.

Remove the bidet and drill ³⁄₁₆" pilot holes at the marks on the floor. Drive the floor bolts (included with the bidet basin) into the holes. Position the bidet so the floor bolts fit into the bolt holes in the base. Tighten nuts onto the floor bolts.

Connect the water supply risers to the bidet faucet using compression unions. Make sure to hook the hot and cold risers up to the correct ports on the faucet.

Hook up the drain line by attaching the P-trap to the drain tailpiece. The trap is then attached to a branch drain line coming out of the wall or floor in the same manner as a sink drain.

Remove the aerator so any debris in the supply line will clear and then turn on the water and open both faucets. Check for leaks in lines and fix, if found. Assemble the bolt caps and thread them onto the floor bolts. *Note: Do not dispose of paper in the bidet—return to the toilet to dry off after using the bidet for cleaning.*

Urinals

Most people consider a urinal to be a commercial or industrial bathroom accessory, so why would you want one in your home—and in your dream bathroom no less? The answer is in the many advantages a urinal has to offer and the fact that most major bathroom fixture manufacturers are now producing urinals designed for residential installation.

A urinal doesn't take up much space and it uses much less water per flush than a standard toilet: .5 to 1.0 gallon of water per flush for the urinal, as opposed to the low-flow toilet's 1.6 gallons of water per flush. You also have the option of a waterless urinal, a real boon in water-scarce areas. A urinal also has the emotional benefit of ending the "up versus down" toilet seat debate. Finally, a urinal is generally easier to keep clean than a toilet because splashing is minimized.

In today's homes with large multiple bathrooms and his and hers master baths, there are plenty of places you can choose to install a urinal. Of course, the perfect place is where it will get used the most: in the bathroom closest to the TV if the guys congregate at your house to watch sporting events; or in the bathroom closest to boys' bedrooms if you've got a passel of them.

Urinals are great water savers and are becoming increasingly popular in today's dream bathroom.

Tools & Materials ▸

Tape measure	Urinal flushometer
Adjustable wrench	Emery cloth
Pencil	Wire brush
Level	Allen wrench
Sealant tape	Drywall
Utility knife	Drywall tape
Drywall saw	Drywall compound
Tubing cutter	2 × 6 lumber
Hacksaw	PVC 2" drainpipe
Miter box	PVC 2" male threaded
Hex wrenches	drain outlet
Smooth-jawed	½ copper pipe
spud wrench	Urinal
Slotted screwdriver	Sealant tape

Waterless Urinals ▶

For the ultimate in water-conservation, you can now purchase a home urinal that uses zero water. A waterless urinal is never flushed, so you'll save about a gallon of water per usage. Naturally, waterless urinals are plumbed into your drain line system. But where typical plumbing fixtures rely on fresh water to carry the waste into the system, the waterless system relies simply on gravity for the liquid waste to find its way out of the fixture and into the drain. The secret is a layer of sealing liquid that is heavier than the water and forms a skim coat over the urine. When the urine enters the trap it displaces the sealing liquid, which immediately reforms on the surface to create a layer that seals in odors. The Kohler fixture seen here (see Resources, page 284) is an example of the sealing liquid system. Other waterless urinals use replaceable cartridges.

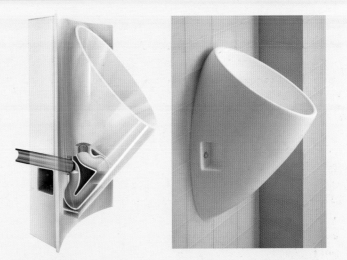

A layer of sealing liquid forms a skim coat that floats on top of the liquid to trap odors.

Flushing Options for Urinals

A manual flush handle is still the most common and least expensive flushing mechanism for urinals. It is reliable but not as sanitary as touchless types such as the Flushometer on page 166.

Motion sensors automatically flush touchless urinals, which is a great improvement in sanitation. These tend to be more expensive, however, and are more likely to develop problems. Also, because they flush automatically when users step away from the fixture they don't allow you to conserve water by limiting flushing.

How to Install a Urinal

Remove the drywall or other surface coverings between the urinal location and the closest water supply and waste lines. Remove enough wall surface to reveal half of the stud face on each side of the opening to make patch work simpler.

2 × 6 mounting board

Following the manufacturer's directions for the urinal and flushometer, determine the mounting height of the urinal, and mark the location of the supply and waste lines. For this, installation, the 2" waste line is centered 17½" above the finished floor. Cut 5½" × 1½" notches in the wall studs centered at 32" above the finished floor surface, then attach a 2 × 6 mounting board.

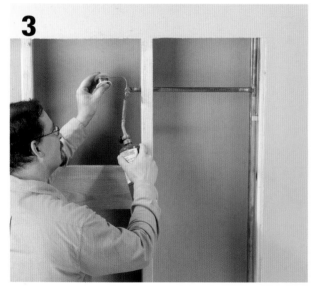

Install the copper cold water supply line according to the manufacturer's specifications. Here, it is 4¾" to the side of the fixture centerline and 45" from the finished floor (11½" from the top of the fixture). Cap the stub-out 3" from the finished wall surface. Install the 2" drainpipe and vent pipe, making sure that the centerline of the drain outlet is positioned correctly (here, 17½" above the finished floor and 4¾" to the side of the supply line).

Attach the male threaded waste outlet to the drain pipe. It should extend beyond the finished wall surface. Replace the wall covering and finish as desired.

Attach the mounting brackets 32" above the floor, 3¼" to the sides of the centerline of the waste outlet.

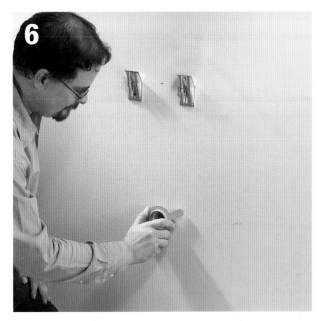

Apply Teflon tape to the waste outlet. Thread the female collar onto the waste outlet until it is firmly seated and the flanges are horizontally level. Place the gasket onto the female collar. The beveled surface of the gasket faces toward the urinal.

Hang the urinal on the brackets, being careful not to bump the porcelain as it chips easily. Thread the screws through the washers, the holes in the urinal, and into the collar. Tighten the screws by hand, then one full turn with an adjustable wrench. Do not overtighten.

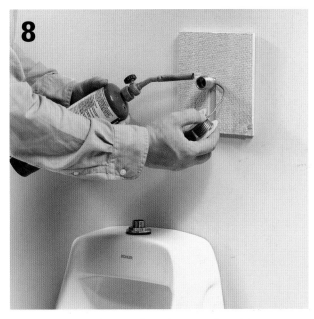

Determine the distance from the centerline of the water inlet on the top of the urinal, called the spud, to the finished wall. Subtract 1¼" from this distance and cut the water supply pipe to that length using a tubing cutter. Turn off the water before cutting. After cutting, deburr the inside and outside diameter of the supply pipe. Attach the threaded adapter to the cut pipe.

(continued)

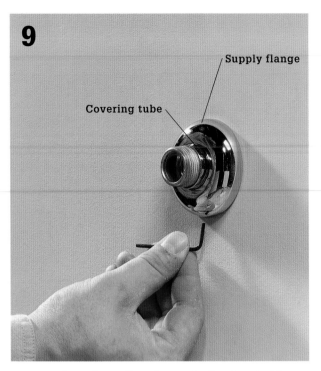

9

Covering tube

Supply flange

Measure from the wall surface to the first thread of the adapter. Using a hacksaw and a miter box or a tubing cutter, cut the covering tube to this length. Slide the covering tube over the water supply pipe. Slide the supply flange over the covering tube until it rests against the wall. Tighten the setscrew on the flange with an Allen wrench.

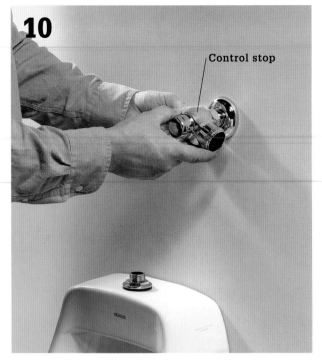

10

Control stop

Apply a small amount of pipe sealant to the adapter threads, then thread the control stop onto the adapter threads. Position the outlet toward the urinal so that it is horizontally level.

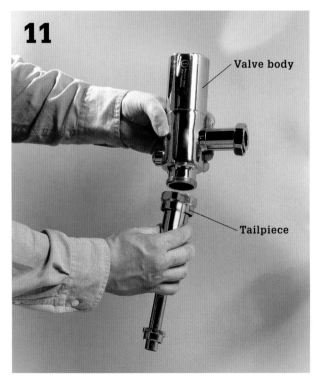

11

Valve body

Tailpiece

Hand tighten the tailpiece into the flushometer valve body.

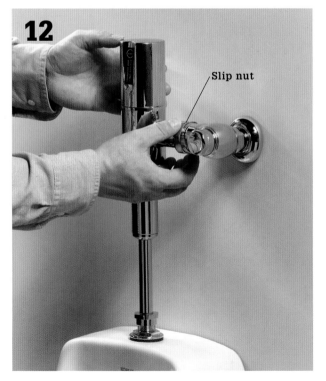

12

Slip nut

Hand tighten the slip nut that connects the valve body to the control stop.

13

Use a smooth-jawed spud wrench to securely tighten the tailpiece, vacuum breaker, and spud couplings.

Tip ▸

For maximum sanitation, choose a urinal flush mechanism with an electronic sensor, like the Kohler Flush-o-meter being installed here. The electronic eye on this type of flush mechanism senses when a user approaches the fixture and then commands the fixture to flush when the user steps away. This eliminates the need to touch the handle before the user has the opportunity to wash his hands.

While testing the flush, adjust the supply stop screw counter-clockwise until adequate flow is achieved.

14

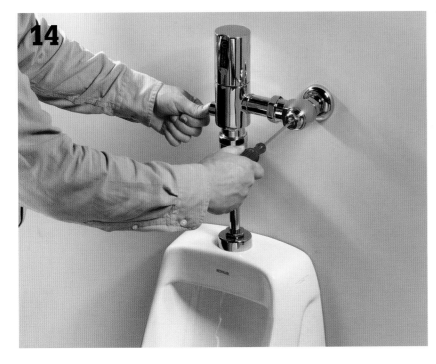

Bathroom Cabinets

When selecting storage and vanity cabinets, you will find there are many materials, styles, and colors to choose from. As you begin combining the units and fixtures, you will find you have an almost infinite number of options.

One of the first decisions to make is between prebuilt or custom-built units and fixtures. Prebuilt cabinets and countertops are available in familiar styles at home centers, and are perfect for renovating half baths, guest baths, and small family bathrooms. For more unique styles in large family bathrooms, master bathrooms, or home spas, you may want to have your cabinets and countertops custom-built by a professional cabinetmaker. Refer to pages 34 to 37 for more information on different styles of cabinets and countertops.

If you are remodeling a bathroom for universal design, there are a number of manufacturers that offer cabinets, countertops, and sinks specifically designed to provide accessibility. For more information on universal design, see pages 48 to 53.

In this chapter:

- Cabinets & Vanity Cabinets
- Stock Cabinets

Cabinets & Vanity Cabinets

Common bathroom cabinets include vanities, medicine cabinets, linen cabinets, and "tank topper" cabinets that mount over the toilet area. See pages 34 to 37 for more information on cabinets.

When installing cabinets in a damp location, like a bathroom, choose the best cabinets you can afford. Look for quality indicators, like doweled construction, hardwood doors and drawers, and high-gloss, moisture-resistant finishes. Avoid cabinets with sides or doors that are painted on one side and finished with laminate or veneer on the other because these cabinets are more likely to warp.

Tools & Materials ▸

Electronic stud finder
Level
Pry bar
Hammer
Screwdriver
Drill
Circular saw
Reciprocating saw
Pencil

Bar clamp
Framing square
Duplex nails
10d common nails
Finish nails
1 × 4 lumber
2½" wood screws
Wood shims

Recessed cabinets conserve space anywhere in the bathroom. Medicine cabinets above vanity locations are the most common recessed cabinets, but linen cabinets and other storage cabinets may be recessed as well.

How to Install a Surface-Mounted Cabinet

1

Locate the wall studs and mark them clearly on the wall surface. Draw a level line at the desired top height of the cabinet body, then measure and mark a second line to indicate the bottom of the cabinet.

2

Attach a temporary ledger board (usually 1 × 4) just below the lower level line using duplex nails. Rest the base of the cabinet on the ledger and hold it in place or brace it with 2 × 4s.

3

Attach the cabinet to the wall at the stud locations by drilling pilot holes and driving wood screws. Remove the ledger when finished, and patch the nail holes with drywall compound.

How to Install a Recessed Cabinet

1

2

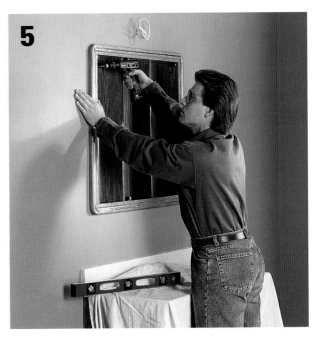

3

Header

Sill
plate

Locate the first stud beyond either side of the planned cabinet location, then remove the wall surface between the studs. (Removing the wall surface all the way to the ceiling simplifies patch work.) Cut along the center of the studs, using a circular saw with the blade depth set to the thickness of the wall surface.

Mark a rough opening ½" taller than the cabinet frame onto the exposed wall studs. Add 1½" for each header and sill plate, then cut out the studs in the rough opening area.

Frame out the top and bottom of the rough opening by installing a header and a sill plate between the cut wall studs. Make sure the header and sill plate are level, then nail them in place with 10d common nails.

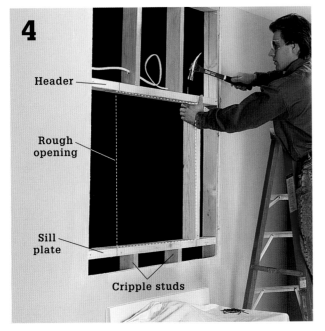

4

Header

Rough
opening

Sill
plate

Cripple studs

5

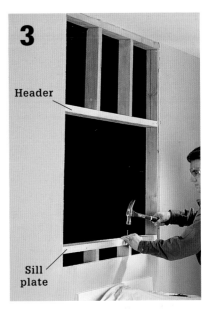

Mark the rough opening width on the header and sill plates, centering the opening over the sink. Cut and nail jack studs between the header and the sill plate, just outside the rough opening marks. Install any wiring for new light fixtures and receptacles, then patch the wall where necessary.

Position the cabinet in the opening. Check it for level with a carpenter's level, then attach the cabinet by drilling pilot holes and driving wood screws through the top and bottom of the cabinet sides and into the wall studs, header, and sill plate. Attach the doors, shelves, and hardware.

How to Install a Vanity Cabinet

1

Measure and mark the top edge of the vanity cabinet on the wall, then use a 4-ft. level to mark a level line at the cabinet height mark. Use an electronic stud finder to locate the framing members, then mark the stud locations along the line.

2

Slide the vanity into position so that the back rail of the cabinet can later be fastened to studs at both corners and in the center. The back of the cabinet should also be flush against the wall. (If the wall surface is uneven, position the vanity so it contacts the wall in at least one spot, and the back cabinet rail is parallel with the wall.)

3

Using a 4-ft. level as a guide, shim below the vanity cabinet until the unit is level.

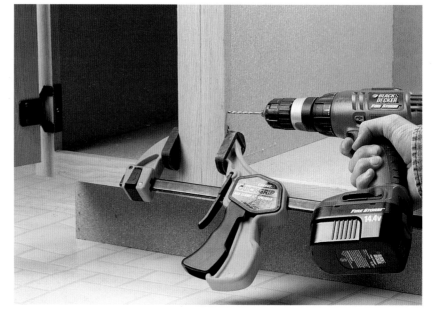

Variation: To install two or more cabinets, set the cabinets in position against the wall, and align the cabinet fronts. If one cabinet is higher than the other, shim under the lower cabinet until the two are even. Clamp the cabinet faces together, then drill countersunk pilot holes spaced 12" apart through the face frames so they go at least halfway into the face frame of the second cabinet. Drive wood screws through the pilot holes to join the cabinets together.

At the stud locations marked on the wall, drive 3" drywall screws through the rail on the cabinet back and into the framing members. The screws should be driven at both corners and in the center of the back rail.

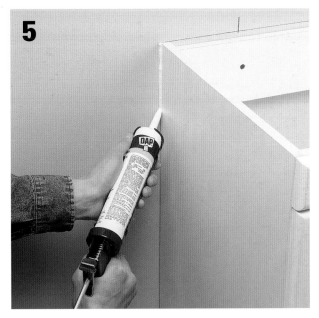

Run a bead of caulk along small gaps between the vanity and wall, and between the vanity and floor. For larger gaps, use quarter-round molding between the vanity and wall. Between the vanity and floor, install the same baseboard material used to cover the gap between the wall and floor.

Variation: Installing a Vanity with a Back

Mark a line on the wall where the top of the vanity will fit, then draw a line down the wall from the midpoint of this line. Draw a corresponding centerline down the back of the vanity.

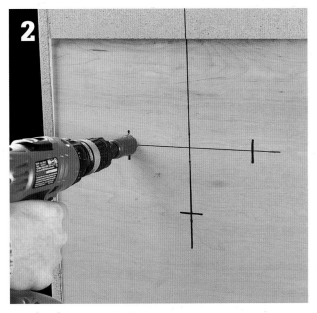

Measure the distance from the supply pipe and drain pipe to the centerline on the wall. Transfer distances to the back of the vanity, measuring from the centerline. Mark pipe cutouts, drill a hole at the center, then cut out with a hole saw or jigsaw.

Stock Cabinets

Cabinets must be firmly anchored to wall studs, and they must be plumb and level when installed. The best way to ensure this is by attaching a ledger board to the wall to assist in the installation. As a general rule, install the upper cabinets first so your access is not impeded by the base cabinets. (Although some professionals prefer to install the base cabinets first so they can be used to support the uppers during installation.) It's also best to begin in a corner and work outward from there.

Tools & Materials ▸

Handscrew clamps
Level
Hammer
Utility knife
Nail set
Stepladder
Drill
Counterbore drill bit
Cordless screwdriver
Jigsaw

Cabinets
Trim molding
Toe-kick molding
Filler strips
Valance
6d finish nails
Finish washers
#10 × 4" wood screws
#8 × 2½" screws
3" drywall screws

Stock cabinets are sold in boxes that are keyed to door and drawer packs (you need to buy these separately). It is important that you realize this when you are estimating your project costs at the building center (often a door pack will cost as much or more than the cabinet). Also allow plenty of time for assembling the cabinets out of the box. It can take an hour or more to put some more complex cabinets together.

How to Fit a Corner Cabinet

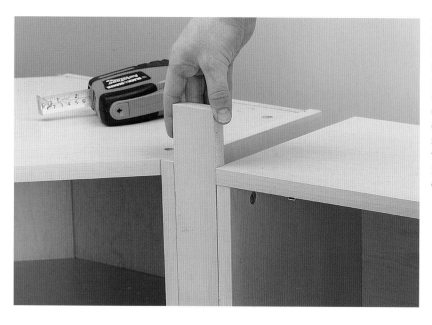

Before installation, test-fit corner and adjoining cabinets to make sure doors and handles do not interfere with each other. If necessary, increase the clearance by pulling the corner cabinet away from the side wall by no more than 4". To maintain even spacing between the edges of the doors and the cabinet corner, cut a filler strip and attach it to the corner cabinet or the adjoining cabinet. Filler strips should be made from material that matches the cabinet doors and face frames.

How to Install Wall Cabinets

1

Position a corner upper cabinet on a ledger and hold it in place, making sure it is resting cleanly on the ledger. Drill ³⁄₁₆" pilot holes into the wall studs through the hanging strips at the top rear of cabinet. Attach the cabinet to the wall with 2½" screws. Do not fully tighten until all cabinets are hung.

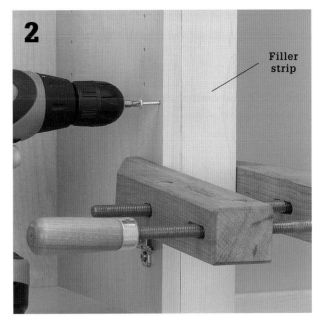

2

Filler strip

Attach a filler strip to the front edge of the cabinet, if needed. Clamp the filler in place, and drill counterbored pilot holes through the cabinet face frame, near hinge locations. Attach filler to cabinet with 2½" cabinet screws or flathead wood screws.

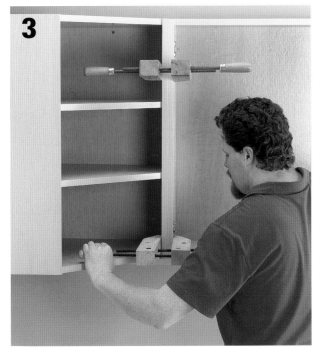

3

Position the adjoining cabinet on the ledger, tight against the corner cabinet or filler strip. Clamp the corner cabinet and the adjoining cabinet together at the top and bottom. Handscrew clamps will not damage wood face frames.

4

Check the front cabinet edges or face frames for plumb. Drill ³⁄₁₆" pilot holes into wall studs through hanging strips in rear of cabinet. Attach cabinet with 2½" screws. Do not tighten wall screws fully until all cabinets are hung.

(continued)

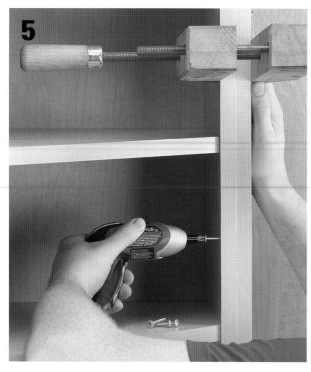

Attach the corner cabinet to the adjoining cabinet. From inside the corner cabinet, drill pilot holes through the face frame. Join the cabinets with sheet-metal screws.

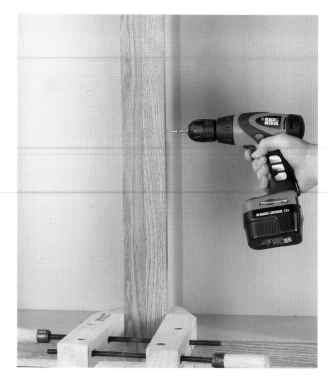

Alternative: Cabinets with face frames. Clamp frames together, and drill counterbored pilot holes through the side of the face frame. Join cabinets with wood screws. Drill ³⁄₁₆" pilot holes in hanging strips, and attach the cabinet to the studs with wood screws.

Join frameless cabinets with #8 × 1¼" panhead wood screws or wood screws with decorative washers. Each pair of cabinets should be joined by at least four screws.

Fill gaps between the cabinet and wall with a filler strip. Cut the filler strip to fit the space, then wedge wood shims between the filler and the wall to create a friction fit that holds it in place temporarily. Drill counterbored pilot holes through the side of the cabinet (or the edge of the face frame) and attach filler with screws.

Remove the temporary ledger. Check the cabinet run for plumb, and adjust if necessary by placing wood shims behind cabinet, near stud locations. Tighten wall screws completely. Cut off shims with utility knife.

Use trim moldings to cover any gaps between cabinets and walls. Stain moldings to match cabinet finish.

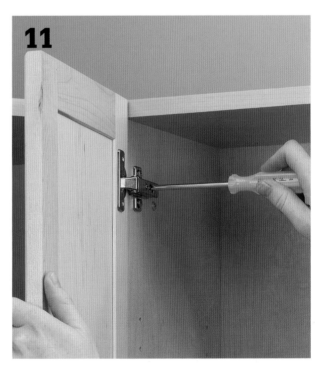

Attach a decorative valance above a window. Clamp the valance to the edge of the cabinet frames, and drill counterbored pilot holes through the cabinet frames into the end of the valance. Attach with sheet-metal screws.

Install the cabinet doors. If necessary, adjust the hinges so that the doors are straight and plumb.

How to Install Base Cabinets

Begin the installation with a corner cabinet. Draw plumb lines that intersect the 34½" reference line (measured from the high point of the floor) at the locations for the cabinet sides.

Place the cabinet in the corner. Make sure the cabinet is plumb and level. If necessary, adjust by driving wood shims under the cabinet base. Be careful not to damage flooring. Drill ³⁄₁₆" pilot holes through the hanging strip and into wall studs. Tack the cabinet to the wall with wood screws or wallboard screws.

Clamp the adjoining cabinet to the corner cabinet. Make sure the new cabinet is plumb, then drill counterbored pilot holes through the cabinet sides or the face frame and filler strip. Screw the cabinets together. Drill ³⁄₁₆" pilot holes through hanging strips and into wall studs. Tack the cabinets loosely to the wall studs with wood screws or wallboard screws.

Use a jigsaw to cut any cabinet openings needed in the cabinet backs (for example, in the sink base seen here) for plumbing, wiring, or heating ducts.

5

Position and attach additional cabinets, making sure the frames are aligned and the cabinet tops are level. Clamp cabinets together, then attach the face frames or cabinet sides with screws driven into pilot holes. Tack the cabinets to the wall studs, but don't drive screws too tight—you may need to make adjustments once the entire bank is installed.

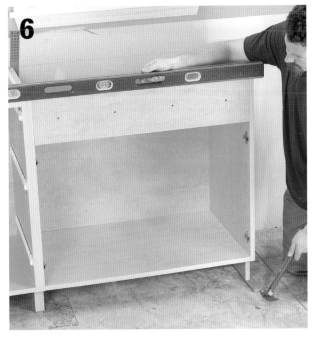

6

Make sure all cabinets are level. If necessary, adjust by driving shims underneath cabinets. Place shims behind the cabinets near stud locations to fill any gaps. Tighten wall screws. Cut off shims with utility knife.

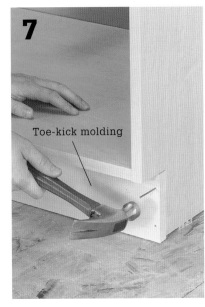

7

Toe-kick molding

Use trim moldings to cover gaps between the cabinets and the wall or floor. The toe-kick area is often covered with a strip of wood finished to match the cabinets or painted black.

8

Hang cabinet doors and mount drawer fronts, then test to make sure they close smoothly and the doors fit evenly and flush. Self-closing cabinet hinges (by far the most common type installed today) have adjustment screws that allow you to make minor changes to the hardware to correct any problems. Add countertops.

Lighting & Ventilation

Lighting plays an important role in every bathroom. Without good lighting placed in strategic areas, we wouldn't be able to conduct most of our bathroom business. Many different types of lighting and a seemingly infinite array of styles are available to light up your dream bath. Unless you're starting from scratch or tearing down the walls is part of your bathroom remodel, be sure to choose fixtures designed for retrofit installations.

Ventilation also plays an important role in every bathroom. It's so important that most building codes require a vent fan in any bathroom lacking natural ventilation. Remodeling your dream bath gives you the perfect opportunity to add a new vent fan or upgrade to a quieter, more efficient model, maybe even one with a built-in heat lamp.

In this chapter:

- Vanity Lights
- Ceiling Lights
- Recessed Lights
- Vent Fans
- Combination Fan/Lights

Vanity Lights

Many bathrooms have a single fixture positioned above the vanity, but a light source in this position casts shadows on the face and makes grooming more difficult. Light fixtures on either side of the mirror is a better arrangement.

For a remodel, mark the mirror location, run cable, and position boxes before drywall installation. You can also retrofit by installing new boxes and drawing power from the existing fixture.

The light sources should be at eye level; 66" is typical. The size of your mirror and its location on the wall may affect how far apart you can place the sconces, but 36 to 40" apart is a good guideline.

Tools & Materials ▸

Drywall saw
Drill
Combination tool
Circuit tester
Screwdrivers
Hammer

Electrical boxes
  and braces
Wall sconces
NM cable
Wire connectors

Vanity lights on the sides of the mirror provide good light.

How to Install Vanity Lights in a Finished Bathroom

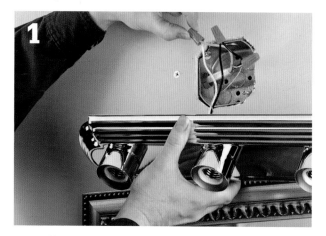

Turn off the power at the service panel. Remove the old fixture from the wall, and test to make sure that the power is off. Undo the connectors, and remove the old fixture. Then, remove a strip of drywall from around the old fixture to the first studs beyond the approximate location of the new sconces. Make the opening large enough that you have room to route cable from the existing fixture to the boxes for the sconces.

Mark the location for the sconces, and install new boxes. Install the boxes about 66" above the floor and 18 to 20" from the centerline of the mirror (the mounting base of some sconces is above or below the bulb, so adjust the height of the bracing accordingly). If the correct location is on or next to a stud, you can attach the box directly to the stud, otherwise you'll need to install blocking or use boxes with adjustable braces (shown).

3

Open the side knockouts on the electrical box above the vanity. Then, drill ⅝" holes in the centers of any studs between the old fixture and the new ones. Run two 14/2 NM cables from the new boxes for the sconces to the box above the vanity. Protect the cable with metal protector plates, and secure the new branch cables at both ends with cable clamps, leaving 11" of extra cable for making the connection to the old box and new sconces. Remove sheathing and strip insulation from the ends of the wires.

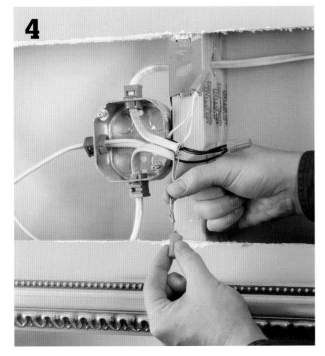

4

Connect the white wires from the new cables to the white wire from the old cable, and connect the black wires from the new cables to the black wire from the old cable. Connect the ground wires. Replace the drywall, leaving openings for the sconces and the old box. Cover the old box with a flat cover, or reconnect and reinstall the original above-mirror fixture after installing the new fixtures.

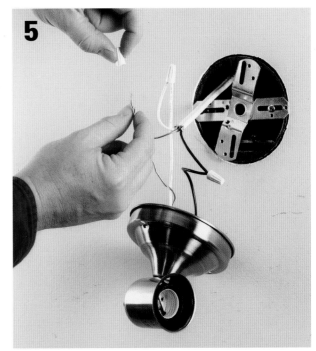

5

Install the fixture mounting braces on the boxes. Attach the fixtures by connecting the black circuit wire to the black fixture wire, and connecting the white circuit wire to the white fixture wire. Connect the ground wires. Position the fixture over the box, and attach with the mounting screws. Restore power and test the circuit.

Ceiling Lights

Ceiling fixtures don't have any moving parts and their wiring is very simple, so, other than changing bulbs, you're likely to get decades of trouble-free service from a fixture. This sounds like a good thing, but it also means that the fixture probably won't fail and give you an excuse to update a room's look with a new one. Fortunately, you don't need an excuse. Upgrading a fixture is easy and can make a dramatic impact on a room. You substantially increase the light in a room by replacing a globe-style fixture by one with separate spot lights, or you can simply install a new fixture that matches the room's décor.

Tools & Materials ▸

Light fixtures
Voltage sensor
Screwdrivers
Wire stripper

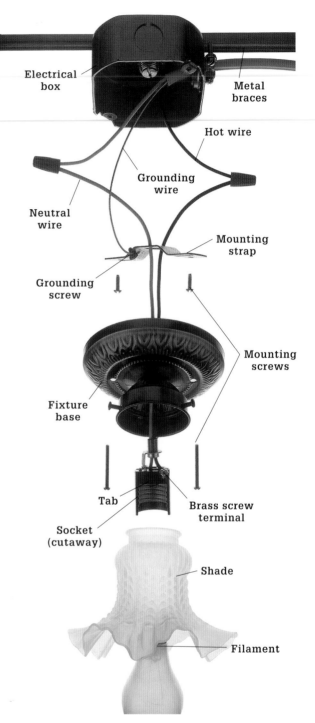

Installing a new ceiling fixture can provide more light, along with an aesthetic lift.

No matter what a ceiling light fixture looks like on the outside, they all attach in basically the same way. An electrical box in the ceiling is fitted with a mounting strap, which holds the fixture in place. The bare wire from the ceiling typically connects to the mounting strap. The two wires coming from the fixture connect to the black and white wires from the ceiling.

How to Replace a Ceiling-mounted Light Fixture

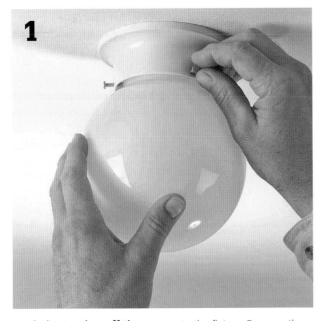

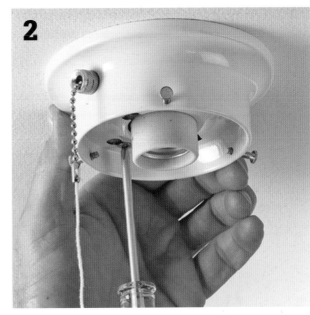

Begin by turning off the power to the fixture. Remove the globe by unthreading the globe (turning it counter-clockwise) or by loosening the three screws that pinch the globe in place (the screws usually go through a collar around the base of the globe). Next, remove the lightbulbs from the fixture.

Detach the old light from the ceiling electrical box. Most traditional fixtures use two long screws to secure the fixture base to the metal electrical box in the ceiling. Have a helper hold the fixture with one hand so it doesn't fall, while you use a screwdriver to remove the two screws. Gently pull the light straight down, exposing the wiring that powers the fixture.

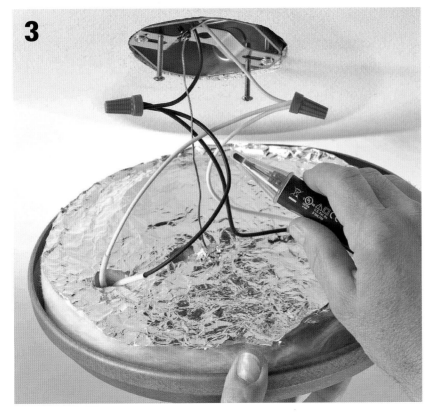

Before you touch the wires that feed the existing light, use a voltage sensor to verify that the circuit is now dead. With the fixture's switch in the on position, insert the sensor's probe into the electrical box and hold the probe within ½" of the black wires inside. If the sensor beeps or lights up, then the circuit is still live, and you'll need to trip the correct breaker to disconnect power to the fixture. If the sensor does not beep or light up, the circuit is dead and you can proceed safely.

(continued)

4

Once you have verified that the power to the light is off at the main panel, remove the fixture by disconnecting the wires. After removing the wire connectors, pull the fixture completely away from the box.

5

Before you install the new fixture, check the ends of the wires coming from the ceiling electrical box. They should be clean and free of nicks or scorch marks. If they're dirty or worn, clip off the stripped portion with your combination tool. Then, strip away about ¾" of insulation from the end of each wire.

6

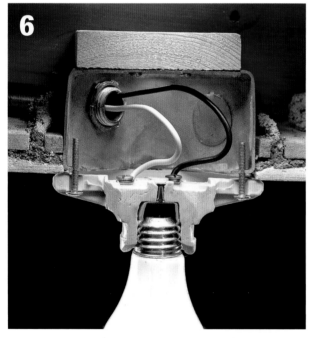

Now, take a look at the electrical box. Most fixtures installed in the last few decades are attached to a mounting strap, a strip of metal reaching from one side of the electrical box to another and attached with two screws. Older light fixtures were often mounted directly to the holes in the box, a less safe installation that doesn't meet current electrical codes.

7

If the box doesn't have a mounting strap, attach one. One might be included with your new fixture; otherwise, you can buy one at any hardware store or home center.

8

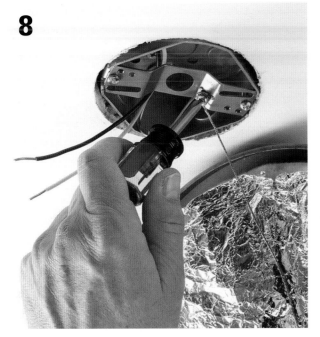

You will probably find a bare copper wire in the box. Connect this wire to the screw near the center of the mounting strap. Wrap the wire clockwise around the screw and turn the screw until it is snug.

9

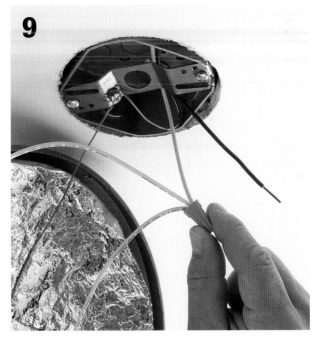

Set the new fixture on top of a ladder or have a helper support it. You'll find two short wires—called leads—coming from the fixture, one white and one black. If the ends of the leads are not already stripped, remove about ¾" of insulation from each wire end. Hold the white lead from the fixture next to the white wire from the ceiling. Push the ends into a wire connector, and twist the connector clockwise until it is snug.

10

Now connect the black wire to the black lead with a wire connector in the same way. Give both connections a gentle tug to make sure the connectors are tight.

11

Tuck the wire connections into the ceiling box on either side of the mounting strap. Secure the light to the ceiling box by driving the fixture's mounting screws through the holes in the fixture base and into the strap.

12

With the fixture secured to the box, you can install the lightbulbs and shades. Each fixture is a little different; follow the manufacturer's instructions. Once the bulbs are in, restore power to the fixture and test it.

Recessed Ceiling Lights

Recessed lights are mounted flush with the ceiling or the wall, making them unobtrusive and a good choice for overall lighting in any style of dream bath. They cast light without drawing attention to themselves, and when attached to a dimmer switch, they can add ambiance for the long, relaxing soaks in your new whirlpool.

Recessed light fixtures should be located where they will best illuminate the activity areas of your bathroom. Any bathroom light fixture should run on a GFCI-protected circuit. If you're uncomfortable working with electricity, hire an electrician to complete the installation.

Tools & Materials ▸

Hammer
Screwdriver
Drill
Utility knife
Cable stripper

Recessed light fixture
Nails
Cable clamps
NM cable
Wire connectors

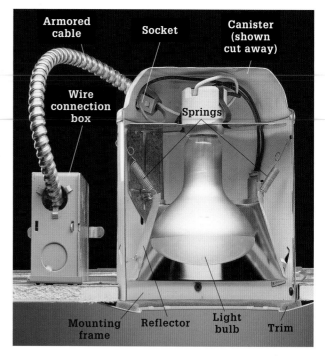

Recessed ceiling lights, often called canister lights or can lights, are perfectly suitable fixtures for providing overhead light in bathrooms. A single can light may be installed in an attic area or even a joist cavity above the bathroom ceiling, but more often several are wired in series.

How to Install Recessed Ceiling Lights

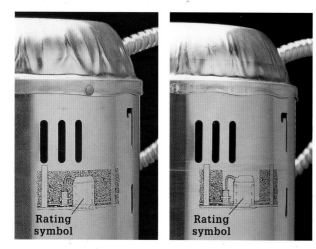

Tip: Choose the proper type of recessed light fixture for your project. There are two types of fixtures: those rated for installation within insulation (left), and those that must be kept at least 3" from insulation (right). Self-contained thermal switches shut off power if the unit gets too hot for its rating. A recessed light fixture must be installed at least ½" from combustible materials.

Extend the mounting bars on the recessed fixture to reach the framing members. Adjust the position of the light unit on the mounting bars to locate it properly. Align the bottom edges of the mounting bars with the bottom face of the framing members, then nail or screw the mounting bars to the framing members.

2

Cable clamp

Open knockout

Remove the wire connection box cover and open one knockout for each cable entering the box. Install a cable clamp for each open knockout, and tighten the locknut using a screwdriver to drive the lugs. Mount any remaining fixtures.

Cutaway view

With the recessed fixtures mounted, install the feeder cable that runs from the service panel to the switch gang box, then install cable to the first fixture in the circuit. Strip the cable sheathing back 6" to 8" from the end using a cable ripper. Insert the cable through a cable clamp and into the wire connection box with ½" of sheathing extending into the box, then tighten the clamp. Cut and install cable to run to any remaining fixtures to complete the circuit. Arrange for the rough-in inspection before making the final connections.

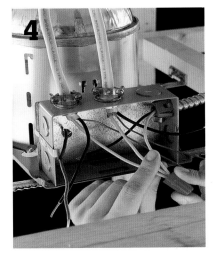

4

Make the final connections before installing drywall (the work must be inspected first). For each fixture, strip ½" of insulation from the white cable wires, then connect them to the white fixture lead using a wire connector.

5

Strip ½" of insulation from the black cable wires, then connect them to the black fixture lead, using a wire connector.

6

Attach a grounding pigtail to the grounding screw on the fixture, then connect all grounding wires. Tuck all wires into the junction box, and replace the cover. Make hookups at the service panel, and arrange for the final inspection.

Vent Fans

For most of us, a dream bathroom does not include foggy mirrors or unpleasant odors. Opening a window, if your bathroom is equipped with one, can help, but vent fans do the best job of clearing the air.

Most vent fans are installed in the center of the bathroom ceiling or over the toilet area. A fan installed over the tub or shower area must be GFCI protected and rated for use in wet areas. You can usually wire a fan that just has a light fixture into a main bathroom electrical circuit, but units with built-in heat lamps or blowers require separate circuits.

If the fan you choose doesn't come with a mounting kit, purchase one separately. A mounting kit should include a vent hose (duct), a vent tailpiece, and an exterior vent cover.

Venting instructions vary among manufacturers, but the most common options are attic venting and soffit venting. Attic venting (shown in this project) routes fan ductwork into the attic and out through the roof. Always insulate ducting in this application to keep condensation from forming and running down into the motor. Carefully install flashing around the outside vent cover to prevent roof leaks.

Soffit venting involves routing the duct to a soffit (roof overhang) instead of through the roof. Check with the vent manufacturer for instructions for soffit venting.

To prevent moisture damage, always terminate the vent outside your home—never into your attic or basement.

You can install a vent fan while the framing is exposed or as a retrofit, as shown in this project.

Tools & Materials ▸

Drill
Jigsaw
Combination tool
Screwdrivers
Caulk gun
Reciprocating saw
Pry bar
Drywall screws
Double-gang retrofit
    electrical box

NM cable (14/2, 14/3)
Cable clamp
Hose clamps
Pipe insulation
Roofing cement
Self-sealing
    roofing nails
Shingles
Wire connectors
Switches

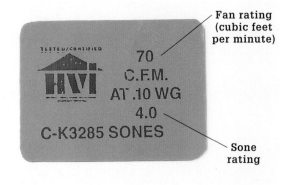

Check the information label attached to each vent fan unit. Choose a unit with a fan rating at least 5 CFM higher than the square footage of your bathroom. The sone rating refers to the relative quietness of the unit, rated on a scale of 1 to 7. (Quieter vent fans have lower sone ratings.)

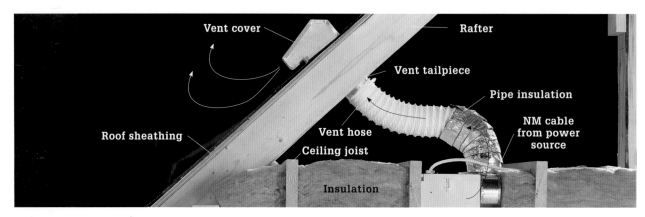

Bathroom vent fans must be exhausted to the outdoors, either through the roof or through a wall. Flexible ductwork is allowed for bath vent fans (but not for clothes dryers).

How to Install a Bathroom Vent Fan

Position the vent fan unit against a ceiling joist. Outline the vent fan onto the ceiling surface. Remove the unit, then drill pilot holes at the corners of the outline and cut out the area with a jigsaw or drywall saw.

Remove the grille from the fan unit, then position the unit against the joist with the edge recessed ¼" from the finished surface of the ceiling (so the grille can be flush mounted). Attach the unit to the joist using drywall screws.

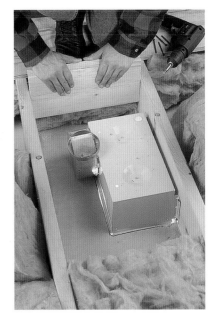

Variation: For vent fans with heaters or light fixtures, some manufacturers recommend using 2× lumber to build dams between the ceiling joists to keep the insulation at least 6" away from the fan unit.

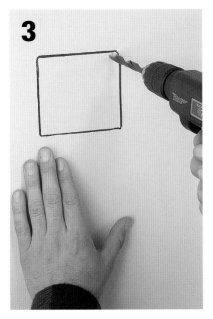

Mark and cut an opening for the switch box on the wall next to the latch side of the bathroom door, then run a 14/3 NM cable from the switch cutout to the fan unit. Run a 14/2 NM cable from the power source to the cutout.

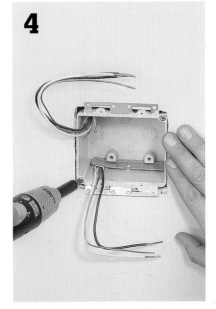

Strip 10" of sheathing from the ends of the cables, then feed the cables into a double-gang retrofit electrical box so at least ½" of sheathing extends into the box. Clamp the cables in place. Tighten the mounting screws until the box is secure.

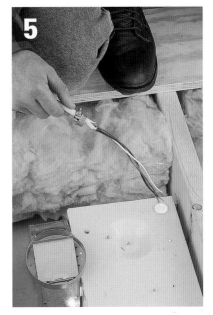

Strip 10" of sheathing from the end of the cable at the vent unit, then attach a cable clamp to the cable. Insert the cable into the fan unit. From the inside of the unit, screw a locknut onto the threaded end of the clamp.

(continued)

Mark the exit location in the roof next to a rafter for the vent hose. Drill a pilot hole, then saw through the sheathing and roofing material with a reciprocating saw to make the cutout for the vent tailpiece.

Remove a section of shingles from around the cutout, leaving the roofing paper intact. Remove enough shingles to create an exposed area that is at least the size of the vent cover flange.

Attach a hose clamp to the rafter next to the roof cutout about 1" below the roof sheathing (top). Insert the vent tailpiece into the cutout and through the hose clamp, then tighten the clamp screw (bottom).

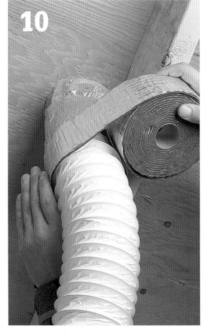

Slide one end of the vent hose over the tailpiece, and slide the other end over the outlet on the fan unit. Slip hose clamps or straps around each end of the vent hose, and tighten the clamps.

Wrap the vent hose with pipe insulation. Insulation prevents moist air inside the hose from condensing and dripping down into the fan motor.

Apply roofing cement to the bottom of the vent cover flange, then slide the vent cover over the tailpiece. Nail the vent cover flange in place with self-sealing roofing nails, then patch in shingles around the cover.

12

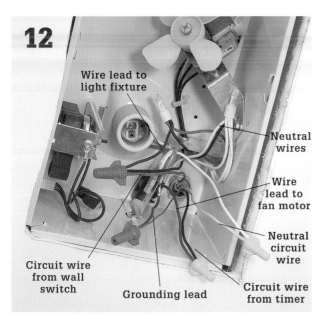

Wire lead to
light fixture

Neutral
wires

Wire
lead to
fan motor

Neutral
circuit
wire

Circuit wire
from wall
switch

Grounding lead

Circuit wire
from timer

13

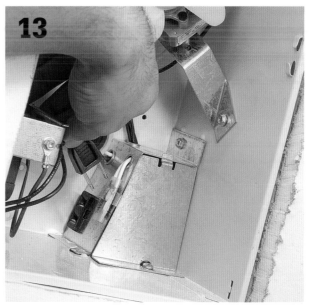

Make the following wire connections at the fan unit: the
black circuit wire from the timer to the wire lead for the fan
motor; the red circuit wire from the single-pole switch (see
step 14) to the wire lead for the light fixture in the unit; the
white neutral circuit wire to the neutral wire lead; the circuit
grounding wire to the grounding lead on the fan unit. Make all
connections with wire connectors. Attach the cover plate over
the unit when the wiring is completed.

Connect the fan motor plug to the built-in receptacle on
the wire connection box, and attach the fan grille to the frame
using the mounting clips included with the fan kit. *Note: If
you removed the wall and ceiling surfaces for the installation,
install new surfaces before completing this step.*

14

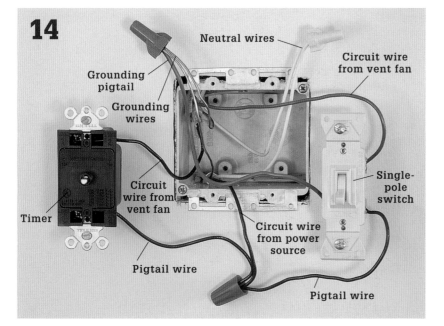

Neutral wires

Grounding
pigtail

Grounding
wires

Circuit wire
from vent fan

Circuit
wire from
vent fan

Single-
pole
switch

Timer

Circuit wire
from power
source

Pigtail wire

Pigtail wire

15

At the switch box, add black pigtail wires to one screw terminal on the timer and
to one screw terminal on the single-pole switch; add a green grounding pigtail to
the groundling screw on the switch. Make the following wire connections: the black
circuit wire from the power source to the black pigtail wires; the black circuit wire
from the vent fan to the remaining screw on the timer; the red circuit wire from
the vent fan to the remaining screw on the switch. Join the white wires with a wire
connector. Join the grounding wires with a green wire connector.

Tuck the wires into the switch box,
then attach the switch and timer to the
box. Attach the coverplate and timer
dial. Turn on the power.

Combination Fan/Lights

Advancing bath fan technology has resulted in smaller, quieter fans with ever more air moving power. It has also brought us interesting new fan combinations. Bath fans with heaters, bath fans that look like a recessed canister light, and whole house fans with in-line boosters are just a couple of examples. In this section we'll show you how to replace an ordinary ceiling light with an attractive light fixture that includes a 70 CFM vent fan (see Resources, page 284).

Because the combo fan seen here is installed in a first-floor master bath, we were able to vent it through the exterior wall just a few feet away. More typically, bath fans are vented through the roof, as seen on pages 194 to 197. We also used inexpensive flexible tubing for the ductwork, but you might consider upgrading to flexible metal or even rigid metal ductwork.

Because this project requires working with electricity, be cautious and do hire a professional if you are not experienced with home wiring.

Tools & Materials ▸

Phillips and straight screwdrivers
Jigsaw or drywall saw
Reciprocating saw
Drill
Electrical tester
Exhaust fan unit
Drywall screws

Self-sealing roofing nails
Wire connectors
Flexible dryer vent duct
Dryer vent clamps
Vent cover
Drywall

This attractive ceiling light has something to hide: It doubles as a 70 cubic foot per minute vent fan cover to keep this bathroom stocked with fresh, dry air.

How to Replace an Overhead Light with a Light/Fan

1

Shut off power to the ceiling light at the electrical service panel. Remove the globe and bulb from the overhead ceiling light, and then disconnect the mounting screws that hold the light fixture to the ceiling box.

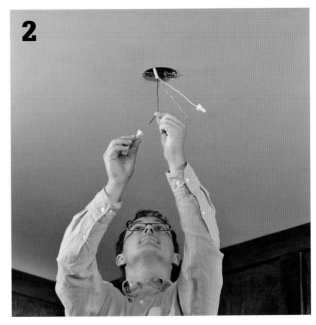

2

Test the wire connections with a current tester to make sure they are not live, and then disconnect the wires and remove the light fixture. Cap the wire ends.

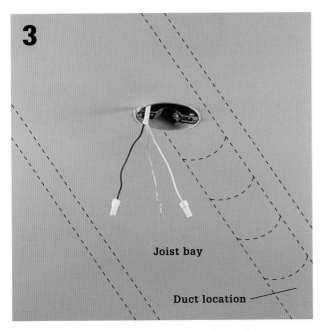

3

Joist bay

Duct location

Plan your exhaust pipe route. In most cases, this means determining the shortest distance between the fan and the outdoors. If the room is located at the top living level, venting through the roof is usually smartest. On lower levels and in basements, you'll need to go through an exterior wall. If you need to route through a wall in a room with a finished ceiling, choose a route that runs through a single ceiling joist bay.

4

Remove ceiling covering in the fan unit installation area and between the joists at the end of the run, next to the wall. You'll need at least 18" of access. If you are running rigid vent pipe or the joist bay is insulated, you'll need to remove ceiling material between the joists for the entire run. Make cuts on the centerlines of the joists.

(continued)

5

Insert flexible vent tubing into one of the ceiling openings and expand it so the free end reaches to the ceiling opening at the wall. A fish-tape for running cable through walls can be a useful aid for extending the tubing.

6

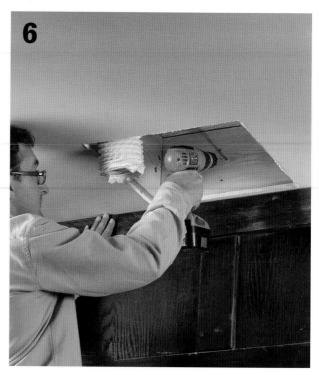

Draw a 4"-dia. circle on the wall framing at the end of the joist bay, marking the exit point for the duct. Choose a long, ¼"-dia. drill bit and drill a hole at the center of the circle. Drill all the way through the wall so the bit exits on the exterior side. This will mark your hole location outside.

7

On the exterior, draw a 4"-dia. circle centered on the exit point of the drill bit. Cut out the opening for the vent cover with a reciprocating saw (or a 4" hole saw if you can find one).

8

Insert the vent cover assembly into the opening, following the manufacturer's directions for fastening and sealing it to the house.

9

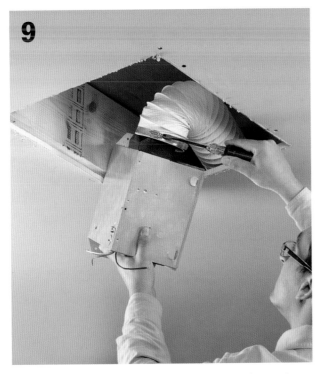

Attach the end of the vent tubing to the outlet on the vent cover unit and secure it with a large pipe clamp.

10

Nail the housing for the light/fan unit to the ceiling joist so the bottom edges of the housing are flush with the ceiling surface.

11

Make the wiring connections in the housing box according to the manufacturer's instructions. In just about every case you should be able to use the existing wires from the original light switch. Once you have connected the wires, restore the power and test the fan.

12

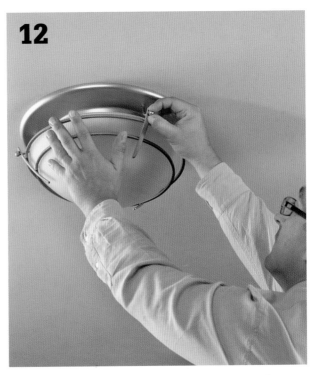

Patch and paint the wall and ceiling in the project area. Mount the light (the model we installed plugs into a receptacle in the fan box), grille, globe, and any other fixture parts.

Accessories & Upgrades

The accessories you choose will put the finishing touches on your dream bath. This is the time to think about adding luxuries such as towel warmers and fog-free mirrors.

Whenever possible, anchor permanently mounted accessories to wall studs or blocking for maximum holding power. If no studs or blocking are located in the area where accessories will be installed, use toggle bolts or molly bolts to anchor the accessories to drywall or plaster walls.

In this chapter:

- Custom Saunas
- Grab Bars
- Tilting Wall Mirrors
- Mirror Defoggers
- Glass Shelving
- Towel Warmers
- Wall-Mount TV Brackets

Custom Saunas

What better way to pamper yourself than by luxuriating in the warmth of your very own sauna. Scandinavians have indulged in this pastime for centuries. The traditional sauna cycle of intense heat followed by a cooling shower helps to soothe, relax, and invigorate the body while providing health benefits such as reduced muscle tension and clean, refreshed skin.

Saunas are typically lined with cedar, redwood, pine, or spruce. Woods that stay comfortable to the touch at high heat, such as abachi, aspen, and hemlock, are often used for the benches and backrests.

Manufactured saunas generally are sold as either prefabricated or custom-cut kits. Both types include the prehung door, benches, electric heater unit, and other accessories. The prefab kits also include finished and insulated wall and ceiling panels, which allow for quick and easy installation.

Custom-cut sauna kits typically are less expensive, but more complicated than prefab kits.

As you plan the location of your sauna, keep in mind that the flooring should be a water-resistant surface such as concrete, resilient flooring, or ceramic tile. Locating the sauna near a floor drain will ease cleaning and allow for bathing.

Check with your manufacturer before attempting to install and connect the electrical wiring for your sauna's systems. Some manufacturers' warranties require that all electrical work be completed by a licensed electrician.

Tools & Materials ▸

Tape measure	Treated 2 × 4s
Chalk line	2 × 4s
4-ft. level	Caulk
Circular saw	Galvanized
Caulk gun	common nails
Powder-actuated	(8d, 10d, 16d)
nailer	3½" unfaced
Hammer	fiberglass
Stud finder	insulation
Plumb bob	1½" pneumatic nails
Stapler	or 4d galvanized
Pneumatic nailer	finish nails
Drill	3" stainless steel
Custom-cut sauna kit	screws

Custom-cut saunas can be tailored to any space or design. This unique hex-shaped sauna includes design elements such as shielded cove lighting, vertical paneling, and mounted backrests.

How to Install a Custom-Cut Sauna

1 Stud layout for 6 × 6-ft. sauna built in this project

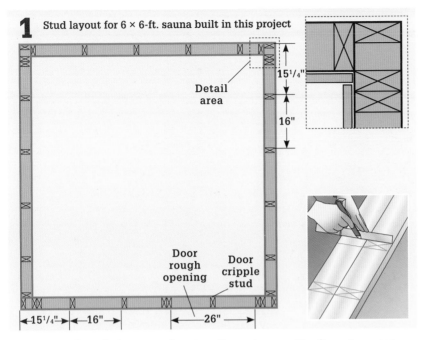

Detail area

15¹⁄₄"

16"

Door rough opening

Door cripple stud

←15¹⁄₄"→ ←16"→ ←26"→

Measure and mark the sauna framing dimensions on the floor, then snap chalk lines to mark your framing layout. Cut bottom plates from treated 2 × 4s, then mark the 16" on-center stud layout onto the plates. Include the door rough opening and extra nailer studs in the corners to allow for fastening the tongue-and-groove boards (detail). Cut top plates to length, pair them with bottom plates, and transfer the stud markings to the top plates (inset). Caulk beneath the bottom plates, then fasten them to the floor using 16d nails (or use masonry screws or a powder-actuated nailer on a concrete floor).

The sauna door requires a double plate to provide a proper sill. Transfer the stud layout markings to another 2 × 4 and install it on top of the front wall plate using 10d nails driven at a slight angle.

3

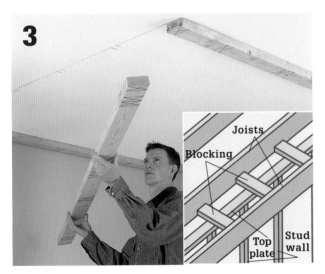

Joists

Blocking

Top plate   Stud wall

Use a stud finder to locate and mark the joists in the area. If a wall falls between parallel joists, remove the ceiling drywall and install 2× blocking between the joists (inset). Use a plumb bob to transfer the plate locations from the floor to the ceiling, then snap chalk lines through the ceiling marks. Attach the top plates to the joists or blocking using 16d nails.

4

Measure and cut the wall studs to length from standard 2 × 4s. Install the studs by toenailing them through the sides of the studs and into the top and bottom plates using 8d nails. On each end, drive two nails through one side of the stud and one more through the center on the other side.

(continued)

5

Install the king studs for the door frame. Use a level to make sure that these studs are plumb. Cut and install a 2 × 4 header flat between the king studs using 16d nails. Cut and install jack studs to fit snugly beneath the header. Cut and install a cripple stud above the header, centered over the rough opening.

6

Measure up 7 ft. from the floor and mark a stud. Use a 4-ft. level to transfer the mark across the studs. Align 2 × 4 nailers on the marks and attach them to the studs with 16d nails. Mark the joist layout onto the nailers using 16" on-center spacing. Cut 2 × 4 joists to fit and fasten them to the nailers using 10d nails. *Note: If the joist span is over 8 ft., use 2 × 6s for the nailers and joists.*

7

Frame openings for the sauna vents according to the manufacturer's directions. Locate the framing for the inlet vent at floor level near the heater. Frame the outlet vent on another wall, located just below the top bench height (about 30"). If you have a wall-mount heater unit, attach 2 × 4 supports between the studs at the heater location according to the manufacturer's directions.

8

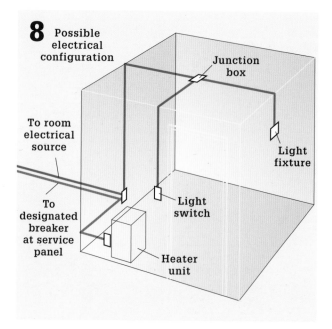

Install electrical boxes and route cable to the lights, switches, and heater unit as directed by the manufacturer. *Note: Some manufacturers or municipalities may require that all electrical work be completed by a licensed electrician.*

9

Install a double layer of 3½" unfaced fiberglass insulation at the ceiling. Lay the first layer on top of the ceiling framing perpendicular to the joists. Install a second layer between the joists. If necessary, drive nails partially into the joists to hold the second layer in place.

10

Install insulation between the studs along the finished walls. For easier access while paneling the sauna, leave the outer walls open until you are ready to panel them. (See Step 15.) Install the included vapor barrier over the insulation on the walls and ceiling and attach it to the framing with ⅜" staples. Begin at the bottom of the walls and overlap the foil pieces as you go up. Repair tears and seal joints with foil tape.

11

Install the precut ceiling boards starting at the back of the sauna. If the boards are slightly shorter than the framing, split the difference and allow equal space on each side. Nail the first board to the joists through its face, then "blind-nail" the board by driving 1½" galvanized pin nails (or 4d galvanized finish nails) at an angle through the inside of the tongue. If you are not using a pneumatic nailer, drive the nail heads below the wood surface with a nail set. For the remaining boards, fit the groove over the tongue of the preceding board and drive nails through the inside of the tongue only.

12

Measure periodically to make sure the boards are straight and parallel to the far wall, adjusting the remaining few boards, if necessary. When you get to the final board, measure the space remaining, rip the board to fit, and face-nail it into place.

(continued)

Check to see if the floor is level by moving a level across the floor. If it is uneven, mark the high point. Measure down from the sauna ceiling to this point and subtract ½". Use this measurement to mark the starting point for the tongue-and-groove wall boards at all four corners. This will allow for a minmum ½" gap between the boards and the floor.

Align the first board with the starting marks along the back wall and attach it to the studs using the blind-nailing techniques shown in Step 11. Trim the boards as necessary to fit around the vent openings. Check the boards for level every few rows, and adjust the next few rows slightly if the boards fall out of level.

Variation: If you are installing the paneling vertically, install 1 × 2 furring strips over the studs, spaced 24" on-center, using 8d nails. Install the boards starting in the corner farthest from the heater. Finish the two walls going toward the heater, then complete the other two walls.

On the open stud walls, finish the exterior with the desired paneling or drywall. Then, install the insulation and vapor barrier, as shown in Step 10. Finish installing the tongue-and-groove paneling on the interior side of the walls.

Measure from the floor and mark the side walls at 12" and 30" for the bench supports. Align the top edge of each support with the marks and fasten them to the wall studs with 3" screws. Install the prebuilt benches by attaching them to the supports with 3" screws.

17

Position the door in the framed opening with the jamb flush with the exterior wall surface. Check that the door is level, plumb, and centered, shimming, if necessary. Fasten the hinge side to the 2 × 4 frame with the included screws. Check the door again for level, then continue to fasten around the frame.

18

Setback

Door jamb extension

If necessary, install the door jamb extensions flush with the interior wall surface, fastening them to the framed opening using 3" screws. Mark a setback to indicate the inside edge of the door casings on each of the jambs. Install the casings around the interior and exterior of the door using 4d galvanized finish nails.

19

Install trim molding to cover the joints at the wall and ceiling corners, cutting the pieces as needed. Fasten the trim with 4d galvanized finish nails. Install the inlet and outlet grills over the vent openings using the included screws.

20

Install the heater unit, control panel, and light fixtures according to the manufacturer's directions. Assemble and install the heater guard around the heater unit, positioning the top edge of the guard just below the exposed rocks. Follow the manufacturer's directions for operating the heater unit.

Grab Bars

Bathrooms are beautiful with their shiny ceramic tubs, showers, and floors, but add water and moisture to the mix and you've created the perfect conditions for a fall. The good news is many falls in the bathroom can be avoided by installing grab bars at key locations.

Grab bars help family members steady themselves on slippery shower, tub, and other floor surfaces. Plus, they provide support for people transferring from a wheelchair or walker to the shower, tub, or toilet.

Grab bars come in a variety of colors, shapes, sizes, and textures. Choose a style with a 1¼" to 1½" diameter that fits comfortably between your thumb and fingers. Then properly install it 1½" from the wall with anchors that can support at least 250 pounds.

The easiest way to install grab bars is to screw them into wall studs or into blocking or backing attached to studs. Blocking is a good option if you are framing a new bathroom or have the wall surface removed during a major remodel (see Illustration A). Use 2 × 6 or 2 × 8 lumber to provide room for adjustments, and fasten the blocks to the framing with 16d nails. Note the locations of your blocking for future reference.

As an alternative, cover the entire wall with ¾" plywood backing secured with screws to the wall framing, so you can install grab bars virtually anywhere on the wall (see Illustration B).

Grab bars can be installed in areas without studs. For these installations, use specialized heavy-duty hollow-wall anchors designed to support at least 250 pounds.

Grab bars promote independence in the bathroom, where privacy is especially important. Grab bars not only help prevent slips and falls, they also help people steady themselves in showers and lower themselves into tubs.

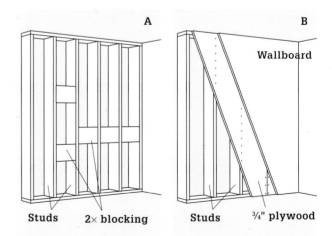

Blocking or backing is required for secure grab bars. If you know where the grab bars will be located, add 2× blocking between studs (Illustration A). You also can cover the entire wall with ¾" plywood backing, which allows you to install grab bars virtually anywhere on the wall.

Tools & Materials ▸

Measuring tape	Masonry bit
Pencil	Grab bar
Stud finder	Hollow-wall anchors
Level	#12 stainless steel screws
Drill	Silicone caulk

How to Install Grab Bars

1

Locate the wall studs in the installation area, using a stud finder. If the area is tiled, the stud finder may not detect studs, so try to locate the studs above the tile, if possible, then use a level to transfer the marks lower on the wall. Otherwise, you can drill small, exploratory holes through grout joints in the tile, then fill the holes with silicone caulk to seal them. Be careful not to drill into pipes.

2

Mark the grab bar height at one stud location, then use a level to transfer the height mark to the stud that will receive the other end of the bar. Position the grab bar on the height marks so at least two of the three mounting holes are aligned with the stud centers. Mark the mounting hole locations onto the wall.

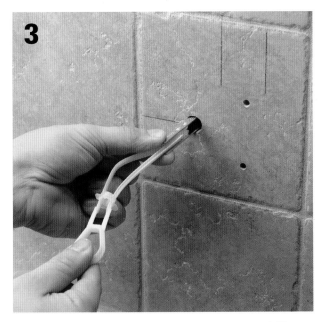

3

Drill pilot holes for the mounting screws. If you are drilling through tile, start with a small bit (about ⅛"), then redrill the hole with the larger bit. For screws that won't hit studs, drill holes for wall anchors, following the manufacturer's directions for sizing. Install anchors, if necessary.

4

Apply a continuous bead of silicone caulk to the back side of each bar end (inset). Secure the bar to the studs using #12 stainless steel screws (the screws should penetrate the stud by at least 1"). Install a stainless steel screw or bolt into the wall anchors. Test the bar to make sure it's secure.

Tilting Wall Mirrors

A mirror is a necessity in any bathroom, but not every bathroom mirror has to be attached to a medicine cabinet. Tilting mirrors and telescoping makeup mirrors are only two of the nearly endless options available.

The most important part of mounting a mirror is accurate placement. A mirror over the vanity should be centered over the centerline of the sink. If you have an asymmetrical sink, center the mirror over the vanity.

Mirror height is also important, especially to those who are especially tall or short. Tilting mirrors are useful if there is a dramatic difference between the tallest and the shortest person in the household. A smaller tilting mirror can take the place of a large stationary mirror.

Extending arm mirrors are handy for shaving or applying makeup. These mirrors typically have two sides with one side providing magnification. Some come with lights and antifogging as well.

Tools & Materials ▸

Level
Drill
Allen wrench
Flat-bladed screwdriver

Tilting wall mirror
Extending
   arm mirror

A tilting wall mirror adjusts to people of varying heights and should be centered over the sink or the vanity. Extending arm mirrors are installed off to the side, since the arm allows the mirror to be drawn closer when needed.

How to Install a Tilting Wall Mirror

1

Determine the height of the mirror mounts by dividing the overall height of the mirror by two and adding the result to the number of inches above the vanity you want the bottom edge of the mirror to be placed. In this case, the mirror came with a mounting template. Tape the template to the wall and drill two 5⁄16" holes at each of the mounting post locations.

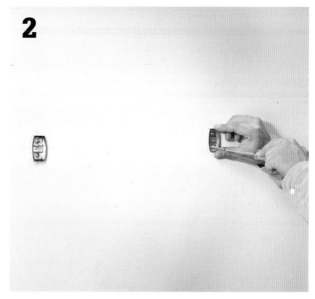

2

Insert the included wall anchors and tap into place. Remove the brackets from the mounting posts by loosening the setscrew. Attach the brackets to the wall at the wall anchor locations.

3

Assemble the mirror if necessary. Make sure the setscrews on the mounting posts are facing downward. Carefully lift the mirror and place the mounting posts over the brackets and slide into place. Tighten the setscrews.

Variation: How to Hang an Extending Arm Mirror. Most extending wall mirrors are surface mounted. Next to the vanity mirror, use a level to mark a vertical line at the eye level of the mirror's main user. Make sure there is sufficient space for the mirror to fold back against the wall. Hold the mirror unit over the line and mark the screw hole locations. Drill two 1⁄4" holes at the marks and insert the wall anchors. Hold the mirror in position and drive in the screws.

Mirror Defoggers

You may not want to deal with the inconvenience of a foggy mirror after your long, hot soak or invigorating shower. Let's face it—no one's dream bath includes inconveniences of any sort. But even with an exhaust fan, your bathroom mirror can get foggy. Instead of wiping off the moisture, which only results in streaks and drips, prevent its formation with a mirror defogger.

A mirror defogger (see Resources, page 284) works by gently heating the mirror to prevent condensation. Typically it is hardwired into the vanity light so that when you switch on the light you're also switching on the defogger. Mirror defoggers come in a number of sizes and with many operating systems. They can be installed under a flat wall-mounted mirror attached to the back of a framed mirror.

Tools & Materials ▸

Measuring tape	Fish tape
Level	Drill
Staple gun	Painter's tape
Stud finder	Mirror defogger
Keyhole saw	

Mirror defoggers are heaters that are installed behind flat wall-mounted mirrors. The heat prevents condensation on the mirror and does away with the inconvenience of a foggy mirror in your dream bathroom.

How to Install a Mirror Defogger

1

Use painter's tape to outline the mirror top and sides on the wall. Carefully remove the mirror and place it in a safe location. Mark the location of the defogger. It should be centered over the sink with the top 6 ft. from the floor. Mark a 4" × 6" box on the wall around the defogger's wire connector. We aligned this mirror's power connection at the top, where it is closest to the power supply. Turn off the circuit breaker for the light fixture.

2

Provide power to the installation area by running cable from a nearby electrical box and into a new box behind the mirror location. If you tie into the electricity at the vanity light (as we have done here), the defogger will turn on and off with the vanity light. If you are not experienced with home wiring, hire an electrician for this part of the job.

3

Patch any holes in the wallboard that will not be covered by the mirror. Position the defogger with the wire connector centered over the access hole and within the lines marked in Step 1. Staple the defogger to the wall surface around the edges only.

4

Make (or have made) the electrical connections according to the manufacturer's instructions. Here, we are re-installing the bathroom vanity light. Remount the mirror with clips (do not use mastic over the defogger).

Glass Shelving

Glass shelving is unobtrusive so it can fit many styles of bathrooms—from sleek modern to elaborate Victorian. You can find a wide variety of shelving available in home stores and online.

Most glass shelves are held in place with metal mounts. How the shelves are secured to the mounts differs and how the mounts are attached to the wall also differs. Most shelves have a hidden bracket that is secured to the wall. The mount then slips over the bracket and is secured with a setscrew. The most basic models may have mounts that are screwed directly into the wall with exposed screws. The directions here are for shelving that uses hidden brackets.

If you are installing shelves on a tiled wall, mount the brackets in grout lines if at all possible to minimize the possibility of cracking the tiles. Many glass shelves have some flexibility in the distance between the mounts.

Tools & Materials ▸

Level   Pencil
Drill   Glass shelves

Glass shelves fit any style and size of bathroom. They are held in place with metal mounts, which can be decorative, that are attached to the wall.

How to Install Glass Shelves

Assemble the shelf and shelf holders (not the brackets). Hold the shelf against the wall in the desired location. On the wall, mark the center point of each holder, where the setscrew is.

Remove the shelves and use the level to extend the mark into a 3" vertical line. Use the level to mark a horizontal line across the centers of these lines.

Center the middle round hole of the bracket over the intersection of the vertical and horizontal lines. Mark the center of each of the oblong holes. Put the bracket aside and drill a ¼" hole at each mark. Insert the included wall anchors in the holes. Replace the bracket and insert the screws into the wall anchors and drive the screws. Repeat for the second bracket.

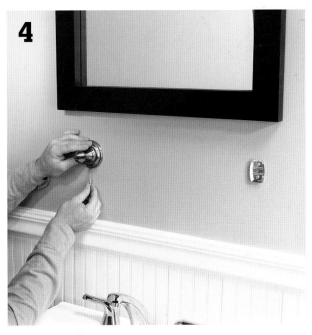

Remove the shelf from the holders. Slide a holder over a bracket, check that the shelf mount is level, and tighten the setscrew. Repeat with the other holder. Insert the shelf and fix in place. Check the shelf for level. If it's not level, remove one holder and loosen the bracket screws. Slide the bracket up or down to make the unit level. Replace the holder and shelf.

Towel Warmers

Here's a little bit of luxury that need not be limited to high-end hotel stays. You can have toasty towels in your own bathroom with an easy-to-install towel warmer. In a relatively cold room, this can make stepping out of the shower a much more pleasant experience.

Heated towel racks are available in a wide range of styles and sizes. Freestanding floor models as well as door- and wall-mounted versions can be plugged in for use when desired. Hardwired wall-mounted versions can be switched on when you enter the bathroom so your towels are warm when you step out of the shower. Although installing them requires some electrical skills, the hardwired models do not need to be located near wall receptacles and they do not have exposed cords or extension cords hanging on the wall. However, if you locate the warmer directly above an existing receptacle, you can save a lot of time and mess by running cable up from the receptacle to the new electrical box for the warmer.

Before installing hardwired models, check your local electrical codes for applicable regulations. If you are not experienced with home wiring, have an electrician do this job for you or opt for a plug-in model.

Tools & Materials ▸

Drill
Level
Keyhole saw
Wiring tools
Phillips screwdriver
Stud finder

Retrofit electrical
   outlet box
Wire connectors
NM cable
Towel warmer
Pencil
Masking tape

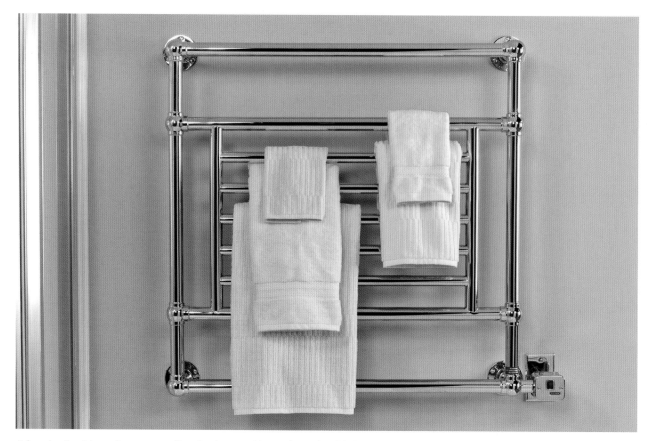

A hard-wired towel warmer offers the luxury of heated towels without the safety concerns of a plug-in device.

How to Install a Hardwired Towel Warmer

Use a stud finder to locate the studs in the area you wish to place the towel warmer. Mark the stud locations with masking tape or pencil lines. Attach the wall brackets to the towel warmer and hold the unit against the wall at least 7" from the floor and 3" from the ceiling or any overhang. Mark the locations of the wall bracket outlet plate (where the electrical connection will be made) and the mounting brackets.

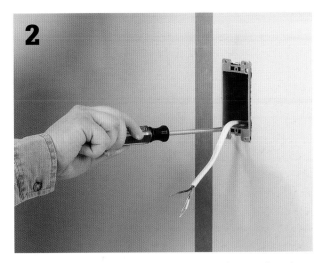

Shut off electrical power at the main service panel. At the mark for the wall bracket outlet, cut a hole in the wallcovering for a retrofit electrical box. Run NM cable from the opening to a GFCI-protected circuit (here, we ran cable down to a receptacle directly beneath it), or install a separate GFCI-protected circuit (you'll need to consult a wiring book or an electrician). Pull the cable through the hole in the retrofit box, and then tighten the cable clamp. Place the box in the hole flush with the wall surface and tighten the mounting screw in the rear of the box. Cut the wires so about 5" extends into the box and strip the insulation off at ⅜" from the end of each wire.

Position the towel warmer over the outlet box and mark the locations of the screw holes for the wall brackets. Make sure the appliance is level. Remove the warmer and drill ¼" pilot holes at the marked locations. If the marks are located over studs, drill ⅛" pilot holes. If not, push wall anchors into the holes. Thread the mounting screws through the brackets. Have a helper hold the towel rack in place and use wire connectors to connect the wires, including the ground wire, according to the instructions.

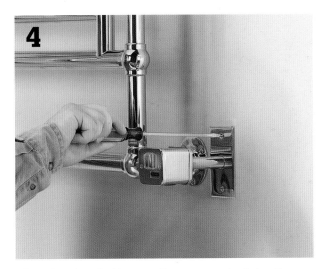

After the electrical connections are made, fasten the towel rack brackets to the wall. Turn on power and test the towel warmer. Finally, attach the electrical cover plate with integral on/off switch.

Wall-Mount TV Brackets

One of America's favorite pastimes is watching TV. We get hooked on dramas, comedies, reality TV, even the news. So why not include a TV in your dream bathroom?

Wall and under-cabinet mounting brackets are available for all types and sizes of TV. For this project we'll install a bracket that can easily hold a 15" flat panel screen. The bracket moves from side to side and swivels to allow viewing from many angles.

You may also want to install an electrical and cable outlet near the bracket to prevent the cords from cluttering your bathroom. These brackets must be mounted to a stud; they cannot be mounted in dry wall with wall anchors.

Tools & Materials ▸

Level	Allen screw
Stud finder	Wrench
Drill	TV bracket
	TV

Wall-mount TV brackets must be secured to studs to support the weight of the TV.

How to Install a TV Mounting Bracket

1

Use a stud finder to find a wall stud in the desired location. Mark a vertical line down the center of the stud. Hold the wall plate against the vertical line so the line is visible through the mounting holes. Mark the location of the mounting holes.

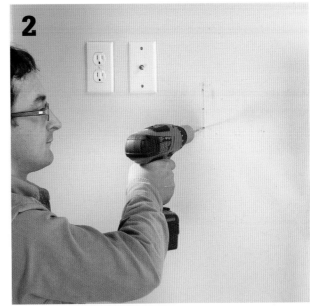

2

Drill pilot holes for the screws at the marks. Do not exceed 2" depth to prevent drilling through hidden pipes or wires.

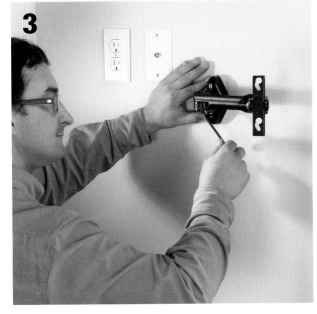

3

Drive the mounting screws through the wall plate into the wall. Place the link assembly over the wall plate and attach with two Allen screws. Secure the television to the bracket according to the manufacturers directions.

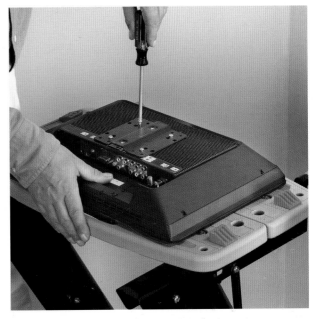

Variation: Flat panel TVs require a different mounting bracket than standard TVs. To mount a flat TV, insert the button head Allen screws into the raised center of the mounting bracket, but do not insert them fully. Remove the stand from the TV. Attach the flat panel mounting bracket to the TV using the attachment screws and the holes from the original stand. Slide the mounting bracket over the link assembly and tighten the Allen screws. Follow the manufacturer's instructions for adjusting arm tension.

Wall Projects

Bathroom walls are easy to ignore because we tend to believe that only practical (and boring) surfaces can be used in bathrooms. After all, they need to be water resistant and easy to clean, right? There are a couple of errors in that assumption.

Yes, a bathroom wall should be water resistant, but that doesn't mean it has to be impervious. The only walls that must be waterproof are tub and shower surrounds. You'd do well to avoid delicate wall surface such as wallpaper or plain drywall with flat paint. But unless you run the steam bath 24/7 you can install most any surface you choose. The other error many homeowners make when considering bathroom walls is to think that wallcoverings that are traditional in bathrooms, such as glazed tile, are necessarily dull and institutional in feel. This is most certainly not true, as the following wall projects will bear out.

In this chapter:

- Installing Drywall
- Installing Cementboard
- Bathroom Wall Tile
- Embellished Wall Tile
- Tile Tub Walls
- Glass Block Windows

Drywall

Drywall panels can be used both to finish new walls and to patch existing wall areas exposed during the installation of a window or door.

You can usually patch smooth plaster walls with drywall, but if you need to match a textured plaster surface, it is best to hire a plasterer to do the work.

Drywall panels are available in 4 × 8-ft. or 4 × 10-ft. sheets, and in ⅜", ½", and ⅝" thicknesses. For new walls, ½" thick is standard. Moisture-resistant greenboard is recommended for use in bathrooms.

Use all-purpose drywall compound and paper joint tape. Lay out drywall panels so that seams fall over the center of openings, not at sides, or use solid pieces at openings. Insulate all framing cavities around each opening.

Tools & Materials ▸

Tape measure
Utility knife
Drywall
T-square
6" and 12"
   taping knives
150-grit sanding sponge

Drywall
Drywall tape
1¼" coarse-thread
   drywall screws
Drywall compound
Metal inside
   corner bead

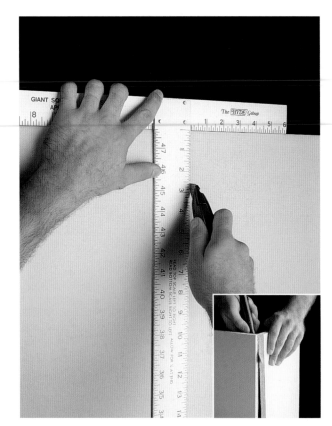

Score drywall face paper with a utility knife, using a drywall T-square as a guide. Bend the panel away from the scored line until the core breaks, then cut through the back paper (inset) with a utility knife, and separate the pieces.

How to Install & Finish Drywall

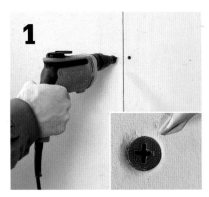

Install panels with their tapered edges butted together. Fasten with 1¼" screws driven every 8" along the edges, and every 12" in the field. Drive screws deep enough to dimple surface without ripping face paper (inset).

Use a 6" taping knife to cover the seam with an even ⅛"-thick bed layer of compound.

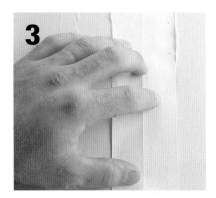

Center drywall tape over the seam and lightly embed it into the compound, making sure it's smooth and straight.

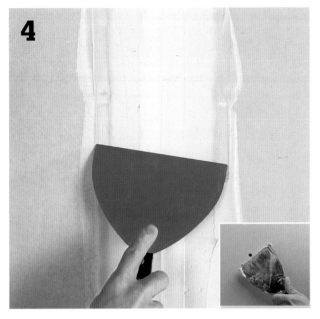

4

Smooth the tape with the taping knife. Apply enough pressure to force compound from underneath the tape, leaving the tape flat and with a thin layer underneath. Cover all exposed screw heads with the first of three coats of compound (inset). Let compound dry overnight.

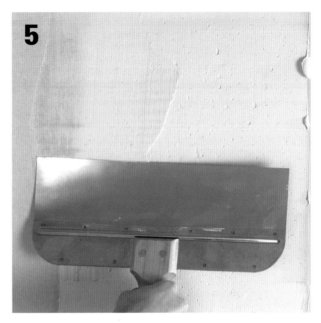

5

Use a 12" knife to second-coat the seams with a thin, even layer of compound. Feather the sides of the compound first, by holding the blade almost flat and applying pressure to the outside of the blade so that it just skims over the center of the seam.

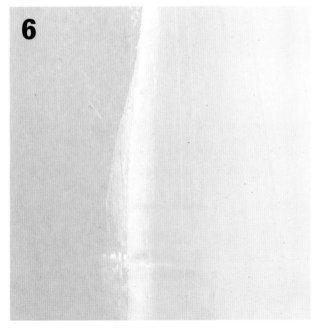

6

After feathering both sides, make a pass down the center of the seam, leaving the seam smooth and even, the edges feathered out to nothing. Completely cover the joint tape. Let second coat dry, then apply a third coat using the 12" knife. After the third coat dries completely, sand the compound lightly with a drywall sander or a 150-grit sanding sponge.

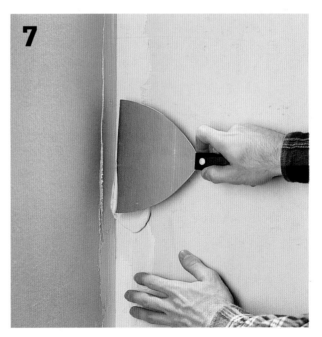

7

Tip: Finish any inside corners using paper-faced metal inside corner bead to produce straight, durable corners with little fuss. Embed the bead into a thin layer of compound, then smooth the paper with a taping knife. Apply two finish coats to the corner, then sand the compound smooth.

Cementboard

Cementboard is one of the three basic types of tile backer board that can be used as a substrate for tile walls in wet areas. The other two are fiber-cement board and Dens-Shield. Unlike drywall, tile backer won't break down and cause damage if water gets behind the tile.

Though water cannot damage either cementboard or fiber-cement board, it can pass through them. To protect the framing members, install a water barrier of 4-mil plastic or 15# building paper behind the backer.

Dens-Shield has a waterproof acrylic facing that provides the water barrier. It cuts and installs much like drywall but requires galvanized screws to prevent corrosion and must be sealed with caulk at all untaped joints and penetrations.

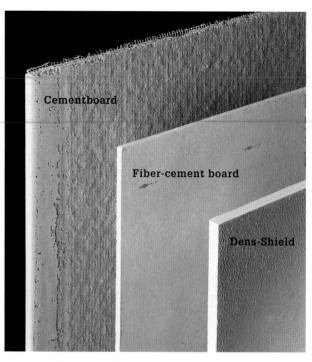

Common tile backers are cementboard, fiber-cement board, and Dens-Shield. Cementboard is made from portland cement and sand reinforced by an outer layer of fiberglass mesh. Fiber-cement board is made similarly but with a fiber reinforcement integrated throughout the panel. Dens-Shield is a water-resistant gypsum board with a waterproof acrylic facing.

Tools & Materials ▶

T-square	Drywall knife
Utility knife	4-mil plastic sheeting
Drill with a small masonry bit	Cementboard
Hammer	1¼" cementboard screws
Jigsaw with a bimetal blade	Cementboard joint tape
	Latex-portland cement mortar

How to Install Cementboard

Staple a water barrier of 4-mil plastic sheeting or 15# building paper over the framing. Overlap seams by several inches and leave the sheets long at the perimeter. *Note: Framing for cementboard must be 16" on-center; steel studs must be 20-gauge.*

Cut cementboard by scoring through the mesh just below the surface using a utility knife or carbide-tipped cutter. Snap the panel back, then cut through the back-side mesh (inset). *Note: For tile applications, the rough face of the board is the front.*

Make cutouts for pipes and other penetrations by drilling a series of holes through the board using a small masonry bit. Tap the hole out with a hammer or a scrap of pipe. Cut holes along edges with a jigsaw and bimetal blade.

Install the sheets horizontally. Where possible, use full pieces to avoid cut-and-butted seams, which are difficult to fasten. If there are vertical seams, stagger them between rows. Leave a ⅛" gap between sheets at vertical seams and corners. Use spacers to set the bottom row of panels ¼" above the tub or shower base. Fasten the sheets with 1¼" cementboard screws driven every 8" for walls and every 6" for ceilings. Drive the screws ½" from the edges to prevent crumbling. If the studs are steel, don't fasten within 1" of the top track.

Cover the joints and corners with cementboard joint tape (alkali-resistant fiberglass mesh) and latex-portland cement mortar (thin-set). Apply a layer of mortar with a drywall knife, embed the tape into the mortar, then smooth and level the mortar.

Variation: How to Finish Cementboard

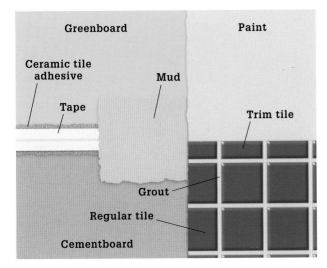

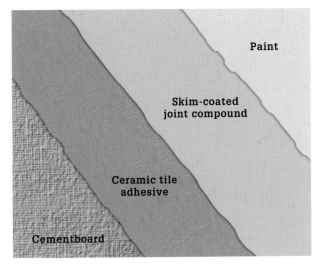

To finish a joint between cementboard and greenboard, seal the joint and exposed cementboard with ceramic tile adhesive, a mixture of four parts adhesive to one part water. Embed paper joint tape into the adhesive, smoothing the tape with a tape knife. Allow the adhesive to dry, then finish the joint with at least two coats of all-purpose drywall joint compound.

To finish small areas of cementboard that will not be tiled, seal the cementboard with ceramic tile adhesive, a mixture of four parts adhesive to one part water, then apply a skim-coat of all-purpose drywall joint compound using a 12" drywall knife. Then, paint the wall.

Bathroom Wall Tile

Tile is an ideal covering for walls in kitchens and bathrooms, but there's no reason to limit its use to those rooms. It's not as common in North American homes, but in Europe, tile has been used in rooms throughout the house for generations. And why not? Beautiful, practical, easy to clean and maintain, tile walls are well suited to many spaces. On the preceding pages, you've seen some design ideas for tile walls. Now it's time to get down to business.

When shopping for tile, keep in mind that tiles that are at least 6" × 6" are easier to install than small tiles, because they require less cutting and cover more surface area. Larger tiles also have fewer grout lines that must be cleaned and maintained. Check out the selection of trim and specialty tiles and ceramic accessories that are available to help you customize your project. (See pages 40 to 41 for information on selecting tile.)

Most wall tile is designed to have narrow grout lines (less than ⅛" wide) filled with unsanded grout. Grout lines wider than ⅛" should be filled with sanded floor-tile grout. Either type will last longer if it contains, or is mixed with, a latex additive. To prevent staining, it's a good idea to seal your grout after it fully cures, then once a year thereafter.

You can use standard drywall or water-resistant drywall (called "greenboard") as a backer for walls in dry areas.

In wet areas, install tile over cementboard. Made from cement and fiberglass, cementboard cannot be damaged by water, though moisture can pass through it. To protect the framing, install a waterproof membrane, such as roofing felt or polyethylene sheeting, between the framing members and the cementboard. Be sure to tape and finish the seams between cementboard panels before laying the tile.

Tools & Materials ▸

Tile-cutting tools	Carpet
Marker	Thinset tile mortar
Tape measure	with latex additive
4-ft. level	Ceramic wall tile
Notched trowel	Ceramic trim tile
Mallet	(as needed)
Grout float	2 × 4
Grout sponge	Carpet scrap
Soft cloth	Tile grout with latex
Small paintbrush	additive
or foam brush	Tub & tile caulk
Caulk gun	Alkaline grout sealer
Straight 1 × 2	Cardboard
Scrap 2 × 4	Story stick/pole

Tile is a practical, easy-to-maintain choice for bathroom walls. The variety of colors, shapes, and sizes ensure there's a tile for everyone. Keep in mind that larger tiles are easier to install, maintain, and clean than smaller tiles.

How to Set Wall Tile

Design the layout and mark the reference lines. Begin installation with the second row of tiles above the floor. If the layout requires cut tiles for this row, mark and cut the tiles for the entire row at one time.

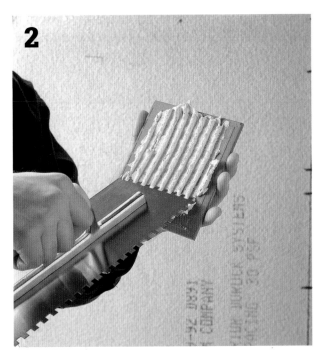

Mix a small batch of thinset mortar containing a latex additive. (Some mortar has additive mixed in by the manufacturer and some must have additive mixed in separately.) Cover the back of the first tile with adhesive, using a ¼" notched trowel.

Variation: Spread adhesive on a small section of the wall, then set the tiles into the adhesive. Thinset adhesive sets fast, so work quickly if you choose this installation method.

Beginning near the center of the wall, apply the tile to the wall with a slight twisting motion, aligning it exactly with the horizontal and vertical reference lines. When placing cut tiles, position the cut edges where they will be least visible.

(continued)

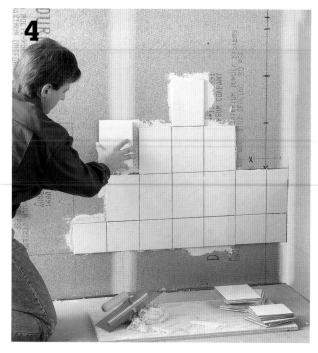

Continue installing tiles, working from the center to the sides in a pyramid pattern. Keep the tiles aligned with the reference lines. If the tiles are not self-spacing, use plastic spacers inserted in the corner joints to maintain even grout lines. The base row should be the last row of full tiles installed. Cut tile as necessary.

As small sections of tile are completed, "set" the tile by laying a scrap of 2 × 4 wrapped with carpet onto the tile and rapping it lightly with a mallet. This embeds the tile solidly in the adhesive and creates a flat, even surface.

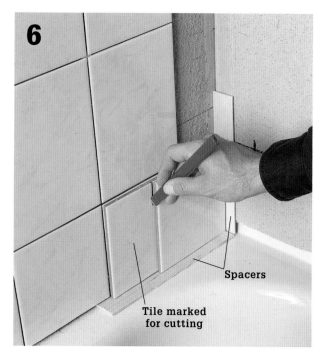

Spacers

Tile marked
for cutting

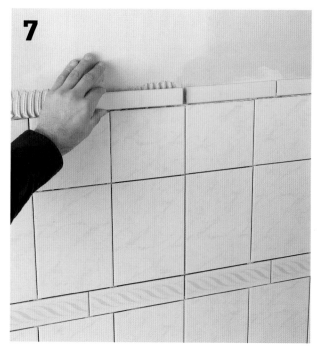

To mark tiles for straight cuts, begin by taping ⅛" spacers against the surfaces below and to the side of the tile. Position a tile directly over the last full tile installed, then place a third tile so the edge butts against the spacers. Trace the edge of the top tile onto the middle tile to mark it for cutting.

Install any trim tiles, such as the bullnose edge tiles shown above, at border areas. Wipe away excess mortar along the top edges of the edge tiles. Use bullnose and corner bullnose (with two adjacent bullnose edges) tiles at outside corners to cover the rough edges of the adjoining tiles.

8

Let mortar dry completely (12 to 24 hours), then mix a batch of grout containing latex additive. Apply the grout with a rubber grout float, using a sweeping motion to force it deep into the joints. Do not grout joints adjoining bathtubs, floors, or room corners. These will serve as expansion joints and will be caulked later.

9

Wipe a damp grout sponge diagonally over the tile, rinsing the sponge in cool water between wipes. Wipe each area only once; repeated wiping can pull grout from the joints. Allow the grout to dry for about 4 hours, then use a soft cloth to buff the tile surface and remove any remaining grout film.

10

When the grout has cured completely, use a small foam brush to apply grout sealer to the joints, following the manufacturer's directions. Avoid brushing sealer on the tile surfaces, and wipe up excess sealer immediately.

11

Seal expansion joints at the floor and corners with silicone caulk. After the caulk dries, buff the tile with a soft, dry cloth.

How to Install Wall Tile in a Bathtub Alcove

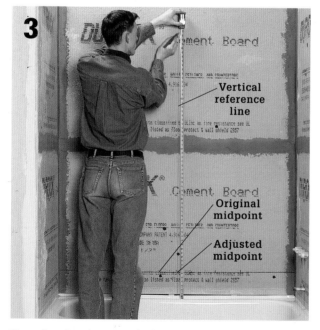

Beginning with the back wall, measure up and mark a point at a distance equal to the height of one ceramic tile (if the tub edge is not level, measure up from the lowest spot). Draw a level line through this point, along the entire back wall. This line represents a tile grout line and will be used as a reference line for making the entire tile layout.

Measure and mark the midpoint on the horizontal reference line. Using a story stick, mark along the reference line where the vertical grout joints will be located. If the story stick shows that the corner tiles will be less than half of a full tile width, move the midpoint half the width of a tile in either direction and mark (shown in next step).

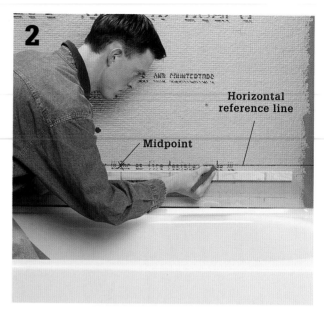

Use a level to draw a vertical reference line through the adjusted midpoint from the tub edge to the ceiling. Measure up from the tub edge along the vertical reference line and mark the rough height of the top row of tiles.

Use the story stick to mark the horizontal grout joints along the vertical reference line, beginning at the mark for the top row of tiles. If the cut tiles at the tub edge will be less than half the height of a full tile, move the top row up half the height of a tile. *Note: If tiling to a ceiling, evenly divide the tiles to be cut at the ceiling and tub edge, as for the corner tiles.*

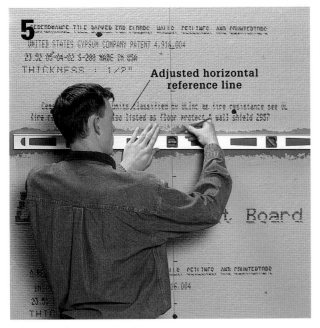

Use a level to draw an adjusted horizontal reference line through the vertical reference line at a grout joint mark close to the center of the layout. This splits the tile area into four workable quadrants.

Use a level to transfer the adjusted horizontal reference line from the back wall to both side walls, then follow Step 3 through Step 6 to lay out both side walls. Adjust the layout as needed so the final column of tiles ends at the outside edge of the tub. Use only the adjusted horizontal and vertical reference lines for ceramic tile installation.

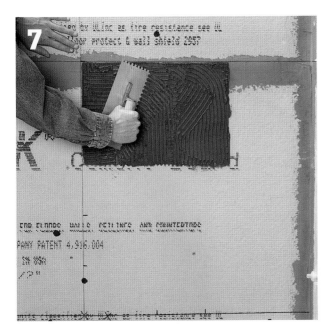

Mix a small batch of thinset mortar containing a latex additive. (Some mortar has additive mixed in by the manufacturer and some must have additive mixed separately.) Spread adhesive on a small section of the wall, along both legs of one quadrant, using a ¼" notched trowel.

Use the edge of the trowel to create furrows in the mortar. Set the first tile in the corner of the quadrant where the lines intersect, using a slight twisting motion. Align the tile exactly with both reference lines. When placing cut tiles, position the cut edges where they will be least visible.

(continued)

Continue installing tiles, working from the center out into the field of the quadrant. Keep the tiles aligned with the reference lines and tile in one quadrant at a time. If the tiles are not self-spacing, use plastic spacers inserted in the corner joints to maintain even grout lines (inset). The base row against the tub edge should be the last row of tiles installed.

Install trim tiles, such as the bullnose tiles shown above, at border areas. Wipe away excess mortar along the top edges of the edge tiles.

Mark and cut tiles to fit around all plumbing accessories or plumbing fixtures.

Install any ceramic accessories by applying thinset mortar to the back side, then pressing the accessory into place. Use masking tape to support the weight until the mortar dries (inset). Fill the tub with water, then seal expansion joints around the bathtub, floor, and corners with silicone caulk.

Variation: Tiling Bathroom Walls

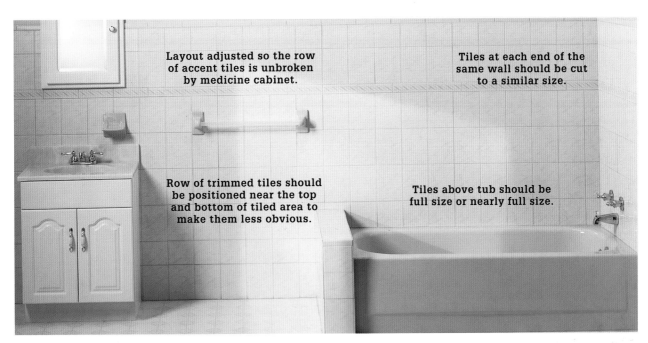

Layout adjusted so the row of accent tiles is unbroken by medicine cabinet.

Tiles at each end of the same wall should be cut to a similar size.

Row of trimmed tiles should be positioned near the top and bottom of tiled area to make them less obvious.

Tiles above tub should be full size or nearly full size.

Tiling an entire bathroom requires careful planning. The bathroom shown here was designed so that the tiles directly above the bathtub (the most visible surface) are nearly full height. To accomplish this, cut tiles were used in the second row up from the floor. The short second row also allows the row of accent tiles to run uninterrupted below the medicine cabinet. Cut tiles in both corners should be of similar width to maintain a symmetrical look in the room.

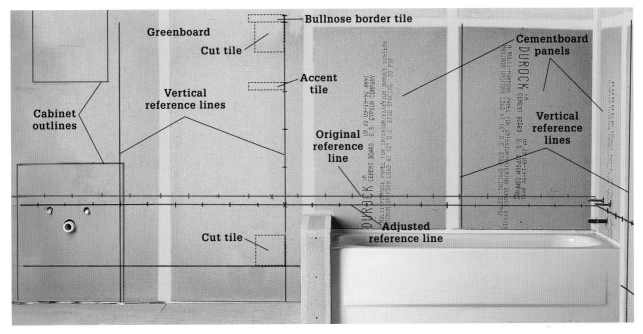

Greenboard

Cut tile

Bullnose border tile

Accent tile

Vertical reference lines

Cementboard panels

Cabinet outlines

Original reference line

Vertical reference lines

Cut tile

Adjusted reference line

The key to a successful wall-tile project is the layout. Mark the wall to show the planned location of all wall cabinets, fixtures, and wall accessories, then locate the most visible horizontal line in the bathroom, which is usually the top edge of the bathtub. Use a story stick to see how the tile pattern will run in relation to the other features in the room. After establishing the working reference lines, mark additional vertical reference lines on the walls every 5 to 6 tile spaces along the adjusted horizontal reference line to split large walls into smaller, workable quadrants, then install the tile. *Note: Premixed, latex mastic adhesives are generally acceptable for wall tile in dry areas.*

Wall tile can be spruced up, even modernized, simply by removing and replacing just a section of it with a decorative accent that suits your style.

Embellished Wall Tile

Many of us live with tile we don't particularly like. It's easy to see why: builders and remodelers often install simple, neutral tile in an effort not to put anyone off. Older homes sometimes have tile that's not quite vintage but certainly no longer stylish. Or, a previous owner might just have had different tastes. Because tile is so long-lasting, new styles and trends often overtake it and make it look dated. Here's a bit of good news: there's a choice beyond simply living with it or tearing out perfectly good tile to start over.

Removing a section of boring tile and replacing it with some decorative accent tile can transform a plain Jane wall into one that makes a unique design statement. And while a project like this requires a bit of demolition, it can be done with very little mess and fuss. Because it involves breaking the seal of the wall surface, it's a better choice for a tiled wall that gets little exposure to water (as opposed to a shower wall or tub deck).

The new tile you install will need to be grouted, and the new grout undoubtedly will be a different color. The only way to blend the new tile into the old is to regrout the entire area. If the project involves only one wall and the same grout color is still available, it is necessary to remove the grout surrounding the tile on the project wall. If you are tiling two or more walls, regrout the whole room.

This project is easier if you don't have to cut any existing tile. It's not especially difficult if you do, but it's always best to know what you're getting into before committing to a project.

Tools & Materials ▸

Tape measure	Masking tape
Grout saw	Safety glasses
Grout scraper	Drywall screws
Flat head screwdriver	Cementboard
Straightedge	Construction adhesive
Utility knife	Drywall screws
Drill	Thinset mortar
¼" notched trowel	Mosaic medallion or
Grout float	decorative tile
Grout sponge	Tile spacers
Buff rag	Grout
Foam brush	Latex additive
Needlenose pliers	Grout sealer
Drop cloth	Dust mask
Grease pencil	

How to Embellish a Tiled Wall

1

Measure the decorative tiles and draw a detailed plan for your project. Indicate a removal area at least one tile larger than the space required. If it will be necessary to cut tile, create a plan that will result in symmetrical tiles.

2

Protect the floor with a drop cloth. So you can patch the tile backer, you'll need to remove a section of tile that's a minimum of one tile all around the project installation area. Using a grease pencil, mark the tiles to be removed, according to the plan drawing. Put masking tape on the edges of the bordering tiles that will remain to keep them from being scratched or otherwise damaged by the grout saw. If you will be reinstalling some of the old tiles, protect them as well.

(continued)

3

Wearing eye protection and a dust mask, use a grout saw to cut grooves in all of the grout lines in the removal area. If the grout lines are soft this will only take one or two passes. If the grout's hard, it may take several. Using a grout scraper, remove any remaining material in the joint. Angle the tools toward the open area to protect the tile.

4

With a flathead screwdriver, pry up the edges of the tile at the center of the removal area. Wiggle the blade toward the center of the tile and pry up to pop it off.

5

Draw cutting lines on the drywall that are at least ½" inside the borders of the area where you removed tiles. Using a straightedge and utility knife, carefully cut out the old drywall. If the tile comes off very easily and the tile backer is not damaged, you may be able to scrape it clean and reuse it.

6

Cut cementboard strips that are slightly longer than the width of the opening. Insert the strips into the opening and orient them so the ends are pressed against the back surface of the tile backer. Drive wallboard screws through the edges of the old tile backer and into the strips to hold them in place.

7

Cut a cementboard patch to fit the opening in the tile backer. Place the patch in the opening and drive drywall screws through the cementboard and into the backer strips. Also drive screws at any stud locations.

8

Cover the edges with wallboard tape. Mix a small batch of thinset mortar. Apply the mortar, using a notched trowel to spread it evenly.

9

10

11

Gently press the accent tiles into the adhesive, smoothing it from the center toward the edges. Let the mortar cure as directed.

Use a damp sponge to soak the protective sheet on the tile. Once wet, slide the sheet off and throw it away.

Mix a batch of grout and fill the joints between tile on the entire wall, one section at a time. (Inset) Clean the tile with a damp sponge. Occasionally rinse the sponge in cool water.

Design Suggestions ▸

Inserts add interest, texture, and color to tile designs. This piece combines tumbled stone with marble in a delicate floral motif.

This stone insert adds a contemporary flair to a simple tile design.

Tile Tub Walls

Your dream bathroom is dressed to the nines, but that alcove bathtub is as plain as can be. You probably appreciated that prefab apron when you were installing the tub, but now it's time to beautify it. One way to improve the appearance of a plain apron and create the look of a built-in tub is simply to build and tile a short wall in front of the tub. All it takes is a little simple framing and a few square feet of tile.

The basic strategy is to construct a 2 × 4 stub wall in front of the tub apron, and then tile the top and front of the wall. One design option is to try and match existing tile, but it's unlikely you'll be able to find the exact tile unless it's relatively new. Choosing complementary or contrasting tile is usually a better bet. Ask your tile retailer to direct you to families of tile with multiple shapes and accessories.

Be sure to include a waterproof backer (cementboard is recommended) and get a good grout seal, since the stub wall will be in a wet area.

Tools & Materials ▸

Stud finder	Cementboard
Tape measure	Drywall screws
Circular saw	Tile
Drill	Thinset mortar
Hammer	Scrap of carpet
Level	Carbide paper
Tile cutting tools	or wet stone
Utility knife	Wide painter's tape
Grout float	Grout
Grout sponge	Silicone caulk
Buff rag	Grout sealer
Foam brush	Permanent marker
2 × 4 lumber	Notched trowel
Construction adhesive	Rubbing alcohol
2½" screws	

An old, boring bathtub can be spruced up to match a newly remodeled dream bathroom by building and tiling a stub wall to dress up the tub apron.

How to Build a Tiled Tub Wall

Measure the distance of the tub rim from the floor, as well as the distance from one wall to the other at the ends of the tub. Allowing for the thickness of the tiles, create a layout and draw a detailed plan of your project, spacing the studs 16" apart on center.

Cut the 2 × 4s to length for the base plate and top plate (58½" long as shown). Cut the studs (five 11" pieces as shown). Set the base plate on edge and lay out the studs, spacing them 16" on center. Make sure the first and last studs are perfectly parallel with the end of the base plate, then drive two 2½" screws through the base plate and each stud.

Draw a placement line on the floor using a permanent marker. Spread a generous bead of construction adhesive on the bottom of the base plate. Align the base plate with the placement line and set it into position. Put concrete blocks or other weights between the studs to anchor the base plate to the flooring and let the adhesive cure according to manufacturer's instructions.

Drive two or three 2½" screws through the studs and into the room walls at each end of the stub wall. If the stub wall does not happen to line up with any wall studs, drive at least two 3" deck screws toenail-style through the stub wall and into the room wall sole plate.

(continued)

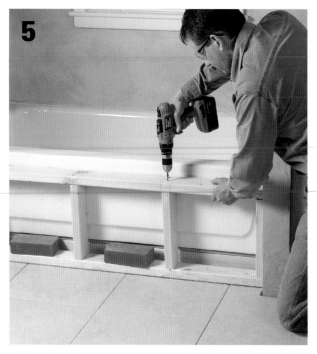

Set the top plate on the stud wall and attach it using two 2½" screws for each stud. Offset the screws slightly to increase the strength of the assembly. The top of the stud wall should be 2½" below the top of the tub.

Cut cementboard to fit the front (14½" as shown). With the factory-finished edge of the cementboard at the top of the wall, attach the cementboard to the studs using drywall screws.

Cut cementboard to fit the top of the stub wall (3½"). With the factory-finished edge facing the tub edge, attach the cement board to the top plate using drywall screws.

Design the layout and mark reference lines on the wall. Draw horizontal and vertical reference lines for the corner tile (used to transition from vertical to horizontal at the top stub wall edge) and the coved base tile (if your project includes them, as ours does). Lay out tile along the floor, including spacers.

9

Start tiling at the bottom of the wall. Lay out the bottom row of tile on the floor, using spacers if necessary. Adjust the layout to make end tiles balanced in size. Mark and cut the tiles as necessary, and then smooth any sharp edges with carbide paper or a wet stone. Mix a small batch of thinset mortar and install the base tiles by buttering the backs with mortar (see page 261).

10

Beginning at the center intersection of the vertical field area, apply mortar using a notched trowel to spread it evenly. Cover as much area as required for a few field tiles. Install the field tiles, keeping the grout lines in alignment.

11

Finish installing the field tiles up to the horizontal line marking the accent tile location.

12

Apply thinset mortar to the backs of the accent tiles and install them in a straight line. The grout lines will likely not align with the field tile grout lines.

(continued)

Install corner tiles to create a rounded transition at the top edge of the wall. Install these before you install the filed tiles in the top row of the wall face or on the top of the stub wall (corner tiles are virtually impossible to cut if your measurements are off). Dry-lay the top row of tiles. Mark and cut tile if necessary.

Fill in the top course of field tile on the wall face between the accent tiles and the corner tiles. If you have planned well you won't need to trim the field tiles to fit. (If you need to cut tiles to create the correct wall height, choose the tiles in the first row of field tiles.)

Remove the dry-lay row of tile along the top of the wall. Shield the edge of the tub with painter's tape, then spread thinset adhesive on the wall and begin to lay tile. Keep the joints of the field tiles on the top aligned with the grout joints of the field tile on the face of the wall.

Mix a batch of grout and use a grout float to force it into the joints between the tiles. Keep the space between the top field tiles and the tub clear of grout to create space for a bead of silicone caulk between the tub and tile.

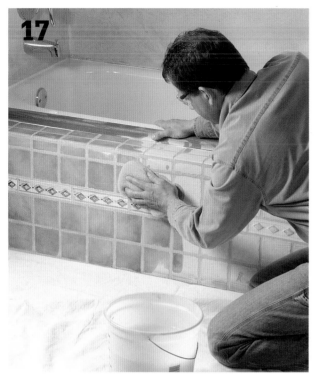

Remove excess grout and clean the tile using a damp sponge. Rinse the sponge often.

After 24 hours, clean the area with rubbing alcohol where the tile and tub meet, then put tape on the edge of the tub and the face of the tile. Apply clear silicone caulk into the gap, overfilling it slightly.

Smooth the caulk with a moistened plastic straw or a moistened fingertip to create an even finish. Make sure this spot is well sealed as it is a prime spot for water to penetrate into the tub wall.

When the grout has cured completely (consult manufacturer's directions), apply grout sealer to the joints.

Glass Block Windows

Probably one of the more enthralling design features that can be added to a dream bath is the glass block window with its tease of light infusion and reduced visibility. It is a highly energy efficient material and offers great security when used for windows. Glass block is a great choice for accent windows and for windows in rooms where privacy is a must.

Glass block is available in a wide variety of sizes, shapes, and patterns. It can be found, along with other necessary installation products, at specialty distributors and home centers.

Building with glass block is much like building with mortared brick, with two important differences. First, glass block must be supported by another structure and cannot function in a loadbearing capacity. Second, glass block cannot be cut, so take extra time to make sure the layout is accurate.

When installing a glass block window, the size of the rough opening is based on the size and number of blocks you are using. It is much easier to make an existing opening smaller to accommodate the glass block than make it larger, which requires reframing the rough opening. To determine the rough opening width, multiply the nominal width of the glass block by the number of blocks horizontally, and add ¼". For the height, multiply the nominal height by the number of blocks vertically and add ¼".

Because of its weight, a glass block window requires a solid base. The framing members of the rough opening will need to be reinforced. Contact your local building department for requirements in your area.

Use ¼" plastic T-spacers between blocks to ensure consistent mortar joints and to support the weight of the block to prevent mortar from squeezing out before it sets. (T-spacers can be modified into L or flat shapes for use at corners and along the channel.) For best results, use premixed glass block mortar. This high-strength mortar is a little drier than regular brick mortar, because glass doesn't wick water out of the mortar as brick does.

Because there are many applications for glass block, and installation techniques may vary, ask a glass block retailer or manufacturer about the best products and methods for your specific project.

Tools & Materials ▸

Tape measure	2 × 4 lumber
Circular saw	16d common nails
Hammer	Glass block
Utility knife	perimeter channels
Tin snips	1" galvanized
Drill	flat-head screws
Mixing box	Glass block mortar
Trowel	Glass blocks
4-ft. level	¼" T-spacers
Rubber mallet	Expansion strips
Jointing tool	Silicone caulk
Sponge	Construction adhesive
Scrub brush	Mortar sealant
Caulk gun	

Glass block windows add both light and privacy to a bathroom, but keep in mind that glass block cannot be cut and it cannot be load bearing.

How to Install a Glass Block Window

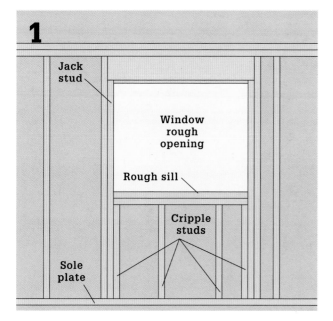

1

Jack stud

Window rough opening

Rough sill

Cripple studs

Sole plate

Measure the size of the rough opening and determine the size of the glass block window you will install (opposite page). Reinforce the rough opening framing by doubling the rough sill and installing additional cripple studs. Cut all pieces to size and fasten with 16d common nails.

2

Cut the perimeter channel to length for the sill and side jambs, mitering the ends at 45°. Align the front edge of the channel flush with the front edge of the exterior wall sheathing. Drill pilot holes every 12" through the channels (if not provided), and fasten the channels in place with 1" galvanized flat-head screws. *Note: Paint the screw heads white to help conceal them.*

3

For the header, cut a channel to length, mitering the ends at 45°, then cut it in half lengthwise using a utility knife. Align one half of the channel flush with the exterior face of the sheathing, and fasten in place with 1" galvanized flat-head screws.

4

Set two blocks into the sill channel, one against each jamb— do not place mortar between blocks and channels. Place a ¼" flat spacer against the first block. Mix glass block mortar and liberally butter the leading edge of another block, then push it tight against the first block. Make sure the joint is filled with mortar.

(continued)

Lay the remainder of the first course, building from both jambs toward the center. Use flat spacers between blocks to maintain proper spacing. Plumb and level each block as you work, then check the entire course for level. Tap blocks into place using the rubber handle of the trowel—do not use metal tools with glass block. Butter both sides of the final block in the course to install it.

At the top of the course, fill any depression at the top of each mortar joint with mortar, insert a ¼" T-spacer, then lay a ⅜" bed of mortar for the next course. Lay the blocks for each course using T-spacers to maintain proper spacing. Check each block for level and plumb as you work.

Test the mortar as you work. When it can resist light finger pressure, remove the T-spacers and pack mortar into the voids, then tool the joints with a jointing tool. Remove excess mortar with a damp sponge, or a nylon or natural-bristle brush.

To ease block placement in the final course, use tin snips to trim the outer tabs off one side of the T-spacers. Install the blocks of the final course. After the final block is installed, work in any mortar that has been forced out of the joints.

9

Expansion strip

Cut an expansion strip for the header 1½" wide and to length. Slide it between the top course of block and the header of the rough opening. Apply a bead of construction adhesive to the top edge of the remaining half of the header channel, and slide it between the expansion strip and header.

10

Clean the glass block thoroughly with a wet sponge, rinsing often. Allow the surface to dry, then remove cloudy residue with a clean, dry cloth. Caulk between glass block and channels, and between channels and framing members before installing the exterior trim. After the molding is installed, allow mortar to cure for two weeks, then apply silicone caulk.

Variation: Glass Block Window Kits

Some glass block window kits do not require mortar. Instead, the blocks are set into the perimeter channels and the joints are created using plastic spacer strips. Silicone caulk is then used to seal the joints.

Preassembled glass or acrylic block windows are simple to install. These vinyl-clad units have a nailing flange around the frame, which allows them to be hung using the same installation techniques used for standard windows.

Flooring Projects

A bathroom floor needs to be water resistant. No matter how much you love carpeting and despite your reasoning that the synthetic fibers are waterproof, you'll soon regret it if you choose to install carpet in your tub or toilet area. Even laminate flooring and traditional wood floors aren't great choices for bathrooms because the water can pool and cause the surface to delaminate or rot.

Better choices for bathroom floors are water resistant, if not impervious, and easy to clean. They also don't trap mold or mildew. Floor tile, sheet vinyl, vinyl tile, and natural stone are all good. Although the vinyl products are popular and practical in many ways, you'll seldom see them installed in a dream bath, so you won't find information on them here. But you will find some very lovely ceramic tile projects that are easily to adapt to natural stone or stone tile. And both tile and stone can be installed over a radiant-heat generating subfloor (which you'll also find in this chapter).

In this chapter:

- Installing a Radiant Heat Floor
- Ceramic Tile Floors
- Glass Mosaic Floors

Radiant Heat Floors

Floor-warming systems require very little energy to run and are designed to heat ceramic tile floors only; they generally are not used as sole heat sources for rooms.

A typical floor-warming system consists of one or more thin mats containing electric resistance wires that heat up when energized, like an electric blanket. The mats are installed beneath the tile and are hardwired to a 120-volt GFCI circuit. A thermostat controls the temperature, and a timer turns the system off automatically.

The system shown in this project includes two plastic mesh mats, each with its own power lead that is wired directly to the thermostat. The mats are laid over a concrete floor and then covered with thinset adhesive and ceramic tile. If you have a wood subfloor, install cementboard before laying the mats.

A crucial part of installing this system is to use a multimeter to perform several resistance checks to make sure the heating wires have not been damaged during shipping or installation.

Electrical service required for a floor-warming system is based on size. A smaller system may connect to an existing GFCI circuit, but a larger one will need a dedicated circuit; follow the manufacturer's requirements.

To order a floor-warming system, contact the manufacturer or dealer. In most cases, you can send them plans and they'll custom-fit a system for your project area.

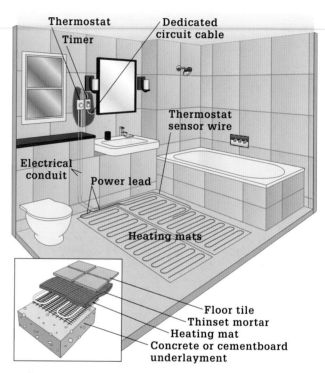

A floor-warming system requires a dedicated circuit to control its heating mats, thermostat, and timer.

Tools & Materials ▸

Multimeter	Single-gang
Drill	electrical box
Plumb bob	½"-dia. thin-wall
Chisel	conduit
Tubing cutter	Setscrew fittings
Vacuum	12/2 NM cable
Chalk line	Cable clamps
Grinder	Double-sided tape
Hot-glue gun	Electrical tape
Fish tape	Insulated cable clamps
Floor-warming system	Wire connectors
Tile	Metal connector plates
Thinset mortar	¼ × ⅜" square-
2½ × 4" double-gang	notched trowel
electrical box	Adapter cover

Floor-warming systems must be installed on a circuit with adequate amperage and a GFCI breaker. Smaller systems may tie into an existing circuit but larger ones need a dedicated circuit. Follow local building and electrical codes that apply to your project.

How to Install a Floor-warming System

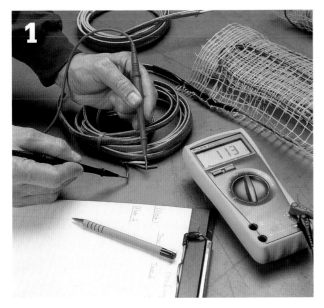

Check the resistance value (ohms) of each heating mat, using a digital multimeter. Record the reading. Compare your reading to the factory-tested reading noted by the manufacturer. Your reading must fall within the acceptable range determined by the manufacturer. If it does not, the mat has been damaged and should not be installed; contact the manufacturer for assistance.

Install boxes for the thermostat and timer at an accessible location. Remove the wall surface to expose the framing, then locate the boxes approximately 60" from the floor, making sure the power leads of the heating mats will reach the double-gang box. Mount a 2½"-deep × 4"-wide double-gang box (for the thermostat) to the stud closest to the determined location and a single-gang box (for the timer) on the other side of the stud.

Use a plumb bob to mark points on the bottom plate directly below the two knockouts on the thermostat box. At each mark, drill a ½" hole through the top of the plate, then drill two more holes as close as possible to the floor through the side of the plate, intersecting the top holes. (The holes will be used to route the power leads and thermostat sensor wire.) Clean up the holes with a chisel to ensure smooth routing.

Setscrew fittings

Cut two lengths of ½" thin-wall electrical conduit to fit between the thermostat box and the bottom plate. Place the bottom end of each length of conduit about ¼" into the holes in the bottom plate, and fasten the top end to the thermostat box, using a setscrew fitting. *Note: If you are installing three or more mats, use ¾" conduit instead of ½".*

(continued)

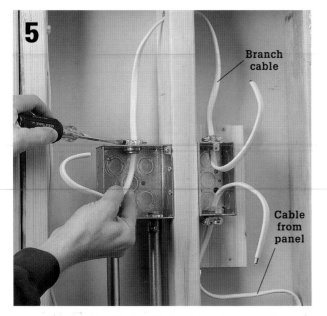

Run 12/2 NM electrical cable from the service panel to the timer box. Attach the cable to the box with a clamp. Drill a ⅝" hole through the center of the stud, about 12" above the boxes. Run a short branch cable from the timer box to the thermostat box, securing both ends with clamps. The branch cable should make a smooth curve where it passes through the stud. Protect the hole with a metal protector plate.

Vacuum the floor thoroughly. Plan the ceramic tile layout and snap reference lines for the tile installation. Spread the heating mats onto the floor with the power leads closest to the electrical boxes. Position the mats 3 to 6" away from walls, showers, bathtubs, and toilet flanges. You can lay the mats into the kick space of a vanity but not under the vanity cabinet or over expansion joints in the concrete slab. Set the edges of the mats close together, but do not overlap them: The heating wires in one mat must be at least 2" from the wires in the neighboring mat.

Confirm that the power leads still reach the thermostat box. Then, secure the mats to the floor, using strips of double-sided tape spaced every 24". Make sure the mats are lying flat with no wrinkles or ripples. Press down firmly to secure the mats to the tape.

Create recesses in the floor for the connections between the power leads and the heating-mat wires, using a grinder or a cold chisel and hammer. These insulated connections are too thick to lay under the tile and must be recessed to within ⅛" of the floor. Clean away any debris, and secure the connections in the recesses with a bead of hot glue.

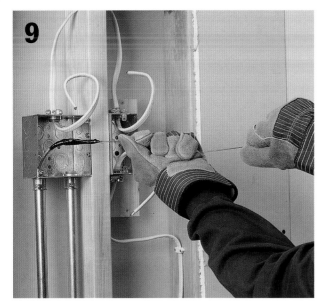

9

Thread a fish tape down one of the conduits, and attach the ends of the power leads to the fish tape, using electrical tape. Fish the leads up through the conduit. Secure the leads to the box with insulated cable clamps. Cut off the excess from the leads, leaving 8" extending from the clamps.

10

Feed the heat sensor wire down through the remaining conduit and weave it into the mesh of the nearest mat. Use dabs of hot glue to secure the sensor wire directly between two blue resistance wires, extending it 6" to 12" into the mat. Test the resistance of the heating mats with a multimeter to make sure the resistance wires have not been damaged. Record the reading.

11

Install the ceramic floor tile. Use thinset mortar as an adhesive, and spread it carefully over the floor and mats with a ⅜" × ¼" square-notched trowel. Check the resistance of the mats periodically during the tile installation. If a mat becomes damaged, clean up any exposed mortar and contact the manufacturer. When the installation is complete, check the resistance of the mats once again and record the reading.

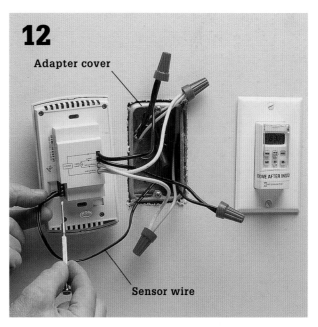

12

Adapter cover

Sensor wire

Install an adapter cover on the thermostat box, then patch the wall opening with drywall. Complete the wiring connections for the thermostat and timer, following the manufacturer's instructions. Attach the sensor wire to the thermostat setscrew connection. Apply the manufacturer's wiring labels to the thermostat box and service panel. Mount the thermostat and timer. Complete the circuit connection at the service panel. After the flooring materials have fully cured, test the system.

Ceramic Tile Floors

Tile flooring should be durable and slip-resistant. Look for floor tile that is textured or soft-glazed—for slip resistance—and has a Class or Group rating of 3, 4, or 5—for strength. Floor tile should also be glazed for protection from staining. If you use unglazed tile, be sure to seal it properly after installation. See pages 40 to 41 for more information on selecting floor tile.

Standard grouts also need stain protection. Mix your grout with a latex additive, and apply a grout sealer after the new grout sets, then reapply the sealer once a year thereafter. Successful tile installation involves careful preparation of the floor and the proper combination of materials. For an underlayment, cementboard is the best for use over wood subfloors in bathrooms, since it is stable and undamaged by moisture (page 226). Thinset is the most common adhesive for floor tile. It comes as a dry powder that is mixed with water. Premixed organic adhesives generally are not recommended for floors.

If you want to install trim tiles, consider their placement as you plan the layout. Some base-trim tile is set on the floor, with its finished edge flush with the field tile; other types are installed on top of the field tile.

Tools & Materials ▶

Chalk line	Foam brush
¼" square-notched trowel	Tile
	Thinset mortar
Drill	Tile spacers
Rubber mallet	2 × 4
Tile-cutting tools	Threshold material
Needlenose pliers	Grout
Utility knife	Latex additive
Grout float	(mortar and grout)
Grout sponge	Grout sealer
Buff rag	Silicone caulk
V-notched trowel	

Ceramic tile floors are a popular choice for the bathroom. Textured or soft-glazed tiles offer slip resistance, an important consideration in a room that is often wet.

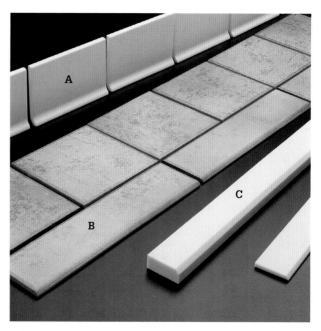

Trim and finishing materials for tile installations include base-trim tiles (A), which fit around the room perimeter, and bullnose tiles (B), used at doorways and other transition areas. Doorway thresholds (C) are made from synthetic materials as well as natural materials, such as marble, and come in thicknesses ranging from ¼" to ¾" to match different floor levels.

How to Install Cementboard Underlayment

1

Starting at the longest wall, spread thinset mortar on the subfloor in a figure-eight pattern. Spread only enough mortar for one sheet at a time. Set the cementboard on the mortar with the rough side up, making sure the edges are offset from the subfloor seams.

2

Fasten cementboard to the subfloor, using 1½" cementboard screws. Drive the screw heads flush with the surface. Continue spreading mortar and installing sheets along the wall, leaving a ⅛" gap at all joints and a ¼" gap along the room perimeter.

Establishing Reference Lines for Floor Tile Installation ▸

To establish reference lines, position the first line (X) between the centerpoints of opposite sides of the room. Snap a chalk line between these points. Next, establish a second line perpendicular to the first. Snap a second reference line (Y) across the room.

Make sure the lines are exactly perpendicular, using the 3-4-5 triangle method.

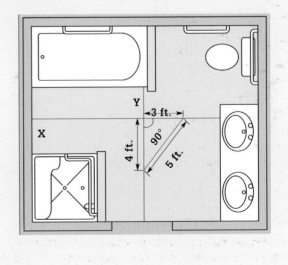

How to Install a Tile Floor

Draw reference lines and dry-fit full tiles along both lines, adjusting the layout as necessary. Mix a batch of thinset mortar, and spread it evenly against both reference lines of one quadrant. Use the notched edge of the trowel to create furrows in the mortar bed. *Note: For large or uneven tiles, use a trowel with ⅜" or larger notches.*

Set the first tile in the corner of the quadrant where the reference lines intersect. When setting tiles that are 8" square or larger, twist each tile slightly as you set it into position.

Using a soft rubber mallet, gently rap the central area of each tile a few times to set it evenly into the mortar.

Variation: For mosaic sheets, use a ³/₁₆" V-notched trowel to spread the mortar, and use a grout float to press the sheets into the mortar. Apply pressure gently to avoid creating an uneven surface.

To ensure consistent spacing between tiles, place plastic tile spacers at the corners of the set tile. *Note: With mosaic sheets, use spacers equal to the gaps between tiles.*

Set tiles into the mortar along the reference lines. Make sure the tiles fit neatly against the spacers. To make sure the tiles are level with one another, lay a straight piece of 2 × 4 across several tiles, and rap the board with a mallet. Lay tile in the remaining area covered with mortar. Repeat Steps 1 through 5, working in small sections, until you reach walls or fixtures.

Measure and mark tiles for cutting to fit against walls and into corners, then cut the tiles to fit. Apply thinset mortar directly to the back of the cut tiles, instead of the floor, using the notched edge of the trowel to furrow the mortar. Set the tiles.

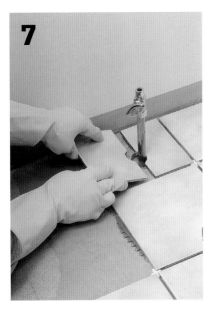

Measure, cut, and install tiles requiring notches or curves to fit around obstacles, such as exposed pipes or toilet drains.

Remove the spacers with needlenose pliers before the mortar hardens. Inspect the joints and remove high spots of mortar that could show through the grout, using a utility knife. Install tile in the remaining quadrants, completing one quadrant at a time.

Install threshold material in doorways. Set the threshold in thinset mortar so the top is even with the tile. Use the same spacing used for the tiles. Let the mortar cure for at least 24 hours.

(continued)

Mix a small batch of grout, following the manufacturer's directions. (For unglazed or stone tile, add a release agent to prevent the grout from bonding to the tile surfaces.) Starting in a corner, pour the grout over the tile. Spread the grout outward from the corner, pressing firmly on the grout float to completely fill the joints. For best results, tilt the float at a 60° angle to the floor and use a figure-eight motion.

Use the grout float to remove excess grout from the surface of the tile. Wipe diagonally across the joints, holding the float in a nearly vertical position. Continue applying grout and wiping off excess until about 25 sq. ft. of the floor has been grouted.

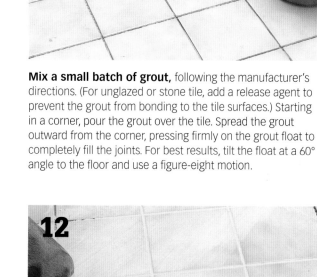

Remove excess grout by wiping a damp grout sponge diagonally over about 2 sq. ft. of the tile at a time. Rinse the sponge in cool water between wipes. Wipe each area only once; repeated wiping can pull grout from the joints. Repeat Steps 10 through 12 to apply grout to the rest of the floor. Allow the grout to dry for about 4 hours, then use a soft cloth to buff the tile surface and remove any remaining grout film.

After the grout has cured completely (check the manufacturer's instructions), apply grout sealer to the grout lines, using a small sponge brush or sash brush. Avoid brushing sealer onto the tile surfaces. Wipe up any excess sealer immediately.

How to Install Base & Trim Tile

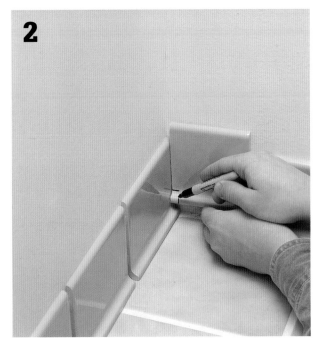

Dry-fit the trim tiles to determine the best spacing (grout lines in base tile do not always align with grout lines in the floor tile). Use rounded bullnose tiles at outside corners, and mark tiles for cutting as needed.

Leaving a ⅛" expansion gap between tiles at corners, mark any contour cuts necessary to allow the coved edges to fit together. Use a jigsaw with a tungsten carbide blade to make curved cuts.

Begin installing base-trim tiles at an inside corner. Use a notched trowel to apply wall-tile adhesive to the back of each tile. Slip ⅛" spacers under the tiles to create an expansion joint. Set the tiles by pressing them firmly onto the wall.

At outside corners, use a double-bullnose tile on one side to cover the edge of the adjoining tile.

After the adhesive dries, grout the vertical joints between tiles, and apply grout along the tops of the tiles to make a continuous grout line. After the grout cures, fill the expansion joint at the bottom of the tiles with silicone caulk.

Glass Mosaic Floors

From the time of the early Greeks and before, mosaic tile has been the design choice for beauty, style, and practicality. More than just a floor and wall covering, mosaic tile is an art form that can reflect nearly anyone's style. In fact, the Latin origins of the word *mosaic* refer to art "worthy of the muses." Mosaic tile is beautiful and durable, and working with it is easier than ever. Modern mosaic floor tile is available in squares that are held together by an underlayer of fabric mesh. These squares are set in much the same way as larger tile, but their flexibility makes them slightly more difficult to hold, place, and move. The instructions given with this project simplify the handling of these squares.

Some manufacturers stabilize mosaic squares with a paper facing on the front of the square. Most facings of this type can be removed with warm water, which we describe here. However, this can vary, so be sure to read and follow the manufacturer's recommendations regarding this facing and its removal.

The colors of mosaic tile shift just as much as any other tile, so make sure all the boxes you buy are from the same lot and batch. Colors often vary from one box to another, too, but mixing tile from boxes makes any shifts less noticeable.

It's also important to know that adhesive made for other tile may not work with glass or specialty mosaic tile. Consult your tile retailer for advice on the right mortar or mastic for your project. Before you start, clean and prepare the floor. Measure the room and draw reference lines. Lay out sheets of tile along both the vertical and horizontal reference lines. If these lines will produce small or difficult cuts at the edges, shift them until you're satisfied with the layout.

Tools & Materials ▸

Tape measure	Tile adhesive
Chalk line	Tile spacers
¼" notched trowel	Grout
Grout float	Latex additive
Grout sponge	Grout sealer
Buff rag	Tile clippers
Sponge applicator	2 × 4
Needle-nose pliers	Scrap carpet
Mosaic tile	Tile cutter

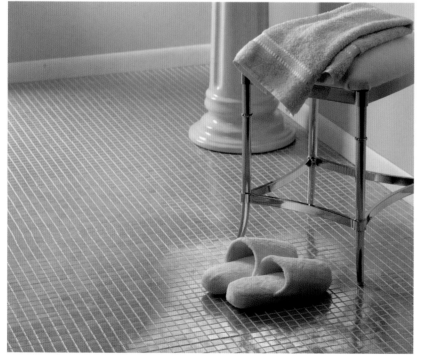

The color of mosaic tile may shift a bit from box to box, so mixing tiles from the various boxes to minimize noticeable color shifts can be as important as purchasing tiles from the same lot and batch.

How to Install a Glass Mosaic Floor

Beginning at the intersection of the horizontal and vertical lines, apply the recommended adhesive in one quadrant. Spread it outward evenly with a notched trowel. Lay down only as much adhesive as you can cover in 10 to 15 minutes.

Stabilize a sheet of tile by randomly inserting three or four plastic spacers into the open joints.

Pick up diagonally opposite corners of the square and move it to the intersection of the horizontal and vertical references lines. Align the sides with the reference lines and gently press one corner into place on the adhesive. Slowly lower the opposite corner, making sure the sides remain square with the reference lines. Massage the sheet into the adhesive, being careful not to press too hard or twist the sheet out of position. Continue setting the tile, filling in one square area after another.

(continued)

When two or three sheets are in place, lay a scrap of 2 × 4 wrapped in carpet across them and tap it with a rubber mallet to set the fabric mesh into the adhesive and force out any trapped air.

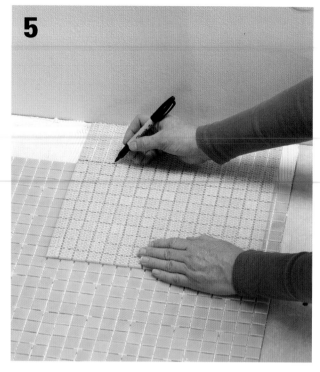

When you've tiled up close to the wall or another boundary, lay a full mosaic sheet into position and mark it for trimming. If you've planned well and are installing small-tile mosaics, you can often avoid the need to cut tiles.

If you do need to cut tiles in the mosaic sheet, and not just the backing, score the tiles with a tile cutter. Be sure the tiles are still attached to the backing. Add spacers between the individual tiles to prevent them from shifting as you score.

After you've scored the tiles, cut them each individually with a pair of tile clippers.

8

Set tile in the remaining quadrants. Let the adhesive cure according to the manufacturer's instructions. Remove spacers with a needle-nose pliers. Mix a batch of grout and fill the joints. Allow the grout to dry according to the manufacturer's instructions.

9

Mosaic tile has a much higher ratio of grout to tile than larger tiles do, so it is especially important to seal the grout with a quality sealer after it has cured.

Working Around Obstacles ▸

1

To work around pipes and other obstructions, cut through the backing to create an access point for the sheet. Then, remove the tiles within the mosaic sheet to clear a space large enough for the pipe or other obstruction.

2

Set the cut sheet into an adhesive bed, and then cut small pieces of tile and fit them into the layout as necessary.

Removal & Demolition

The teardown phase is one of the least glamorous aspects of a remodel. But without it, unless you're working from scratch, you can't get started on creating your dream bathroom.

Begin this phase of your project by removing fixtures located near the door. Even if you plan to keep these items, get them out of the way so they are not damaged, and to clear the way for removing other fixtures. Also remove cabinets, vanities, electrical fixtures, and accessories.

Remove old bathtubs and shower stalls only after you have created a clear path to get them out. Trim and wall and floor surfaces may need to be removed first. Label all items you plan to reuse, then store them where they won't be in the way. Get help when removing heavy fixtures like a bathtub.

Turn off water supply and electrical power to the bathroom before removing electrical and plumbing fixtures or cutting into walls or ceilings.

Work safely: wear eye protection, dust masks, and heavy gloves during any demolition and removal process.

In this chapter:

- Removing Toilets
- Removing Sinks & Cabinets
- Removing Showers & Tubs

Removing Toilets

Turn off shutoff valves, mounted near fixtures on the water supply lines, before disconnecting water pipes. Sinks and toilets usually are equipped with easily accessible shutoff valves, but many bathtubs and showers are not.

Turn off the main shutoff valve when there are no individual shutoff valves at the fixture being removed. Main shutoff valves usually are located in your basement, near the water meter.

Cut corroded bolts with a hacksaw if you cannot loosen the nut with a wrench and you wish to remove the old fixture intact. Often, floor bolts on toilet bowls must be sawed off.

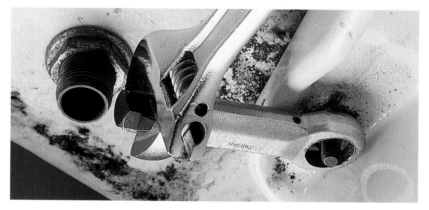

Crack corroded nuts with a nut splitter if you cannot reach the bolt with a hacksaw or wrench. Bolts that connect toilet tanks and bowls (above) and coupling nuts that connect faucets to supply lines can be difficult to reach. Nut splitters are sold at most automobile parts stores.

Plug drain pipes with a rag or pipe cap if they will be open for more than a few minutes. Uncovered waste pipes allow dangerous sewer gases to escape into your home.

How to Remove a Toilet

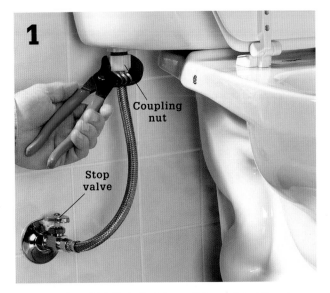

1

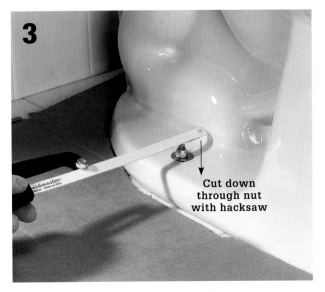

Coupling nut

Stop valve

Remove the old toilet. First, turn off the water at the stop valve. Flush the toilet holding the handle down for a long flush, and sponge out the tank. Unthread the coupling nut for the water supply below the tank using channel-type pliers if needed. If you have a wet vac, use it here and in Step 3 to clear any remaining water out of the tank and bowl.

2

Grip each tank bolt nut with a box wrench or pliers, and loosen it as you stabilize each tank bolt from inside the tank with a large slotted screwdriver. If the nuts are stuck, apply penetrating oil to the nuts and let it sit before trying to remove them again. You may also cut the tank bolts between the tank and the bowl with an open-ended hacksaw (inset). Remove and discard the tank.

3

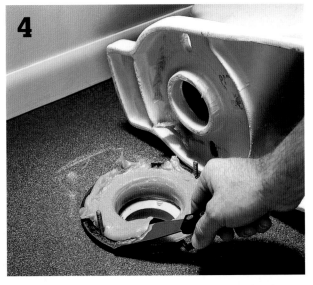

Cut down through nut with hacksaw

Remove the nuts that hold the bowl to the floor. First, pry off the bolt covers with a screwdriver. Use a socket wrench, locking pliers, or your channel-type pliers to loosen the nuts on the tank bolts. Apply penetrating oil and let it sit if the nuts are stuck, then take them off. As a last resort, cut the bolts off with a hacksaw by first cutting down through one side of the nut. Tilt the toilet bowl over and remove it.

4

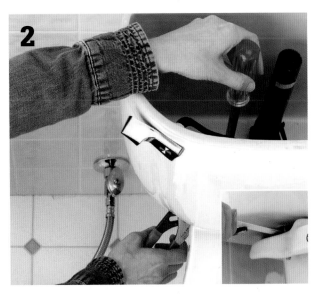

Removing an old wax ring is one of the more disgusting jobs you'll encounter in the plumbing universe (the one you see here is actually in relatively good condition). Work a stiff putty knife underneath the plastic flange of the ring (if you can) and start scraping. In many cases the wax ring will come off in chunks. Discard each chunk right away—they stick to everything. If you're left with a lot of residue, scrub with mineral spirits. Once clean, stuff a rag in a bag in the drain opening to block sewer gas.

Removing Sinks & Cabinets

Replacing bathroom sinks, countertops, and cabinets are a quick and relatively inexpensive way to give your bathroom a fresh, new look.

First, disconnect the plumbing, then remove the sink basin or integral sink/countertop unit. Next, take out any remaining countertops. Finally, remove the cabinets and vanities.

Tools & Materials ▸

Bucket
Channel-type pliers
Adjustable wrench
Basin wrench
Reciprocating saw

Hacksaw
  or pipe cutter
Screwdriver
Utility knife
Flat pry bar

Cut apart cabinets and vanities to simplify their removal and disposal. A reciprocating saw or jigsaw works well for this job. Wear eye protection.

How to Disconnect Sink Plumbing

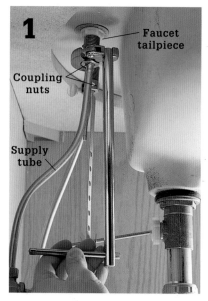

1

Faucet tailpiece

Coupling nuts

Supply tube

Turn off the shutoff valves, then remove the coupling nuts that connect the supply tube to the faucet tailpieces using a basin wrench. If the supply tubes are soldered, cut them above the shutoff valves.

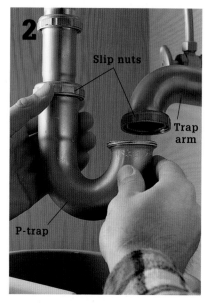

2

Slip nuts

Trap arm

P-trap

With a bucket beneath, remove the P-trap by loosening the slip nuts at both ends. If the nuts will not turn, cut out the drain trap with a hacksaw. When prying or cutting, take care to avoid damaging the trap arm that runs into the wall.

3

Pop-up drain linkage

Retaining nut

Disconnect the pop-up drain linkage from the tailpiece of the sink drain by unscrewing the retaining nut.

Shown in cross-section for clarity

Mounting clips

Self-rimming sink: Disconnect the plumbing, then slice through any caulking or sealant between the sink rim and the countertop using a utility knife. Lift the sink off the countertop.

Rimless sink: Disconnect the plumbing, including the drain tailpiece. To support the sink, tie wire around a piece of scrap wood and set the wood across the sink opening. Thread the wire down through the drain hole and attach it to another scrap of wood. Twist the wire until taut, then detach the mounting clips. Slice through any caulking, slowly loosen the wire, then remove the sink.

Wall-mounted sink: Disconnect the plumbing, slice through any caulk or sealant, then lift the sink off the wall brackets. For models attached with lag screws, wedge 2 × 4s between the sink and floor to support it while the screws are removed.

Pedestal sink: Disconnect the plumbing. If the sink and pedestal are bolted together, disconnect them. Remove the pedestal first, supporting the sink from below with 2 × 4s. Lift the sink off the wall brackets (photo, left).

Integral sink/countertop: Disconnect the plumbing, then detach the mounting hardware underneath the countertop. Slice through any caulk or sealant between the countertop and wall, and between the countertop and vanity. Lift the sink/countertop unit off the vanity.

How to Remove a Medicine Cabinet

Remove the cabinet doors and mirrors, if possible. If the cabinet has electrical features, see the variation shown below.

Remove screws or any other anchors that hold the sides of the cabinet to the wall studs.

Pull the cabinet out of the wall cavity. Pry the cabinet loose with a pry bar, or grip the face frame of the cabinet with pliers to pull it out.

Variations for Wall-Mounted Cabinets

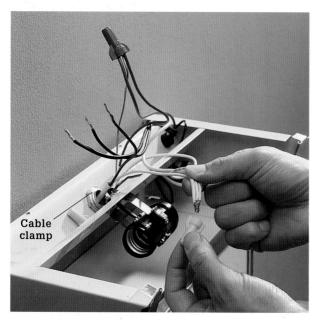

Cable clamp

Cabinets with built-in electrical features: Shut off the power, then disconnect the built-in lights or receptacles. Unscrew the cable clamp on the back of the connection box so the cable is loose when the cabinet is removed.

Surface-mounted cabinets: Support the cabinet body from below with 2–4 braces, then remove the mounting screws to free the cabinet from the wall. When removing a large cabinet, have a helper hold the cabinet while you work.

How to Remove a Countertop & Vanity

Disconnect the plumbing, then cut through any caulk or sealant between the backsplash and the wall.

Detach any mounting hardware, located underneath the countertop inside the vanity.

Remove the countertop from the vanity, using a pry bar if necessary.

Turn off the main water supply, then remove the shutoff valves, preserving as much of the supply pipe as possible. Cap the supply pipes or install new shutoff valves after the vanity is removed, then turn the water supply back on.

Remove the screws or nails (usually driven through the back rail of the cabinet) that anchor the vanity to the wall.

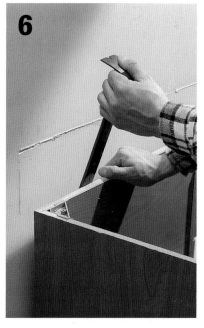

Cut through any caulk or sealant between the vanity and wall, using a utility knife, then pry the vanity away from the wall.

Removing Showers & Tubs

Bathtubs and showers are heavy and bulky fixtures, so they pose special problems for removal. Unless the tub or shower has unique salvage value, cut or break the unit into pieces for easy removal and disposal. This technique allows one person to handle most of the disposal chores. Always wear eye protection and heavy gloves when cutting or breaking apart fixtures.

For most tubs and showers, you need to remove at least 6" of wall surface around the tub or shower pan to gain access to fasteners holding it to the wall studs. Maneuvering a tub out of an alcove is also easier when the wall surfaces are removed. If you are replacing the entire wall surface, do all the demolition work before removing the tub.

Disconnect the faucet through the access panel, usually located on the wall surface behind or next to the tub faucet and drain. (If the tub does not have an access panel, add one.) Turn off the shutoff valves, then cut the shower pipe above the faucet body. Disconnect or cut off the supply pipes above the shutoff valves.

Tools & Materials ▸

Reciprocating saw	Hammer
Channel-type pliers	Masonry chisel
Screwdriver	Wire cutter
Hacksaw	Eye protection
Adjustable wrench	Utility knife
Flat pry bar	2 × 4 or 1 × 4 lumber
Wrecking bar	Rag

How to Remove Handles & Spouts

1 **Shut off the water supply,** then remove the faucet handles by prying off the covers and unscrewing the mounting screws.

2 **Remove the tub spout** by inserting a screwdriver into the spout and twisting counterclockwise until it unscrews from the stub-out that extends from the wall plumbing.

3 **Unscrew the collar nut** to remove the showerhead. Loosen the escutcheon, then twist the shower arm counterclockwise to unscrew it from the wall plumbing.

How to Disconnect Drain Plumbing

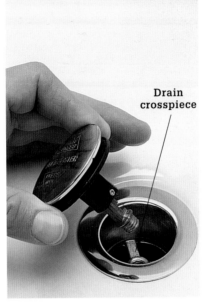

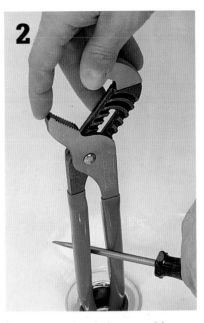

Remove the drain plug. Most bathtub plugs are connected to drain plug linkage that is lifted out along with the plug.

Spring-mounted drain plugs: Remove the plug by unscrewing it from the drain crosspiece.

Disconnect the drain assembly from the tub by inserting a pair of pliers into the drain opening and turning the crosspiece counterclockwise. Insert a long screwdriver between the handles and use it to twist the pliers.

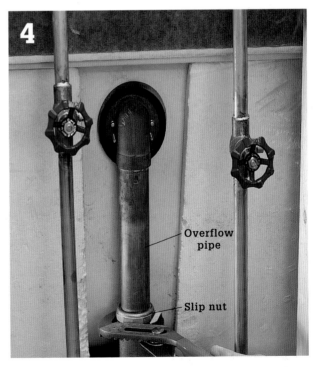

Remove the screws in the overflow coverplate (top photo). Remove the coverplate along with any attached drain plug (bottom photo).

Remove the overflow pipe by unscrewing the slip nut that holds it to the rest of the drain assembly, then lifting out the pipe. Stuff a rag into the waste pipe after the overflow pipe is removed to keep debris from entering the trap.

How to Remove a Shower Stall

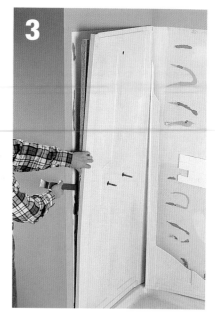

After disconnecting the faucet handles, spout, and showerhead, remove the shower curtain rod or shower door, molding or trim, and any other accessories.

Slice the caulking around each shower panel using a utility knife. Remove any screws holding the panels together. *Note: Tiled shower walls are removed in the same way as any ceramic tile wall.*

Pry shower panels away from the wall using a flat pry bar. If the panels are still intact, cut them into small pieces for easier disposal using a jigsaw or a sharp utility knife.

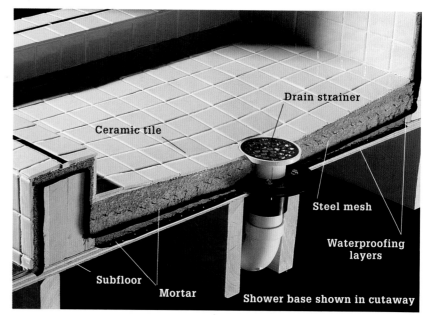

Drain strainer

Ceramic tile

Steel mesh

Waterproofing layers

Subfloor

Mortar

Shower base shown in cutaway

Fabricated shower bases (fiberglass or plastic): Slice the caulking between the base and the floor, then unscrew any fasteners holding the base to the wall studs. Pry the base from the floor with a wrecking bar.

Ceramic-tile shower base: Remove the drain strainer then stuff a rag into the drain opening. Wearing protective equipment, break apart a section of tile with a hammer and masonry chisel. Cut through any steel mesh reinforcement using a wire cutter. Continue knocking tile and mortar loose until the waterproofing layers are exposed, then scrape off the layers with a long-handled floor scraper.

How to Remove a Bathtub

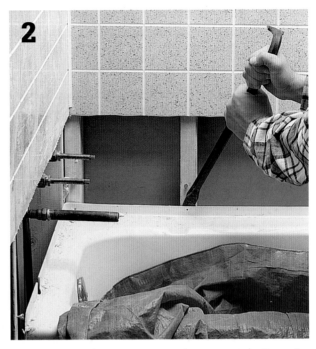

Use a reciprocating saw to cut away at least 6" of the wall surface above the tub on all sides. Before cutting into a wall, be sure faucet handles, spouts, and drains are all disconnected.

Remove the fasteners that hold the tub flanges to the wall studs, then use a wrecking bar or a piece of 2 × 4 to pry the bathtub loose.

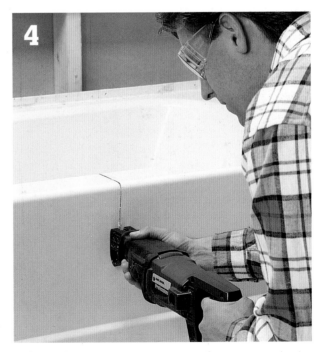

Lift the edge of the bathtub and slip a pair of 1 × 4 runners beneath the tub apron. Pull the tub away from the wall using the runners as skids. Have helpers when removing steel and cast-iron tubs.

Cut or break the bathtub into small pieces for easy disposal. Fiberglass, reinforced polymer, or pressed steel tubs can be cut with a reciprocating saw. Cast-iron and steel tubs should be carried out.

Appendix: Plumbing Codes & Permits

The Plumbing Code is the set of regulations that building officials and inspectors use to evaluate your project plans and the quality of your work. Codes vary from region to region, but most are based on the National Uniform Plumbing Code, a highly technical, difficult-to-read manual. More user-friendly code handbooks are available at bookstores and libraries. These handbooks are based on the National Uniform Plumbing Code, but they are easier to read and include diagrams and photos.

Sometimes these handbooks discuss three different plumbing zones in an effort to accommodate state variations in regulations. Remember that local plumbing code always supersedes national code. Your local building inspector can be a valuable source of information and may provide you with a convenient summary sheet of the regulations that apply to your project.

As part of its effort to ensure public safety, your community building department requires a permit for most plumbing projects. When you apply for a permit, the building official will want to review three drawings of your plumbing project: a site plan, a water supply diagram, and a drain-waste-vent diagram. If the official is satisfied that your project meets code requirements, you will be issued a plumbing permit, which is your legal permission to begin work. As your project nears completion, the inspector will visit your home to check your work.

Note: These specifications may not conform to all building codes; check with your local building department regarding regulations in your area.

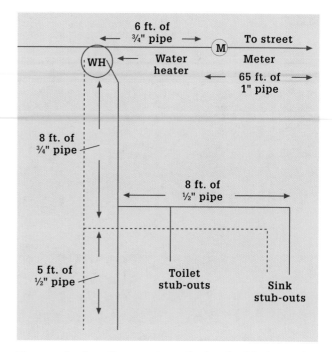

The supply riser diagram shows the length of the hot and cold water pipes and the relation of the fixtures to one another. The inspector will use this diagram to determine the proper size for the new water supply pipes in your system.

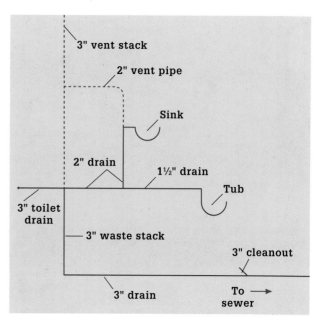

A DWV diagram shows the routing of drain and vent pipes in your system. Indicate the lengths of drain pipes and the distances between fixtures. The inspector will use this diagram to determine if you have properly sized the drain traps, drain pipes, and vent pipes.

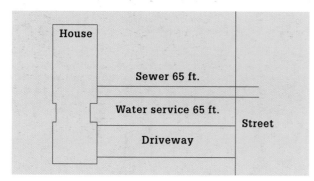

The site plan shows the location of the water main and sewer main with respect to your yard and home. The distances from your foundation to the water main and from the foundation to the main sewer should be indicated on the site map.

Fixture Supply Pipe & Trap Sizes

Fixture	Unit Rating	Min. branch pipe size	Min. supply tube size	Min. trap size
Toilet	3	½"	⅜"	n/a
Vanity Sink	1	½"	⅜"	1¼"
Shower	2	½"	⅜"	2"
Bathtub	2	½"	½"	1½"

To determine the minimum size of supply pipes and fixture drain traps, you must know the fixture's unit rating, a unit of measure assigned by the plumbing code. *Note: Branch pipes are the water supply lines that run from the distribution pipes toward the individual fixtures. Supply tubes carry water from the branch pipes to the fixtures.*

Sizes for Horizontal & Vertical Drain Pipes

Pipe size	Maximum fixture units for horizontal branch drain	Maximum fixture units for vertical drain stacks
1¼"	1	2
1½"	3	4
2"	6	10
2½"	12	20
3"	20	30
4"	160	240

Drain pipe sizes are determined by the load on the pipes, as measured by the total fixture units. Horizontal drain pipes less than 3" in diameter should slope ¼" per foot toward the main drain. Pipes 3" or more in diameter should slope ⅛" per foot. *Note: Horizontal or vertical drain pipes for a toilet must be 3" or larger.*

Maximum Hole & Notch Sizes

Framing member	Maximum hole size	Maximum notch size
2 – 4 loadbearing stud	1⁷⁄₁₆" diameter	⅞" deep
2 – 4 non-loadbearing stud	2½" diameter	1⁷⁄₁₆" deep
2 – 6 loadbearing stud	2¼" diameter	1⅜" deep
2 – 6 non-loadbearing stud	3⁵⁄₁₆" diameter	2³⁄₁₆" deep
2 – 6 joists	1½" diameter	⅞" deep
2 – 8 joists	2⅜" diameter	1¼" deep
2 – 10 joists	3¹⁄₁₆" diameter	1½" deep
2 – 12 joists	3¾" diameter	1⅞" deep

The maximum hole and notch sizes that can be cut into framing members for running pipes is shown above. Where possible, use notches rather than bored holes to ease pipe installation. When boring holes, there must be at least ⅝" of wood between the edge of a stud and the hole, and at least 2" between the edge of a joist and the hole. Joists can be notched only in the end one-third of the overall span; never in the middle one-third of the joist. When two pipes are run through a stud, the pipes should be stacked one over the other, never side by side.

Pipe Support Intervals

Type of pipe	Vertical support interval	Horizontal support interval
Copper	6 ft.	10 ft.
ABS	4 ft.	4 ft.
CPVC	3 ft.	3 ft.
PVC	4 ft.	4 ft.
Galvanized Iron	12 ft.	15 ft.
Cast Iron	5 ft.	15 ft.

Minimum intervals for supporting pipes are determined by the type of pipe and its orientation in the system. Use only brackets and supports made of the same (or compatible) materials as the pipes. Remember that the measurements shown above are minimum requirements; many plumbers install pipe supports at closer intervals.

Wet Venting

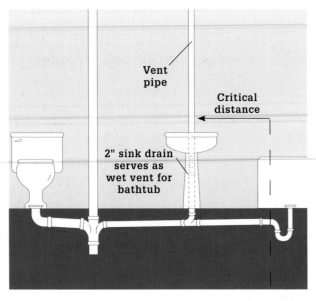

Vent pipe

Critical distance

2" sink drain serves as wet vent for bathtub

Wet vents are pipes that serve as a vent for one fixture and a drain for another. The sizing of a wet vent is based on the total fixture units it supports: a 3" wet vent can serve up to 12 fixture units; a 2" wet vent is rated for 4 fixture units; a 1½" wet vent, for only 1 fixture unit. *Note: The distance between the wet-vented fixture and the wet vent itself must be no more than the maximum critical distance.*

Auxiliary Venting

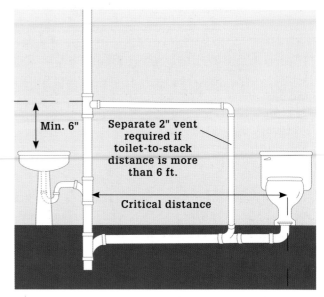

Min. 6"

Separate 2" vent required if toilet-to-stack distance is more than 6 ft.

Critical distance

Fixtures must have auxiliary vents if the distance to the main waste-vent stack exceeds the critical distance. A toilet, for example, should have a separate vent pipe if it is located more than 6 ft. from the main waste-vent stack. This secondary vent pipe should connect to the stack or an existing vent pipe at a point at least 6" above the highest fixture on the system.

Vent Pipe Sizes, Critical Distances

Size of fixture drain	Minimum vent pipe size	Maximum trap-to-vent distance
1¼"	1¼"	2½ ft.
1½"	1¼"	3½ ft.
2"	1½"	5 ft.
3"	2"	6 ft.
4"	3"	10 ft.

Vent pipes are usually one pipe size smaller than the drain pipes they serve. Code requires that the distance between the drain trap and the vent pipe fall within a maximum *critical distance,* a measurement that is determined by the size of the fixture drain. Use this chart to determine both the minimum size for the vent pipe and the maximum critical distance.

Vent Pipe Orientation to Drain Pipe

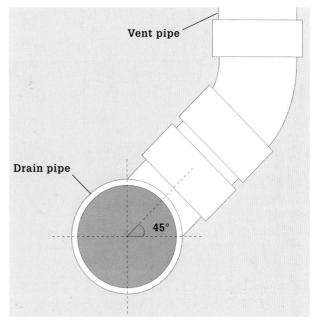

Vent pipe

Drain pipe

45°

Vent pipes must extend in an upward direction from drains, no less than 45° from horizontal. This ensures that waste water cannot flow into the vent pipe and block it. At the opposite end, a new vent pipe should connect to an existing vent pipe or main waste-vent stack at a point at least 6" above the highest fixture draining into the system.

Appendix: Wiring Codes & Permits

To ensure public safety, every community requires that you get a permit to install new wiring and have the completed work reviewed by an appointed inspector. Electrical inspectors use the National Electrical Code (NEC) as the primary authority for evaluating wiring, but they also follow the local building code and electrical code standards.

As you begin planning new circuits, call or visit your local electrical inspector and discuss the project with him or her. The inspector can tell you which of the national and local code requirements apply to your job, and may give you a packet of information summarizing these regulations. Later, when you apply to the inspector for a work permit, he or she will expect you to understand the local guidelines as well as a few basic NEC requirements.

The NEC is a set of standards that provides minimum safety requirements for wiring installations. It is revised every three years.

In addition to being the final authority of code requirements, inspectors are electrical professionals with years of experience. Although they have busy schedules, most inspectors are happy to answer questions and help you design well-planned circuits.

As with any project, if you are uncomfortable working with electricity, hire a professional electrician to complete new wiring installations and connections.

The bathroom requirements listed below are for general information only. Contact your local electrical inspector for specific wiring regulations:

- A separate 20-amp receptacle circuit for small appliances is required.
- All receptacles must be GFCI protected.
- Light fixtures and switches must be on a separate circuit. (A minimum 15-amp circuit.)
- All fixture and appliance switches must be grounded.
- There must be at least one ceiling-mounted light fixture.
- Whirlpools and other large fixtures or appliances are required to be on a dedicated circuit.

The manufacturers of some home spa fixtures, such as saunas and whirlpools, may specify that a certified electrician make the electrical connections for their product. Make sure to follow these directions, as doing otherwise may result in the warranty being voided.

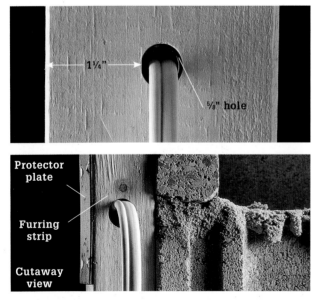

Cables must be protected against damage by nails and screws by at least 1¼" of wood (top). When cables pass through 2 – 2 furring strips (bottom), protect the cables with metal protector plates.

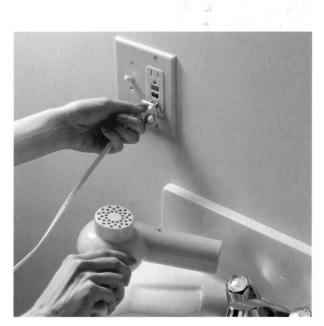

Kitchen and bathroom receptacles must be protected by a GFCI. Also, all outdoor receptacles and general use receptacles in an unfinished basement or crawlspace must be protected by a GFCI.

Metric Conversion Chart

Lumber Dimensions

Nominal - U.S.	Actual - U.S. (in inches)	Metric	Nominal - U.S.	Actual - U.S. (in inches)	Metric
1 × 2	¾ × 1½	19 × 38 mm	1½ × 4	1¼ × 3½	32 × 89 mm
1 × 3	¾ × 2½	19 × 64 mm	1½ × 6	1¼ × 5½	32 × 140 mm
1 × 4	¾ × 3½	19 × 89 mm	1½ × 8	1¼ × 7¼	32 × 184 mm
1 × 5	¾ × 4½	19 × 114 mm	1½ × 10	1¼ × 9¼	32 × 235 mm
1 × 6	¾ × 5½	19 × 140 mm	1½ × 12	1¼ × 11¼	32 × 286 mm
1 × 7	¾ × 6¼	19 × 159 mm	2 × 4	1½ × 3½	38 × 89 mm
1 × 8	¾ × 7¼	19 × 184 mm	2 × 6	1½ × 5½	38 × 140 mm
1 × 10	¾ × 9¼	19 × 235 mm	2 × 8	1½ × 7¼	38 × 184 mm
1 × 12	¾ × 11¼	19 × 286 mm	2 × 10	1½ × 9¼	38 × 235 mm
1¼ × 4	1 × 3½	25 × 89 mm	2 × 12	1½ × 11¼	38 × 286 mm
1¼ × 6	1 × 5½	25 × 140 mm	3 × 6	2½ × 5½	64 × 140 mm
1¼ × 8	1 × 7¼	25 × 184 mm	4 × 4	3½ × 3½	89 × 89 mm
1¼ × 10	1 × 9¼	25 × 235 mm	4 × 6	3½ × 5½	89 × 140 mm
1¼ × 12	1 × 11¼	25 × 286 mm			

Metric Conversions

To Convert:	To:	Multiply by:	To Convert:	To:	Multiply by:
Inches	Millimeters	25.4	Millimeters	Inches	0.039
Inches	Centimeters	25.4	Centimeters	Inches	0.394
Feet	Meters	0.305	Meters	Feet	3.28
Yards	Meters	0.914	Meters	Yards	1.09
Square inches	Square centimeters	6.45	Square centimeters	Square inches	0.155
Square feet	Square meters	0.093	Square meters	Square feet	10.8
Square yards	Square meters	0.836	Square meters	Square yards	1.2
Ounces	Milliliters	30.0	Milliliters	Ounces	.033
Pints (U.S.)	Liters	0.473 (Imp. 0.568)	Liters	Pints (U.S.)	2.114 (Imp. 1.76)
Quarts (U.S.)	Liters	0.946 (Imp. 1.136)	Liters	Quarts (U.S.)	1.057 (Imp. 0.88)
Gallons (U.S.)	Liters	3.785 (Imp. 4.546)	Liters	Gallons (U.S.)	0.264 (Imp. 0.22)
Ounces	Grams	28.4	Grams	Ounces	0.035
Pounds	Kilograms	0.454	Kilograms	Pounds	2.2

Counterbore, Shank, & Pilot Hole Diameters

Screw Size	Counterbore Diameter for Screw Head (in inches)	Clearance Hole for Screw Shank (in inches)	Pilot Hole Diameter	
			Hard Wood (in inches)	Soft Wood (in inches)
#1	.146 (⁹⁄₆₄)	⁵⁄₆₄	³⁄₆₄	¹⁄₃₂
#2	¼	³⁄₃₂	³⁄₆₄	¹⁄₃₂
#3	¼	⁷⁄₆₄	¹⁄₁₆	³⁄₆₄
#4	¼	⅛	¹⁄₁₆	³⁄₆₄
#5	¼	⅛	⁵⁄₆₄	¹⁄₁₆
#6	⁵⁄₁₆	⁹⁄₆₄	³⁄₃₂	⁵⁄₆₄
#7	⁵⁄₁₆	⁵⁄₃₂	³⁄₃₂	⁵⁄₆₄
#8	⅜	¹¹⁄₆₄	⅛	³⁄₃₂
#9	⅜	¹¹⁄₆₄	⅛	³⁄₃₂
#10	⅜	³⁄₁₆	⅛	⁷⁄₆₄
#11	½	³⁄₁₆	⁵⁄₃₂	⁹⁄₆₄
#12	½	⁷⁄₃₂	⁹⁄₆₄	⅛

Resources

American Standard
800 442 1902
www.americanstandard-us.com
p. 41 (top), 94

Armstrong Floors
717 397 0611
www.armstrong.com
p. 41

Brizo
www.brizo.com
p. 43 (right)

Bricor
830 624 7228
www.bricor.com
p. 127

Broan-NuTone
800 558 1711
www.broan.com
p. 8, 18 (top left), 38 (right), 39 (right and inset)

Ceramic Tiles of Italy
www.italiatiles.com
p. 10 (top), 11 (top & lower), 12 (top & lower right), 13 (top & lower), 14 (lower right), 15 (all), 16 (lower right), 41 (lower left), 78, 85 (all), 130, 137 (top right) 228, 250

Cherry Tree Design
Shoji pocket doors
www.cherrytreedesign.com
p. 52 (lower)

Crossville, Porcelain Stone
931 484 2110
www.crossvilleceramics.com
p. 186 (top)

Diamond Cabinets
www.diamond2.com
p. 19 (lower left), 34, 36 (right), 37 (top), 172

Economic Mobility, Inc
800 342 8801
www.toiletlift.com
p. 49 (lower left)

Elkay
630 574 8484
www.elkay.com
p. 50 (left)

Encore Cabinetry, Inc.
email: info@encoreceramics.com
www.encoreceramics.com
p. 27 (lower left), 40 (left),

Finnleo
800 346 6536
www.finnleo.com
p. 43 (left), 204

Ginger
888 469 6511
www.gingerco.com
p. 50 (right)

Hakatai Enterprises, Inc.
888 667 2429
www.hakatai.com
p. 64, 136, 236, 262

Harrell Remodeling, Inc.
www.harrell-remodeling.com
p. 51, 210

ICI Paint
www.icipaints.com
p. 92 (lower)

Ideal Standard International
www.idealstandard.com
p. 42

International Assoc. of Plumbing & Mechanical Officials
20001 E. Walnut Dr. South
Walnut, CA 91789
www.iapmo.org

International Conference of Building Officials
5360 Workman Mill Rd.
Whittier, CA 90601
800 284 4406

Jacuzzi
909 606 1416
www.jacuzzi.com
p. 10 (lower), 17 (top), 19 (lower right), 24, 26 (right), 31 (lower left middle), 52 (top)

Kohler
800 4 KOHLER
www.kohlerco.com
p. 16 (lower left & middle), 17 (lower), 18

(lower), 19 (top), 20, 22, 23 (all), 25-26 (all), 28-29 (all), 31 (top three & lower left), 33 (top left & right, lower right), 48, 49 (lower right), 92 (lower left & right), 98, 126, 137 (lower left & right), 167 (top left & right), 167 (lower right)

National Kitchen & Bath Association (NKBA)
800 843 6522
www.nkba.org

Options by Design
908 322 8989
www.optionsbydesign.com

Pittsburgh Corning
800 624 2120
www.pittsburghcorning.com
p. 246

Price Pfister
800 732 8238
www.pricephister.com
p. 30

Seattle Glass Block
425 483 9977
http://sgb.glassblk.com
p. 27 (lower right), 40 (right), 86, 91 (lower three)

Swanstone
800 325 7008
www.swanstone.com
p. 27 (top), 51, 102 (top), 140

Toto
800 350 8686
www.totousa.com
p. 49 (top), 163 (lower right)

Velux Windows
800 888 3589
www.veluxusa.com
p. 46 (right)

Walker Zanger
732 697 7700
www.walkerzanger.com

Credits

p. 12 (lower left), 16 (top), 18 (top right)

Wellborn Cabinet, Inc.
800 336 8040
www.wellborn.com
p. 36 (left)

Alamy / www.alamy.com
p. 266 photo © Hugh Threifall / Alamy

Eric Roth
p. 46 (left), 47 (top & lower), 60, 174 photos © Eric Roth

Fotolia / www.fotolia.com
p. 116 photo © Fotolia / www.fotolia.com

Istock / www.istock.com
p. 6 photo © Dean Turner, 14 (top) photo © Alexey Kuznetso & (lower left) photo ©

istock, 32 photo © Terry J. Alcorn & 33 (lower left) photo © Martí Sáiz, 35 (left) photo © Robert Perron & (right) photo © Pamela Moore, 37 (lower) photo © Justin Horrocks, 38 (left) photo © Tor Lindqvist, 44 photo © Gary Woodard, 54 photo © Alistair Scott, 142 photo © Dean Turner, 154 photo © George Mayer, 132 photo © Nicola Gavin, 167 (lower left) photo © Auke Holwerda, 184 photo © Bernardo Grijalva, 202 photo © istock, 222 photo © Krzysztof

Index

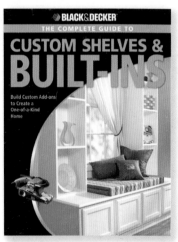
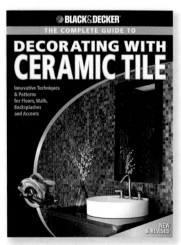